M000048649

THE TRIUMPH BOOK

Raising Wheels

Melanie Davis
& Melissa Copp

Copyright © 2019 by Melanie Davis & Melissa Copp. All rights reserved.
ISBN 978-1-68454-630-5

No part of this book may be reproduced or transmitted in any form or by
any means, electronic or mechanical, including scanning, photocopying,
recording, or by any information storage and retrieval system, without
permission in writing from the publisher.

The Triumph Book: RAISING WHEELS published by Triumph Press

10 9 8 7 6 5 4 3 2 1

Dedicated to
Gracie Kiltz
and
Robert Fraga

This book is a thank you letter...

Jody, my husband, thank you for your unwavering loyalty to our family. We couldn't have gone through the long days at the hospital or the hours upon hours waiting in a small specialist office without your sense of humor, funny voices or long hugs. Thank you for being an incredible father which makes me an incredible mother. We are a team like no other.

Calan and Lawson, my sons, thank you for the struggle that has turned out to be the biggest blessing on earth. The journey that allowed me to be your mother has given me the most amazing perspective on life. I don't sweat the small stuff and live life to the fullest. Not many people can say that right out of the gate. You are an inspiration to me every waking moment and while we fight an unknown prognosis, the future is so bright.

Lesley, my twin sister, thank you for your compassion and support during a confusing but beautiful mess of a journey into adulthood and motherhood. You have been by my side through our highs and lows and there is no doubt that some of my strength comes from you.

Our many friends that have become family, thank you for bringing meals, sending essentials, reaching out when we needed it the most and for advocating for our family so many times. You'll never know how much we appreciate the support and why we will forever be indebted to each of you.

Chip, Jo and Tim, our angels, we could never thank you enough in words for what you have done for our family. Our home called Hope was made possible by you which has provided us the first glimpse into a real future with the boys.

My mom and dad and in-laws, thank you for the proper upbringing that has allowed us to take on such a monumental task of raising two medically fragile, but strong-willed boys. Mom, I lost you so long ago, but I imagine you beaming with pride that your daughter is a fighter.

The brave contributors in this book, thank you for sharing your story so other families won't feel so alone. Wear your bravery as a badge of honor.

With love,

Your Wife, Your Mom, Your Sister, Your Friend and Your Daughter Melissa

Contents

Introduction
How I'm Raising Wheels

Melanie Davis

Everyone has disabilities. Some are hidden deep within our minds or hearts while others are easy to see. Our challenges can actually become great assets when they serve as a well-spring for strengths and abilities which inspire and uplift as they influence and change the world. The stories in this book demonstrate this truth. While each story serves as a guide and support to those who have a mobility challenge, or whose children are differently abled, their power and impact is much farther reaching as they assist readers to recognize the incredible Triumph that exists around us. At a time when there is excessive, agenda-driven focus

on what's wrong in the world, we need to be reminded of all that is right. What may appear on the surface to be a physical or mental defect is actually a source of greatness we can cling to for hope and encouragement.

Brynn Marie Davis

In our society, we tend to categorize adversities. I could easily be pegged simply as a "SIDS Mom" because I have suffered the unexpected death of a baby daughter at seven months old. In accepting this label, I might believe that only mothers who have experienced a crib death can understand my pain and, in so doing, narrow the circle in which I accept help, or give it.

I have never seen my tragedy in such a limiting way, but I can't

Brynn Marie Davis give myself credit for that. On the day of Brynn's passing, I felt a profound sense of purpose and have full faith that God has given me a unique blessing. My heart has been covered and protected me from feeling the depths of grief and loss like most mothers when they have to bury their babies.

If you asked me how I would react to losing a child before Brynn's death, I would have said, "Lock me in a dark room and throw out the key!" It is still unimaginable today for me to think of losing any of my four living children, but when that "mother's worst nightmare" happened to me, I discovered I can get through anything. Losing such a beautiful, happy, joy-of-my-life didn't incapacitate me like I thought it would, and that is ONLY because God has protected my heart and given me a calling in exchange for what He has temporarily taken from me (because I KNOW I will hold my baby daughter again one day).

So, what is this "calling" God has given to me? Honestly, it's taken many years to discover what I'm meant to do with my tragedy, and I would like to share a little of this journey with you here as I explain *How I'm Raising Wheels.*

I enjoy writing, especially journaling, and believe it contains great intrinsic value. The notable scientist, Galileo, conveyed it well when he said, "Of all other stupendous inventions, what sublimity of mind must have been his who conceived how to communicate his most secret thought to any other person, though very far distant either in time or place, speaking with those who are not yet born, nor shall be this thousand or ten thousand years? And with no greater difficulty than the various arrangement of two dozen little signs upon paper? Let this be the seal of all the admirable inventions of man." (*Fingerprints of the Gods*, Graham Hancock, Three Rivers Press, 1996, pg. 32)

Isn't that amazing?! We all have free access to the GREATEST invention of man...the ability to write and convey thoughts to generations so far into the future, it's impossible to comprehend! I find that invigorating and well worth my time.

When I became a mother, I started a meaningful tradition. After each ultrasound, I went to the bookstore and bought a journal...blue with sailboats and teddy bears or pink with flowers and hearts, depending if my new joy was to be a girl or boy. I would begin writing in the journal,

2

bringing it with me to the delivery room to have the footprints inked inside right after birth. Then, still in the hospital, I would write a mother's first message to her child.

I continued writing in each of these journals (five in all), capturing the cute and funny things my little ones would do that I knew I'd forget if I didn't write them down. For example, when my oldest boy, Danny, was three, he flushed a toothbrush down the toilet. Sitting next to the porcelain bowl, flustered as I tried to fish it out, my son put his chubby arm across my shoulders, patted my face and said, "It's OK Mom. I still have a red one!"

Recently, I sat on the couch with my 13-year-old son, Carson, the "baby of the family," reading his journal together, shocked at how much I had completely forgotten. When he was a toddler, I couldn't get him to stay in his crib at bedtime, so I put a white mesh canopy over it which zipped closed. Carson managed to pry holes into the mesh in various places from which he would eject Hot Wheels and other small toys. These holes also became part of our bedtime ritual as he wouldn't lay down until I had given him a kiss through each one of them. Reading this journal from his babyhood together was a bonding experience, especially at an age when it can be difficult to have such meaningful moments. All of my children treasure the journals I wrote during their early years. It gives them a sense of confidence and esteem to see themselves through my eyes.

In the journal I kept for Brynn, I continually wrote of her sweetness. It was stated over and over. She really did have an angelic presence which I inadvertently captured as I wrote about her, and could clearly recognize upon rereading her journal after she died. Brynn rarely slept, as if she knew she didn't have long on the earth. She almost never cried, but I sure did... *"Please sleep, Brynn! I'm sooo tired!"*

Looking back, it's easy to see Brynn was an angel who seemed to know her time on earth would be short, and so she didn't want to waste it. On February 6, 2002, at 5 a.m. I woke with an instant sense of alarm. I leaped out of bed and ran to Brynn's room to find her buried under the covers. Turning on the light of a musical toy fish bowl that hung on the slats of the crib, I could see in the moving colored shapes going 'round that things weren't right. As I lifted Brynn out from under the covers, her body was lifeless. Running with her out into the light of my bedroom, my brain struggled to process what I saw.

The SIDS death of my daughter became my life's greatest sorrow but would lead to unspeakable joy. Months after her death, I picked up Brynn's journal and wrote about the experience of finding her dead in the crib, the ambulance ride, praying she would make it, but knowing Brynn was already gone. I described being interviewed in the interrogation room of the police station as part of the protocol when there's a death in the home, which happened only hours after leaving the hospital and the pronouncement of death. I preserved the memory of the breakdown of our minivan on our way to the funeral, driving between San Jose, California and Carson City, Nevada where she would be buried. I stood in the middle of a rest area parking lot, high in the Sierra Nevada Mountains, watching our van being towed away along with my daughter inside her casket.

Some months after her death, I picked up Brynn's journal again and wrote all that I learned, which is that God is real and will support us through our adversities. For me, knowledge of God's existence goes beyond faith because I *FELT* His presence and comfort during my initial grief in a way that is hard to describe, but was physically tangible. I wrote with an audience in mind, my children and posterity, so they would know about Brynn, but also to teach them not to fear the challenges that will come, to give assurance they can find purpose and meaning in all sorrows, as I had learned through this tragedy.

I am so grateful I had that tradition of keeping a journal. It has proven to be a priceless tool, not only in my own healing, but for many others as I

discovered the power of narrative therapy in writing and sharing stories of adversity with others on their journey through sorrow. Because I handled my loss so well, people would come to me, asking for advice on how to help their loved one or friend suffering child loss. In the course of time I discovered the online technology to publish a storybook full of Brynn's pictures, along with my journal of her life and death. I printed a copy of this glossy book whenever someone needed to read my experience. I would give it freely with the suggestion that there might be something in my story that can comfort or help a grieving loved one. Over time, I literally gave out 100 copies and realized that the more I was able to share my story, the more purpose I found in Brynn's passing.

Eventually, I drew from this experience and authored *The Triumph Program*, a workbook and narrative therapy process assisting people to discover, write and share their Triumph Stories. It's made up of seven sections containing reading, writing, art therapy and other activities which help participants take on the perspective of a researcher into their own lives, recognizing the new strengths and abilities gained from tragedy and the potential for doing good in the world because of it. *The Triumph Program* is an evolution from darkness to light as it begins by guiding the development of the tragedy story and ends with a vision for the future with new-found purpose and hope. It is based on two principles: 1) The more purpose you find in tragedy, the less painful it becomes; and 2) there's powerful healing found in service to others.

Initially, I facilitated the 12-week program primarily in bereavement and retirement communities which included writing in the workbook during the week and then meeting once a week in small peer group settings to share the stories and discoveries with each other. I would tell the participants, "You can overcome grief!" Of course, overcoming grief is how you define it. I describe it as being able to find purpose and joy again in life, not being continually stuck in sorrow. That isn't to say you won't ever feel the pain of loss; however, life can still be meaningful and happy.

There must be a standard position taught when counselors study bereavement which states that people don't "overcome grief" because, to a person, every counselor I worked with when facilitating *The Triumph Program* pulled me aside to tell me not to say that. Instead they instructed me on the acceptable catch phrases I should use such as, "In time, you will find a new normal" or "There is no time-line for grieving, take all the time

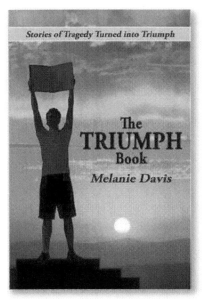

you need." I believe this attitude must be a systemwide knee-jerk reaction to people in grief being pushed back to "normal life" too soon or not being granted space to grieve at all. But the idea that we may never get over our sorrow and be stuck in pain all our lives is setting the bar too low. My response to this dysfunction in bereavement counseling was to write *The Triumph Book*, a collection of 20 stories from people who have endured severe tragedies and who have found purpose and joy in life *BECAUSE* of what they went through. The stories vary widely, from death-loss to illness and disability, as well as suffering violence and murder. Most were in the media when they first happened because the situations are so sensational, but the book shares "the rest of the story" which are ALL stories of overcoming and triumph! Chapter One is essentially Brynn's Journal, allowing me to share her story more widely and affordably than the glossy storybooks I had been printing previously.

The Triumph Book is the first collection in what has become *The Triumph Book Series*. (You are now reading the third anthology of stories in the series, with more topics coming!) After writing this initial book, I enjoyed the process so much I wanted to compile another collection of stories, this time from veterans. I have always been drawn to the personal narratives of our military heroes and wanted to increase patriotism by sharing their experiences, because who loves our country more than those who are willing to die for it? As I interviewed veterans who represent battles from WWII up through our recent conflicts, I discovered I had been an ignorant civilian having no idea the battles they face upon return. Out of this realization, and with the initial publishing of *HEROES* on 11/11/11 (I couldn't pass up that Veteran's Day date!), I started the national campaign, *Love Your Veterans*. We owe veterans more than the passing "thank you" for what they have done for us. Each person who lives in freedom should anxiously support our war heroes through their struggles in gratitude for all their costly sacrifices.

Veterans showed their love when they were willing to die for us. I feel strongly that we will never care for them the way they need or deserve until we *love* them in return. To truly love another person, you need to know him and understand his heart. The best way to love our veterans is to know their stories!

 USMC LCPL Matthew Brown's story is featured in *The Triumph Book: HEROES*. He was a machine gunner during the Invasion of Fallujah who was shot on Veteran's Day. His description of being shot is so visceral, you almost know what it feels like. Matt's serious wound caused permanent disability and plunged him into debilitating PTSD until he found his way through the suicidal tendencies, the drug and alcohol abuse, the fear, anger and hopelessness, becoming a Triumph Story not only for veterans, but anyone suffering life-altering trauma. After capturing his story for the book, I asked Matthew to help me co-author a version of *The Triumph Program* to heal the hidden wounds of our veterans.

In the course of writing and publishing these books, I founded Triumph Press. Through this publishing imprint, I have also been able to publish other noteworthy books from people who have overcome extreme hardships or who have something important to teach. This is how I met Tamara Simmons, author of *The Funding Guide for Children with Disabilities*.

Triumph Press published her valuable resource helping parents learn how to become a funding source recipient or raise money for accessible technology. So many children are in need, but often times insurancewon't cover these expensive costs. *The Funding Guide* teaches how to run community fundraising events or effectively use crowdfunding platforms. It has a directory of over 200 funding sources which helps parents quickly identify the best matches for their children, substantially shortening the research time as well as providing step-by-step instructions for winning a grant. Working with Tammy on her Funding Guide drew me in, and I wanted to become more involved in the marketing and distribution of something so important.

We decided to give the ebook version of *The Funding Guide* free through her website: *www.DisabilityFundingSpecialist.com*, so it can be readily available to all who need it. This is made possible by many supportive sponsors which are featured on the website and in the book. We were also assisted in our mission as the Abilities Expo gave us a booth in the center of their events, called "The Meet-Up Zone," where we provided free consultations to all who signed up for an appointment. In this meeting we assessed fundraising goals and helped design a plan to achieve them based on the many approaches taught in *The Funding Guide*.

It was at the Abilities Expo in Houston that Tammy Simmons and I met the Copp Family, who scheduled an appointment with Tammy to be mentored in ways they could raise funds for their accessible dream home. At this time, I was exploring the idea of creating a Funding eCourse where we could show how to fundraise by filming the process of conducting different fundraising approaches, which could be a companion to *The Funding Guide*. It can be much easier to learn a skill by watching it being done successfully.

8

The Copp Family meeting with Tamara Simmons in
the Meet-Up Zone of the Abilities Expo

After meeting the Copp Family and hearing their passion to achieve their accessible home, I knew this was the story I needed for the eCourse and the Copps excitedly agreed to participate. A month later, I traveled to Waco, TX and met with the family in their former home, filming their explanation of the many challenges the house presented and outlining their plans for the new home that would be renovated to be fully accessible for their two boys in wheelchairs. Later, we filmed a committee meeting with those who volunteered to help with the fundraising plans in order to chronicle the process for future viewers to follow. After weighing many different suggestions, we decided to put together what we dubbed "The Giving Trees Festival," which is a display of gorgeous donated Christmas trees decorated by businesses, organizations and individuals wanting to help the cause. We would charge an entrance fee for people to walk through the stunning display as well as auction the trees with the potential of raising tens of thousands of dollars. We modeled the event on similar benefits which have been established in large cities, usually by children's hospitals which often raise hundreds of thousands of dollars. We figured this event had the best potential of raising the kind of money needed to buy and remodel a home to be perfectly wheelchair friendly.

The planning and preparation went flawlessly as Melissa Copp's talents shine brightest when she's organizing! She was able to secure a large room in the Waco Convention Center where a parade would conveniently pass right by our festival on the day of the event, bringing masses of onlookers just outside the doors. There was substantial media and enthusiasm for the festival including many local newspaper and magazine articles, as well as bright flashing billboards promoting this new holiday festival along the busiest freeways of Waco, all supporting these darling little boys.

On the day before *The Giving Trees Festival* opened to the public, the convention center was alive with the sounds of merry music as tree after tree was meticulously decorated in the most creative themes imaginable. I was able to film the decorators/donors standing beside their trees, talking about the uniqueness of their submissions as well as their reasons for participating. One craftsman hand-welded a metal tree which had taken a total of sixty hours to complete! The conference room was enchanting and everyone was certain this would be just the event we needed to help the Copp Family achieve their accessible home, and that I needed to produce an eCourse teaching how to put on successful events.

Success in all of our goals would surely have been the result...except for the weather. It rained so hard the parade was canceled and few ventured out. Those who did come were in awe of what was accomplished. (Did I mention that Melissa and her crew pulled this together in just three months!?) Some of the trees were sold at the event and others were moved for display and sale at additional locations raising around $15,000, which was far from what we expected or needed.

Not long into the new year, after this Christmas-time fundraiser, the Copp Family moved out of their boundary-ridden home and into a small apartment, as they had sold that house in hopes of buying and designing the wheelchair friendly new one. I don't think Melissa will mind me sharing that, at this time, she was quite disheartened. The Copps had no idea how long they would be living in these cramped, inconvenient quarters as they struggled to find their way home. (There wasn't even accessible parking for their van.) While talking with Melissa, I told her about *The Triumph Book Series* and discussed the idea of compiling a book full of inspiring stories from those who are achieving greatness while living with unique abilities. I suggested to Melissa that we could write such a book together. She would help find the stories as well as share her own, which would be a profound resource for anyone seeking inspiration. It could also become a much needed, virtually nonexistent guide for parents raising children with physical challenges.

After some excited discussion, Melissa offered the title "Raising Wheels," and now you are reading the fulfillment of the plans we made on that day. This chapter is titled *How I'm Raising Wheels* because while I'm not the mother of such special children, I am an enthusiastic champion for accessibility and hope this book will do much to *RAISE* awareness of the need for accessibility while *RAISING* funds to assist families, like the Copps, to be able to achieve more accessible lives. I am one of the co-founders of the Raising Wheels Foundation, along with Melissa and Jody Copp and the first board members. I have since moved to the advisory board in order to put my focus on the promotion and distribution of this *RAISING WHEELS* book with the purpose of supporting the mission of the foundation, which you will learn more about in this book.

While *The Giving Trees Festival* was not the success we had planned and hoped for, all the publicity surrounding the event, along with Melissa's continuous hard work towards their goals, contributed to the Copp Family being chosen to receive their accessible dream home on HGTV's Fixer Upper with Tim Tebow guest starring on that special episode. The rest of the story is Melissa's to tell in the next chapter, however, I would like to point out that sometimes what seems like failure is actually an important stepping stone towards success beyond what we could ever envision.

The process of compiling this book and coming to know each of the contributing authors has been an enriching and life-changing experience. Their wisdom provides a roadmap, not only for thriving on wheels, but as a support for traversing any adversity we may face. It is my hope that as you read these stories you will be encouraged to look into your own life and heart for that Triumph which is the ultimate reward for all we endure.

the **FUNDING GUIDES**

download for **FREE**

www.thefundingguides.com

A Home Called Hope

Melissa and Jody Copp

Melissa:

We sat on a cold steel bench in front of our apartment complex motionless, frozen by what was just told to us. It was a little after 9:00 p.m. on a Thursday evening. Calan was inside sleeping while Lawson lay drowsy in Jody's arms. "I'm sorry, can you repeat that?" I asked. "Melissa, Jody...you are FINALLY going to get the wheelchair accessible home of your dreams for your boys!" Not many moments in my life have left me speechless, but this was one of them. Earlier that day I had received a call from the Executive Director of the Magnolia Foundation saying he had some urgent news and that he wanted to meet with us in person right away. I told him that the boys had a Challenger Little League baseball game, and we wouldn't be home until later that evening. After we arrived back home and got the boys ready for bed, we met him outside and sat down on one of the wooden benches in front of the apartment building that we had been living in for the past 14 months. Never in a million years would I have predicted what we were going to be told that night. The previous nine years of heartache and unbearable pain flashed before my eyes. Was it really going to get better? Was it finally our time? We sat face to face with the news that changed our lives forever in the most amazing of ways.

Up until this point, good news was not familiar to our family. In fact, we started to expect bad news being told to us at every specialist appointment and hardships became the norm. It was just easier to expect it than to fight against it. After Jody and I got married, we knew we wanted children but not until we found a house in which we could start a life. We found an amazing home in a quiet neighborhood with three bedrooms and a big yard our dogs and future children could play in. It was perfect. Within a few months after moving into our first home, we found out I was pregnant. We couldn't contain our excitement! How wonderfully scary it was to be part of this exclusive club of parenthood where life is temporarily filled with diapers, baby wipes and self-doubt. We had normal checkups and the baby was developing at a normal rate. Ha, normal. What is normal anymore? I look

back now and remember how naïve I was about everything, thinking that if I read, "What to Expect When Expecting," it was going to give me a heads up on motherhood. Not a chance. I went to every appointment with Jody by my side and every single appointment went by the book. I gained roughly 30 pounds during the pregnancy and had consistent morning sickness that lasted all day and every month of the pregnancy. Besides being sick all the time, I was still eating, drinking and working out like usual.

Jody:

While not saying it publicly, I never wanted to have children until I met Melissa. I've always wanted a FAMILY, but the thought of little kids running around scared the absolute tar out of me. I have to be responsible for someone else? No deal, I can barely take care of myself, let alone a baby! I was great at spoiling my dog, Cocoa, but she could use the doggy door and all I really had to do was keep her fed and watered and let her lay in my lap and she was good.

I remember Melissa telling me she had cooked supper and it was time to eat. As I got to the table, right alongside the plates and silverware was a pregnancy test. I was shocked to say the least, even though we had been trying to have a baby. I'm glad I didn't have someone filming me because I'm sure it wasn't the exact response Melissa wanted, but I was genuinely excited and gave her a huge hug saying "I can't believe it!" over and over.

As soon as the week of my due date hit, we were ready to meet our little man. I remember going to the mall so we could walk around to induce labor on my own when all of a sudden, my water broke right there in the middle of the mall. We went immediately to the hospital and after about 12 hours of labor, our son arrived at 2:46 a.m. on August 12, 2008. We named him Calan. Without knowing the fate of our son, we gave him a name that was unique because we felt that he deserved it. Oh, how fitting that really was! He weighed 6 pounds 13 oz. and started nursing right away. We became inseparable.

We took all the recommended parenting classes and bought every single thing off those must-have lists for newborns...so we should have been prepared, right? Wrong. They don't prepare you for the ambiguous, black hole abyss of what our family was about to fall into...

Shortly after bringing Calan home, I noticed that I was changing his clothes 8-10 times in a day because of the amount of spit-up he would have. He would SCREAM, SCREAM and SCREAM for hours. Days turned into nights and nights turned into days without comprehension. The colic was so bad and he would cry so hard that his legs would kick out and remain stiff. "What is going on?" I kept asking myself time and time again. I couldn't remember what day or time it was. I wasn't living anymore. I was just keeping my son from crying all day and all night. We didn't take fun walks in the neighborhood or have lunch dates with friends while Calan slept beside me. I longed for those memories instead of the nightmare that ensued. He would cry incessantly throughout the day and night and would only stop crying to feed. I felt imprisoned inside my own home for fear of Calan not being able to be soothed. His little body was rigid and stiff with pain. I was awake roughly twenty out of the twenty-four hours in the day while he was home with me. I had never felt the pain of exhaustion like that before. It was a beautiful mixture of torture and life.

Melissa wanted to breastfeed. Calan had no issues nursing and seemed to be getting full, but soon he began to exhibit strange behaviors, even when nursing. He would latch and begin nursing immediately, but then push away and begin screaming. Again, he would latch and nurse, then push away and scream. When we would bring up this behavior to his primary care physician, they initially said he was just hungry and to try again. Melissa would often call me at work and tell me something was wrong, but I was doing all I could to balance little sleep at night and work. I kept thinking we were just bad at this because family and friends would often tell us, "Don't worry, this is normal, y'all are just first-time parents and haven't found a routine yet."

I would help when I got home from work, but we were both zombies. I remember Calan would often be fine when I got home and Melissa feared that I didn't believe her. We would only get that one golden hour in the evening between 5:30 p.m. and 6:30 p.m., then the crying would begin again. In one of Melissa's darkest moments, I heard her sobbing in the middle of the night. Even though I had to work the next day, I went into the room, put my arms around her and said "It's going to be alright, we'll get through this together." I took Calan the rest of the night so she could get some sleep and passed out with him lying next to me. We knew this couldn't be normal and had to get relief for all of us, for our sanity. Melissa was doing everything she could but the stress of being home with Calan day and night was taking a toll on her, mentally and physically.

Finally, the doctor suggested Calan might be allergic to Melissa's breast milk. So we began the tedious task of trying to find a formula and bottle combination that would work. I'd go to the store weekly and purchase at least two different formulas, powdered and liquid form, and just about every type of bottle and nipple combination available. We would try the formulas for at least seven days at a time to be sure the old formula had exited his system. Oftentimes, we thought we had found a winner, only to be met with more days and nights of screaming before we could try a new formula, all the while experimenting with different bottles to find a solution. Our life during this time was excruciating, and we were oftentimes at each other's throats because the stress was so high. We just wanted to fix whatever was happening to our son.

After going through numerous brands and types of formulas, bottles and nipples, we found a formula and bottle combination. We referred to it as "liquid gold." We would buy cases at a time and make sure at least two bottles were in the refrigerator at all times. This was our first introduction into the many medical expenses we would incur without warning. Travelling was difficult because the formula had to stay cold. Once we had a formula he could digest, the doctor also suggested giving him Zantac to aid with his reflux. We had tried everything to ease his pain and finally appeared to have an answer.

While we hoped for the best and thought that was the only mountain we were meant to climb as parents, it was just the tip of the iceberg which was preparing us for the difficult road ahead. During the few times Calan was awake and not screaming, we noticed that he had very rapid movement in both eyes (called *nystagmus*) but didn't think much of it since we had bigger problems at hand. The end of my maternity leave was also fast approaching and soon Calan was going to a daycare facility and I was going back to work. He was eight weeks old. I was crushed. I felt robbed. I didn't have the storybook maternity leave I so desperately wanted or thought I'd earned. I could feel the bitterness set in. It would not leave me for another four years.

At three months old, our baby, who was in so much pain before, smiled for the FIRST time because of the combination of the reflux medicine and formula which finally relaxed his little body. Seeing him finally smile was so warming that it all-but-erased the hardship we had gone through, almost. The colic lessened by this point and that's when we noticed Calan's gross motor development was delayed. Something in our gut was instantly on fire. "Oh God, please let everything be ok with my baby after all this." I pled with God every single day. Soon, we would find out that it wasn't going to be.

At around five months old, Calan's daycare provider pulled me aside and said that Calan was not holding his head up like the other same-aged infants in the class, and wanted to let me know. We noticed at home that he was weaker than what he should be, so we worked on tummy time a lot, which we had avoided in his first three months since the colic was so bad. Around that time, Calan got his first virus which prompted a visit to his pediatrician and then the emergency room due to coughing, wheezing and fever. He got treated and released and was better in the next few days. I also scheduled Calan to see an ophthalmologist for his nystagmus as well as a neurologist for the developmental delay. Someone had to provide us the answers to these mysteries. They were starting to mount.

Melissa had been telling me about Calan's eyes darting back and forth and his inability to focus on things like toys or other objects. I didn't want to believe it, but I began to notice it too. It didn't always happen, but it began to happen with enough regularity that there was no denying something was going on with his eye movement.

Only six months after Calan was born, we had our first consult with an ophthalmologist about 37 miles away. During the visit, he noticed the unusual eye movement and suggested that Calan might have "probable bilateral optic nerve hypoplasia" and recommended getting a brain MRI to check to see if his optic nerves were intact and fully formed. The hairs on my arms stood up and goosebumps formed all over when he mentioned the words "brain MRI." Did I have any idea what that entailed? No. Did that get covered by a chapter in the "What to Expect When Expecting?" book? No. The worry started to set in. We told the ophthalmologist that due to Calan's low muscle tone; we had already made an appointment with a neurologist the very next week. He wanted us to see if the neurologist would recommend getting an MRI as well, and until then we would follow up with him every six months. Now the nerves set in. I remember the sick feeling in my stomach and how we remained very quiet in the exam room. How could we feel after getting slammed with news like this? After all, this would all be curable, *right*?

A week later, as planned, we drove another 118 miles away, a 236-mile round trip, to a hospital in Dallas to see our first neurologist. I told myself, "Ok, we'll go in. It will be quick. He'll do a physical exam and tell us it's something easily fixable, and we'll get out of there and head back home." I couldn't have been more wrong. The neurologist did a physical exam of Calan. He noticed he had overall weak muscle tone and that he was having trouble tracking items with his eyes. I heard a lot of "hmmm" sounds during the evaluation. He recommended that we start Calan on physical therapy sessions due to his weak muscle tone. As he was still holding onto his legs during the exam, the neurologist quietly mentioned that "sometimes children have low muscle tone and nystagmus due to a brain tumor. We need to see if that is what is causing this." Did I just hear him correctly? I looked at Jody for confirmation. His face was in complete disbelief. I don't remember uttering a single word the rest of this day, just the feeling of pure shock. He called to get us into the rotation to do an immediate brain MRI as soon as possible, right there in the hospital. There we were, six months into parenthood, sitting in a small, sterile exam room in Dallas being told our son might have a possible brain tumor or brain abnormality causing his muscle weakness and unusual eye movements. This day ended up being one of the most excruciatingly painful days to date. We waited ten more hours to get a brain MRI performed on our infant son due to a backlog of emergencies. All the while, the words "brain tumor" were repeating in my head over and over and over and over.

> *As if everything we had endured up to this point wasn't enough, this day would prove to test our mettle. Our appointment had been a mid-morning appointment. Calan had been fed before seeing the neurologist and once the MRI request had been made, we were informed Calan would need to fast for at least 6-8 hours before the MRI could be completed. When we were given that information, I looked at Melissa and said, "Great, now we have to starve our poor child." The hospital also wouldn't perform the MRI without immediate payment, so out came the credit card as there was no way we could afford what they were asking on the spot. And then the waiting began.*
>
> *The hospital has a foyer with wooden animals covered by carpet in the shape of a carousel for the children to play on. There are also benches and a gift shop. Calan was due to have his MRI at 6:00 p.m. that evening. I tried to keep Calan as comfortable as possible and insisted on carrying and holding him the entire time to try to keep him satisfied and sleeping as much as I could. By the end of the day my arms were cramping so bad I thought they were going to fall off, but I also felt incredibly guilty for having to do this to him and knew Melissa was exhausted from what we had been going through, so I put it out of my mind. We hadn't eaten all day for fear that the smell of food would trigger Calan's appetite and he'd start to cry. By the time we were called into the MRI prep area, it had been well over 10 hours since Calan's last meal and he was absolutely inconsolable. This was not a colic cry that we had heard before. It was different. Everything was different.*

> Due to hospital protocol, we were not allowed to go back to the MRI area and could only watch as they strapped him down on the gurney and administered anesthesia. Watching our infant son go lifeless on a table is something we will never forget. It's scary. It's out of body. It was scarring. The scars were adding up. We were told to "go get a bite to eat in the cafeteria downstairs." After not having anything to eat all day ourselves, we tried to force down a burger, all the while wondering what was happening to our baby boy. When we got the call to come back to the recovery room, we found Calan trying to wake up from the anesthesia. We couldn't leave until he held down a certain amount of fluid, so we waited for him to recover enough to be discharged. By the time we left the hospital and got back home it was well into the early morning hours, only to get back up and go to work the next day as though nothing had happened. We couldn't afford to take any additional time off with the unknown of what was to come. It was a combination of shock and disbelief that this was becoming the norm, and we didn't know how to explain this in words to our families, or anyone really. We kept everyone in the dark, even ourselves.

Waiting for the results was excruciating. I couldn't concentrate. I was in a state of disbelief that this was actually happening. I tried to keep myself distracted, so I signed up to attend a professional lunch meeting. I had just pulled in to park and my phone rang with a Dallas area phone number. I knew this was it. My hands were shaking so bad I could barely press the answer button. I sat there in the middle of the parking lot trembling as I answered the phone with my vehicle turned off. "Is this Melissa Copp, Calan's Mom?" asked the neurologist. "Yes, it is." I exhaled with barely enough breath to say the words. "Ma'am, your son's brain is fully formed with no sign of abnormality of the soft tissue. His optic nerves are also fully formed and connected to the brain with no sign of issue as well." He uttered the words so matter of fact that instant relief came pouring over me. With tears streaming down my face, shivering with emotion, I asked, "Are you 100% sure?" He replied, "Yes. The scans were seen by several radiologists and myself." It was like a brand-new start, a new beginning into parenthood! But then I was quickly snapped out of it, being jolted by the reality that something wasn't right. Why was Calan not strong enough to hold his head up or sit unsupported or hold his bottle? Something was wrong. Very wrong. If it wasn't a brain abnormality, then what was it? We certainly thought that if we weren't dealing with a cancer diagnosis or a brain abnormality, we could handle whatever came our way. We certainly never expected where our journey would take us next...

Three months went by after that fateful day of hearing that our son's brain scan was normal. Per the neurologist's recommendations, we got Calan evaluated for physical therapy at the local hospital in Waco which had an outpatient rehabilitation clinic. I still remember his very first physical therapy appointment. It's like a mixture of military boot camp and torture devices in the shape of toys being used to increase muscle tone in your body. Our nine-month-old son had already endured months of colic, acid reflux, lactose intolerance, a brain MRI and was now doing physical therapy sessions several times a week with no cause in sight for his issues. We started physical therapy right away in hopes that he would build up his strength. Our weeks were now dictated by a therapy schedule and our milestones were dictated by therapy standards instead of the typical developmental milestone chart you see in a pediatrician's office. There were no support groups I felt comfortable going to, nowhere that we seemed to fit for fear of judgment. We avoided the "why" questions from family, friends and strangers. "Why is he not crawling yet?" "Why is he not reaching for toys?" "Why? Why? Why?" We started to feel isolated, scared and broken. In between weekly therapy sessions, we kept adding a different specialist to the mix to find out the reasons for Calan's low muscle tone and gross motor delays. The yearning for an answer to these questions became the driving motivation for never giving up. We survived these days one by one, without hesitation. That is what we had to do for our son, for each other. It became a mission as his mother to find out the cause. I would not stop until we had answers.

By the time Calan was 1½ years old, he had seen a half dozen specialists in genetics, neurology, endocrinology, ophthalmology, speech pathology and audiology. We also learned about and enrolled Calan in a program through the state called Early Childhood Intervention (ECI). A case worker came every two weeks to our house. This ended up being one of the only programs we qualified for which is just a consult-based program until the child ages out at three years old. We didn't find any value in this program at all, but it was something. He was barely able to hold his own head up at this point and could sit assisted. Every now and then I would find myself daydreaming of Calan running into my arms to give me a hug. I was curious what that felt like. Other friends who were having children were all typical-developing and with every day that passed, we were distancing ourselves from a typical life. This was a recurring dream that I had throughout his first years. I longed to see Calan strong enough to sit unassisted or babble. He wasn't even able to say "momma" yet. During this time, we saw a fighter though. He fought hard. It kept us going.

He cried at every therapy appointment, through every uncomfortable position, all the while spending 30-45 minutes several times a week with a physical therapist building up his muscle tone one molecular cell at a time. As we were adding specialists every month to his roster, we racked up over 700 miles driving to all the out-of-town appointments. We saw the ugly side of medical insurance since most tests and therapy appointments weren't covered under our plan. He had undergone two brain MRIs, an EEG to check for seizure activity and had several blood draws for various tests to find answers; the answers we wouldn't get for over four more years. Everything kept coming back normal, ruling out dozens of probable medical conditions one at a time. This wasn't the childhood I predicted for my son. No one predicts this. Interestingly, when I was pregnant with Calan I never had any dreams imagining what my child would look or be like, what kinds of things we would do together. Not one dream. I know so many soon-to-be moms have vivid dreams of pushing their baby in a swing or holding hands with them as they learn to walk. It was odd to me that never happened and now I know why. God was preparing me for a life not expected but earned. Not only did we have the expenses of a new baby, but we had the expenses of an unexpected and undiagnosed medical condition. We earned our parent badges through the blood, sweat and tears of raising a medically fragile child. Nothing was ever given to us, but earned over time. Looking back, I'm grateful for these intense moments because it prepared me to be smarter, stronger and more responsible for my family.

> *Normal is a word we came to hear quite often, and a word I began to loathe. Test after test came back normal. What I quickly learned regarding medicine is how many tests are designed to find out what you DON'T have, more so than what you do. It was obvious Calan wasn't normal by the typical definition, but as Melissa said, he was, and still is, a fighter.*

As the days turned into weeks and the weeks turned into months and the months turned into years, we saw new specialist after new specialist. We even tried taking Calan to see a pediatric dietician which helped us figure out how to bulk up his little muscles, but overall it was just another task added onto our laundry list full of caretaking items we were given. After mounting frustrations with each specialist, we were given a blanket diagnosis of Hypotonic Cerebral Palsy, but we didn't take that as the answer. Heck, the neurologist that gave it to us didn't even feel comfortable giving that diagnosis to us. This was the first time a specialist told us that we may never find out what was truly the cause of the symptoms. It was also the first time my gut told me that we had to keep fighting to find answers, even if specialists would tell us otherwise. Thank goodness, I listened.

> *I attended every single therapy visit. Thinking about it now, it just seems like a dream. When you're deep in the middle of life, sometimes it's hard to realize how difficult a time it was. I was Calan's cheerleader. I pushed him; I coached him along. Therapy was difficult, and I insisted on going alone as much as possible because I didn't want Melissa to hear the crying, and sometimes screaming, as Calan worked so hard to obtain his goals; goals that seem so simple to a typically developing child: roll over; reach across your body to grab an item on the left side of your body with your right hand, and vice versa; try to stand independently for two seconds without falling; and eventually, try to take steps in the parallel bars so as to eventually move on to using a walker or other assistive device.*
>
> *I developed a rapport with our physical therapist and I kept her in the loop on all the specialists seen and tests being conducted. During one of our appointments she looked at me and said, "Calan may be a million-dollar baby. Sometimes all the testing in the world never truly finds an answer." That thought continued echoing in my head each and every time a test came back "normal."*

As the years went by, difficulties increased and frustrations magnified. Medical bills kept piling high. No help in sight. At this point, we averaged a medical appointment every three to four days continuously throughout the year. Both of us worked full time jobs, trying to keep a low profile. We kept up our mental and physical strength to continue life as "normal" while we knew in our hearts it was going to be different than anyone we know. We hadn't met anyone else raising a medically fragile child. We kept most of our anguish, frustration and stress due to our medical journey with Calan a secret. At my job, any time anyone would ask me about Calan, I dodged the question and quickly changed the subject. Not that I was embarrassed by him or our situation, but the honest truth was we were living an unconventional life that not many people could understand so avoided discussion in hopes of making it more bearable. This meant we could stay in our own little world and keep the struggles private for as long as possible just to stay sane. It was dangerous to keep in, but we knew that if we didn't understand this ourselves, how were we going to explain it to our family, friends and employers? We kept most of the appointments under the radar, taking turns so we didn't take too much time off work.

During this time, I discovered there was a supplemental health care plan through the government you could apply for called Medicaid, and we could possibly qualify through a waiver program called the Medically

Dependent Children's Program (MDCP). It would help cover the voluminous amount of medical expenses we were enduring. I expected to fill out a form and we would get an approval letter soon. I couldn't have been more wrong about this process. This was the first of many failed attempts at getting the help my family so desperately needed. We received a call saying a nurse was going to come by to see if Calan met the medically necessary criteria for the program. She came. She accessed. She left. The very next week, we got a certified letter mailed to us saying we were denied due to not meeting the medically dependent criteria. We were heartbroken, not just for Calan, but for our family. We weren't sure how we were going to survive financially, mentally and physically without supplemental help. It kept going like this for another three years. I would apply for a governmental program or join a list and no help came. Without hesitation. Without break. Without an understanding as to why. All the while, continuing the desire to do whatever it took for our son to live life to the fullest.

> *Frustration does not BEGIN to explain how I felt. I was so angry inside that with all of the issues we'd been dealing with, no program was out there that could help our family. I had seen other families in therapy that were getting new equipment, equipment we NEEDED to assist Calan, yet they didn't have to pay for it as it was covered under a program. Meanwhile, we were having to prioritize every expense and determine just how beneficial a suggested piece of equipment would be. While we wanted to do everything in our power to help Calan, without financial assistance, there were just some items we knew could help him that we were unable to purchase on our own.*
>
> *I began to pick the brain of any therapist, Assistive Technology Professional (ATP) or parent that would listen, to try and figure out how their child met the requirements of various programs. Every program I would tell Melissa about, she had either already applied for and been denied, or we didn't meet the requirements to begin with.*
>
> *It was around this time I was told something I still find appalling to this day, which immediately grounded me. Trying to help, someone told me our best bet was to get a divorce, one of us quit our job and the other take a minimum wage job, and then we should be able to obtain assistance. They were aware of others that had to make the decision to destroy their families in order to survive. That day solidified my resolve to NEVER let that happen to our family. Melissa and I made a vow to God that we would live as husband and wife until death do us part, and NO government program was worth breaking that vow!*

You would think after being in countless hospitals, seeing dozens of specialists and having experienced a voluminous amount of medical appointments that we would have seen a social worker by this time, but that did not happen. We learned the hard way that undiagnosed and untreated conditions rarely, if ever, see a social worker unless a medical condition is discovered in utero and the child undergoes either surgery or treatment for a condition right away. We went undetected in the support side of the hospital and health insurance for many years. It wasn't until Calan was four years of age that I started to research grants to apply for so we could survive financially. I was so incredibly naive to the process before but became an expert as I went. This is one time I wish my gut had told me to stand up for my family sooner. In so many ways, I felt like I had let them down. Our debt was massive, our anguish was mounting, and a wave of guilt stayed with me like a dark cloud over my head that I couldn't fix it. This feeling of guilt would end up becoming my driving force to work harder than I've ever worked before to get my son the medical help he deserved. This drive inside me hasn't stopped to this day.

Calan was now wearing ankle-foot orthosis to help with stability and using devices like a posterior walker and a manual wheelchair to aid in mobility. Everything felt like a blur. Appointments were running together and only a handful of family and close friends knew what was happening. It seemed like we were constantly scheduling and going to one doctor or specialist after another. Trying to balance work and medical appointments was a real struggle. Calan was having trouble with posture, muscle movement, incontinence, speaking, choking when eating and drinking, aspiration and had countless visits to the hospital and ER for difficulty breathing and fever. We were on our second neurologist, added a child development specialist, endocrinologist, an otolaryngologist and countless others. We were seeing up to 12 specialists at once racking up over 800 miles in driving to each location and no one could figure out the cause of Calan's medical issues.

During one of the appointments, a neurologist we hadn't seen before came in to the exam room in a state of complete disbelief. He couldn't believe that the child sitting in front of him was the same child in the medical file he was holding in his hands. His chart was full of words like "hypotonia" and "floppy baby syndrome," so he expected to see a child needing help breathing and other basic functions through medical devices. This was the first time that a specialist mentioned that we may never find out the cause of his issues and that he may never walk independently. It was the first time we felt we were given an honest opinion, but knew that we needed to continue looking for answers. We moved onto researching another neurologist for a third opinion. Although the news never got better over time, and it was increasingly frustrating to hear that specialists in their field had absolutely no idea what Calan was born with, we never lost hope that one day we would find out. It was important to remember why we continued to fight for Calan. That he was earning his mobility one successful goal at a time through his therapy sessions, so we could at least do this for him. We needed to continue searching for answers. He was fighting for his life, so we kept fighting too.

Calan was getting stronger. Goals he had worked years on in therapy were finally progressing. He was gaining enough balance and control to be able to take steps in his posterior walker. Someone had to be hovering around him at all times for safety, and his stamina was such that he could only go for short stints, but his determination was so inspiring. He would look at me proudly, but inside I was conflicted. I was beaming with joy with what he had accomplished, but I never allowed myself to truly deal with the anguish of seeing my son struggle so much.

This might have sounded like an absolute worst time to have another baby to most people, but we knew in our hearts it was the perfect time. In all honesty, we were waiting for Calan to walk on his own, but it wasn't looking good. He was doing so great in physical therapy and using the support of a pediatric posterior walker for his mobility, but we knew we didn't want to wait any longer. We knew we wanted to have another child and for Calan to have a sibling to share life with. Even though we were feeling heartache and anguish about Calan's situation, we still had absolutely no idea the cause of his medical condition. Throughout some of the conversations with our genetic counselor and geneticist, there was a chance this could be a genetic condition that has still gone undetected. There was no way to know for sure, especially since none of the tests were coming back abnormal. But we knew in our hearts that no matter what, we would accept whatever child God created for us to raise. We knew our family would be perfect the way it was. That was one of the only things we knew for certain.

After finding out about my second pregnancy, we decided to continue our diagnostic journey for Calan and see a third neurologist in Austin, about 96 miles away, 192 miles round trip. We still wanted answers. We were determined not to give up, especially now with another child on the way. During the initial physical exam, the neurologist observed Calan had zero reflexes and low muscle tone. He noticed that when he pushed and tried to create a reflex reaction in Calan's body, his muscles were stagnant. We had already performed all major diagnostic tests at this point, except one. The neurologist was certain this was a muscle condition since all the tests that have ever been taken by all the specialists were normal. Typically, when trying to diagnose a medical condition, there are 12 basic tests to be performed which should result in a diagnosis, unless it's never been seen before and can't be detected. The most invasive diagnostic test is the muscle biopsy, and we left it as a last resort, hoping we would have found answers already. We were out of options. We were hoping we could avoid this test for Calan, but it was looking like it was our last shot at finding any answers. We were mentally and physically drained, however, as we had been going at this for years and years and hit a level of exhaustion that could not be powered through. We needed a break. We hit the proverbial medical fatigue wall with the hundreds and hundreds of appointments, tests, therapies and consults we had just experienced without pause for the last three years. We were also extremely financially strained with no help in sight, and were expecting our second son later that Spring. Yes! A second son! We were beyond thrilled. We decided to wait until after the baby was born to have Calan do the muscle biopsy surgery.

> *Learning a second son was on the way was truly a gift, but I was concerned about how we were going to be able to make it as a family. The enormous financial pressure we were under with the costs of equipment, medical bills and normal living expenses were piling up. The expenses had pinched us so much we decided we had to sell our first home and find a house with a lower mortgage payment. So, in September of 2011 we put our home on the market and began looking for another. We were giving up our very first home we purchased together so we could make it. We knew we had to sacrifice in more ways than we wanted so we could continue as a family. It is so easy to look back now and understand that God has always been directing us, even when we couldn't see it. Our home sold in a few months and we were in a new home by November, right before the holidays. It had more room to grow as a family and was closer to Calan's school.*

A few months before our second son was born, Calan became very ill. He had another battle with pneumonia and RSV that caused him to be so incredibly weak that we took him back to the hospital where he also got treated for bronchitis a few days later. His body was having a hard time fighting, so the doctors intervened to help him as much as they could. It was during this hospital visit that we knew we had to let go of some of the dreams we had for our family. We might not be able to ever go on vacation or be able to buy nice things for each other, but as long as we were in this together, that was all we needed. This sacrifice continued daily. We identified things that we no longer needed or weren't necessary and lived without them. We truly let go of those dreams and replaced them with new ones. No matter where we were or what hospital room we were in, as long as we were together, the rest didn't matter.

On March 15, 2012, Calan became a big brother to our son Lawson. My pregnancy with Lawson was also normal with no complications, just the extended morning sickness that lasted the entire pregnancy. He was measuring a little bigger than normal so my Ob/Gyn induced me on his due date. He came into this world with a loud cry at a whopping nine pounds, ready to let us know he was here to complete our family.

> *The arrival of Lawson was a very bittersweet moment for me. Melissa and I had been dealing with so much and felt like we were all alone. Our marriage had been pushed to the breaking point, and we each had so much pent up anger and resentment; Melissa feeling guilty for not being able to fix all our financial problems, me mourning the loss of getting to experience "normal" activities with Calan, like sports. But more than that, I was scared I could never love another child as much as I loved Calan. During Melissa's pregnancy, Calan was having issues going to sleep on his own, so I would hold him every night until he fell asleep and then put him to bed. I had bonded so deeply with Calan through therapy and holding him at night, I couldn't imagine having another child that would compete for my love and attention. But once I saw Lawson, I felt the same joy all over again about being a daddy.*

After bringing Lawson home, he demonstrated extremely similar issues that Calan showed during the first few months of feeding. Lawson's legs would stiffen, and he would occasionally cry in pain while feeding. This time I was calm. This time I was armed with experience. This time I knew what to do. After about six weeks into breastfeeding, Lawson having colic the entire time, I decided to take him to the hospital to get an x-ray. He was diagnosed with silent reflux and was put on Zantac, the same as Calan.

We also switched Lawson to "liquid gold" right away, which was a special formula that we knew aided with super-sensitivities and had worked with Calan. It almost instantly made a difference to Lawson's demeanor.

We had a happy baby for the first time, and his colic almost dissipated thereafter. When that happened, we were able to discover that Lawson was showing the same symptoms: low muscle tone, nonexistent reflexes, missed milestones and a slew of other issues. I decided to advocate for Lawson as soon as possible with his pediatrician. We intervened with physical therapy and started sessions when he was six months old. This time there wasn't the frustration or loneliness. You saw a family fight together, a family that felt whole, a family that felt powerful in strength and commitment. We could let this define us in a negative way or a positive way. We rolled up our sleeves and said to each other, "We don't know what we are up against and that's ok, we just do this 110%." So that's exactly what we did.

On our seventh wedding anniversary, October 8, 2012, we took both boys to the neurologist for a follow up appointment. It was typical for us to book appointments on birthdays, anniversary dates and other special occasions. Sacrifices like this would happen every day from here on out. We traded anniversary dinners for specialist appointments and tried to squeeze in giving a card to each other every once in a while. These days became harder for me to accept. I tried not feeling angry about it or sorry for myself, but I will admit that these days were harder for me to accept than others. We had a new normal way of celebrating and that had to be ok. We couldn't afford fancy dinners or gifts to each other, but our commitment to being there, hearing whatever harsh reality we were dealt that day, was done together. Offering me his strength in lieu of presents ended up being the best gift Jody has ever given me to this day. We were determined to be there for the boys, together. Determination is a powerful tool. It's what we see in each other. It's what we see in our boys. By now Lawson had mimicked a lot of the same issues Calan had in infancy, so we knew at this point it was likely they shared a genetic condition. The neurologist shared the same assessment, but still wanted us to continue with the muscle biopsy before performing any other tests. He felt certain it was going to come back with positive results for "congenital myopathy" as a possible diagnosis. We spent another year on and off going to see more specialists, including a new geneticist which mentioned a test called *whole exome sequencing*, a genetic test that was brand new on the market.

It was a blood test that was performed to dissect whole genomes down to the microscopic level for deletions, additions and mutations of genes. She said insurance companies were not known to cover this test and it was close to $30,000 to perform, so we tabled it for the time being and put our energy into the muscle biopsy.

> *The decision to follow the advice of the neurologist to perform the muscle biopsy was heart-wrenching. Melissa and I had discussed at length, many times, about how we did not want to do ANYTHING invasive if we didn't have to. After hearing from two geneticists about the whole exome sequencing test and the high cost (and that was only if insurance approved), we agreed this may be our only option to determine what was causing the issues with the boys. As is the case in life, you have to play with the cards dealt to you. Due to the issues we had already experienced with insurance, we fully expected to be denied for the test altogether, or that the cost of the test would be too much for us to handle based on estimates we had been given.*

There aren't many times in my life that I wish I could turn back time to rethink a decision. I usually stand by what I decide without hesitation. I am tedious in my research and confident when making a choice. However, I really wish I could turn back time and change my decision to do the muscle biopsy. It was not only scarring for us to go through, but changed our five-year-old Calan in so many ways after he had this surgery performed. He remembers everything. We remember everything. The difficulty coming out of anesthesia, the vomiting, the angst and worry. Want to take a guess what the test results were? You guessed it! Normal. Again. It was now five years into our diagnostic journey and we still had no answers except knowing all the conditions they tested negative for. Finding out these normal tests results yet again has taken a toll. It took our breath away every single time we heard it. We logged over 2,600 miles to hear "normal" over and over and over again, but when we got home, we didn't experience "normal." We still changed diapers due to medical incontinence. We still assisted with feedings due to aspiration and choking. We still carried and lifted and transferred the boys to move from one place to the other. This wasn't normal and there was no explanation for it. How was this possible? Jody and I would often fight and scream due to our frustration and the pain coming out. Why were we having to go through all this pain and suffering just to find out that no answers existed? I often talked to God during these times and wanted to hear something back, but I didn't. I know now that I wasn't ready to talk. I wasn't ready to hear the answers.

Melissa and I struggled with everything. We were so exhausted mentally and physically that it felt as though we were ships in the night. When we would try to communicate, it either came out wrong or the other person misinterpreted what the other was trying to say. We are a very active family and sometimes Melissa would inundate us with trips and events just to keep us busy and our mind off our struggles. We openly talked about divorce and discussed if we would be better off, but deep down each of us KNEW God put us together for a reason and to just grind it out. It's still tough, but our love is deeper than we ever thought possible and knowing we aren't alone in this journey has saved us many times.

There were so many difficult parts to our journey, but one of the hardest ones to face on a daily basis was answering the same question over and over when someone would stop us. "Excuse me, can I ask why your boys can't walk? What is wrong with their legs?" I always answered the same way I do today. "There isn't anything wrong with them, but they do have a condition that weakens their muscles and requires them to use assisted devices for their mobility." We try to always stay positive around the boys. We make sure they know that nothing is WRONG with them, and they are perfect the way they were born. They love using their devices to this day because it gives them their independence and mobility to life. Without them, they would have to rely on someone else for everything, including getting from here to there all day long. We avoid using the terms "disabled," "handicapped" or "wheelchair bound" because we see them as able bodied, just differently abled.

We have come to learn that our boys are NOT wheelchair bound, but only bound by the barriers they come across. I looked around and saw barriers everywhere. They were in our house. I was cleaning up the kitchen and we had transferred the boys outside on the screened in porch so they could feel the breeze and watch the birds in the backyard as we often let them do. Calan was in his walker looking out and Lawson was strapped in his gait trainer on wheels so it would assist him upright to look out. I don't know why, but this moment stopped me in my tracks and became the reason I knew something better was out there for them. It drove me to find a better life for them where barriers wouldn't prevent them from playing in their own backyard. Life took on a different meaning from this moment on. We began to focus on the boys' ability and the joy we found in that.

Being new to the special needs community, as many special needs parents can relate, we felt isolated and alone at first. We were inundated with so many appointments and tests the first five years that we hardly had time to focus on activities that were fun. What made it worse was not knowing what our children's condition was, leaving us feeling helpless. We began to wonder what type of life our boys would live. But then God began working in our lives in a much different way. Melissa struck up a conversation with a woman at a local health fair one day and mentioned the boys. She told Melissa about their basketball program and said there was a league for special needs children. With Melissa and I both growing up playing sports, we decided we needed to give it a try and expose Calan to as much as possible. This was the beginning of a much brighter future.

We enjoyed having this new connection with Calan, but more importantly, we began to make connections with other families in the special needs community. We finally began to feel accepted and were surprised to see the vast array of children and diagnoses in our area. Calan had been using a posterior walker, but could only go for small amounts of time due to his stamina. So, around this time, we got Calan his first wheelchair. We had internally fought the idea of a wheelchair for a little while, afraid it would be a negative, but oh how we were mistaken! We were shocked and amazed at how quickly he was able to grasp the use of his chair and the freedom and independence he was finally able to experience! It truly began to open our eyes to what the future would hold for us, but unfortunately, we also began to really see the lack of accessibility for those using wheelchairs in the community.

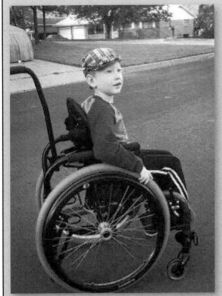

Through these activities, we started connecting more and more with our community which led us to another program called Challenger Little sports leagues began to take away some of the tension of the financial crunch, but of course, the issue was always in the back of my mind. Since the boys have never had monetary assistance, we were unsure of what to do and were too proud to really let anyone know what was going on and ask for help. We would mention we didn't receive assistance and people were shocked, most of the other families in our new community did receive assistance of some sort. So even in a new circle, we still felt somewhat isolated in that regard.

We received denial letter after denial letter in the mail for all government assisted programs. I knew there had to be a way that families could survive financially, so I started researching grant options through other organizations. This was a tough pill to swallow, asking for help, but a necessary evil to survive. The biggest lesson I have learned in this journey is not to wait on someone else to help you, but learn to help yourself by initiating it. Arm yourself with options. Arm yourself with assistance and know where to go for the right help. Help exists. You just have to find it. I found several organizations that assisted us through these next few years. It would never erase the financial debt that accrued the first five years or so, but it was a start. Our hardest time was when we found ourselves raising not one, but two medically fragile children who were denied all government assisted programs with both of us working full time jobs and battling 24-hour exhaustion. We still found energy to fight like our two boys did every day. We knew help was out there, so we went to conferences, symposiums and expos learning what resources existed. We started seeing a light where there was no light before.

When so many gave up on us in the past, there were that many waiting to help us and more. We started getting more confident in taking this monster

of a mission on and tackling the unobtainable, the unimaginable. I started writing grants and submitting applications for equipment and diagnostic tests for the boys, and they started getting approved little by little. We began getting the much-needed help we were so desperately seeking. It provided us the courage to continue searching for a medical diagnosis for our boys. All the specialists that we had gone to had already discharged us without answers because there was nothing else, medically, they knew to do. However, I did not stop. I would not stop. A few days later, a friend gave me an article clipping entitled "Gene Scans Solve Mystery Diseases" in the local paper. In the article, it discussed a study that focused on sequencing of DNA that was done by a specialist in Houston. It evaluated 250 patients that had little-to-no diagnosis and the sequencing test proved fruitful for providing some answers in the patient's gene flaws. I knew this was our next step in trying to find answers for our boys. I couldn't wait to call the very next day to get a referral. I found out that the specialist was out of the Department of Pediatric Medicine in Genetics at Texas Children's Hospital in Houston, 196 miles away. We were now almost six years into our diagnostic journey hoping for answers soon so that we could provide better specialized care that the boys needed to survive.

Our initial consult with a geneticist at Texas Children's Hospital was six months later. By now we knew the drill: physical exam, genetic counseling, medical history review and recommendations on genetics testing. The only difference this time was that during the clinic visit, the geneticists predicted that the most likely diagnosis for the boys is "hereditary spastic paraplegia." They were extremely confident that this was our diagnosis... with utmost certainty. For testing, he recommended doing *whole exome sequencing* to see if it would support the diagnosis. This is the test that came up a year before, but we were told was not covered by insurance. We had to make the decision to risk piling up more medical debt or possibly never finding answers. So, we went for it. For now, the geneticist suggested doing bloodwork on Calan with both Jody and I providing a blood sample for comparison-testing. We all agreed that if it wasn't necessary for Lawson to provide a blood sample at this time, then we would wait to see what the first round of tests revealed. Up until now, we had been able to spare Lawson on all diagnostic tests and didn't want to expose him to unnecessary tests if we didn't have to.

By now Melissa and I had been to numerous doctors and specialists and heard many of the same questions, so we had a pretty good routine down. We never really knew what to expect, but we were pleasantly surprised with the amount of time the geneticist spent with us, really listening to our answers and what we were telling them about the boys. We ended up meeting two geneticists and three of their staff during the initial consult. They were brainstorming between themselves, throwing out tons of medical terms. Surprisingly, Melissa and I kept up with their conversation rather well. We knew more medical jargon than the average person and it started rolling off our tongues just as articulately. When the geneticist finally suggested the whole exome sequencing test, we were both relieved to know yet another geneticist was in agreement for the test, but worried about the cost as we had already been warned how expensive the test can be, and that many insurances wouldn't cover it because it was still relatively new. But we knew we had to go for it if we wanted a shot at finding out what was causing our boys' medical condition.

We made a trip to Houston once more to do the blood draws in September of 2014. We were all scared, but determined. It would take about three months to get the results back. I did everything to keep my mind off the fact that we were waiting for test results that would possibly change our lives. This is when I realized something about myself. All the times before, I was hoping that the results would come back normal so that I would have proof that nothing was wrong with my child, but this was the first time that I was wanting test results to come back positive. I knew if I didn't face this head on, then my sons didn't have a chance. I needed to know what we were dealing with here. The months went by one excruciating month at a time and Calan fell very ill almost three months after the blood draws occurred. We transported him to the local hospital by ambulance because his situation was very dire. He was diagnosed with the H1N1 virus and bronchitis. He was treated and released. I later regretted not forcing his admittance. We were not armed with the knowledge that we have now.

This was one of the scariest episodes to date. I had dropped off Lawson at daycare and was on my way to work when I received a frantic phone call from Melissa saying Calan had a nosebleed that wouldn't stop, and he was unresponsive. I raced home to find Melissa sitting on the floor, soaked in blood, and Calan lying across her lap with labored breathing. After a quick

> *discussion on the best course of action, we decided to call the ambulance so they could quickly administer whatever might be needed and get Calan to the hospital immediately. It was a very long morning and our anxiety was at an all-time high because he had been throwing up so much blood, something we never experienced. We were told it was because he had swallowed so much blood from the bloody nose, but it was terrifying.*

The very next day as I was caring for Calan having just been released from the hospital, my phone rang. It was the genetics counselor with Texas Children's Hospital with the lab results from the whole exome sequencing done on Calan, myself and Jody. My heart started racing and I barely had any breath to answer hello. The genetics case worker advised me that they had found two genetic changes in the PNPT1 gene which was also present in both parents as well. They call this change "combined oxidative phosphorylation deficiency type 13" and recommended just doing target testing on Lawson to see if it comes up on his DNA evaluation. She mentioned that this genetic mutation isn't linked to any known syndrome at this time. There were no mentions of it in medical journals or published articles. Before we let this information even sink in, we made arrangements for Lawson to get his blood drawn. We make our third 196-mile trip to Houston on Valentine's Day 2015 to get the final piece of our puzzle completed. Lawson provided a blood sample to the lab, and we wait another six weeks to find out if it's in fact what has been plaguing our sons since birth.

> *In between all the doctor and specialist visits, adaptive sports leagues and work, we had a different type of incident, one that changed our lives for the better. In January of 2015, right before Lawson had his blood draw, I was involved in a vehicle accident in my crew cab pickup, our family truck because it was the only vehicle we had large enough to transport our family and the two wheelchairs. Luckily, I had just dropped Calan off at school and was driving alone when another pickup didn't see me and pulled out in front of me. I was unhurt, but the damage to the pickup was substantial and my vehicle ended up being totaled. As if our stress levels weren't high enough already, this just upped the ante.*
>
> *I had been researching vehicles for years prior to the accident and knew our next vehicle would need to be a minivan for our family. When the accident occurred, I immediately began thinking about how we could get a minivan to give us the flexibility that type of transportation offered. The only problem was the cost. Since the accident was 100 percent not my fault,*

we knew the money would be going towards a new van. But we also knew what we were getting from insurance wasn't enough to get our payments low enough, and we were running out of time as the rental would only be covered by insurance for a short period.

Up to this point, Melissa and I had been pretty quiet and reserved in what we told people about our life. Only a few of our closest friends and family truly knew what we were going through, but even they never really understood our hardships and we had plenty of "advice" on how we should be handling our situation. But Melissa and I knew this was bigger than us, and after much prayer and a few late night "talks," we finally made the decision to ask for help.

Melissa and I work together as a team so well because we're yin and yang. Honestly, I'm a pretty skeptical person and just didn't see how anyone would be willing to help us, whereas Melissa has a very positive, nothing-can-stop-us attitude and felt others would understand our need, and it was desperate at the moment. Melissa finally persuaded me to create a GoFundMe account and boy was I wrong! I quickly learned the power of social media and how much our family was loved, restoring more faith in humanity than I ever thought possible. Within three days, friends, family and strangers had generously donated over $18,000.00! We couldn't believe it. We were shocked and stunned, me much more than her. But because of the love and generosity of others, we were able to bridge the gap and get manageable payments so we could purchase a new minivan as our family vehicle!

As promised, we received a call from the genetics counselor when the results came in about six weeks after Lawson had his blood draw. She didn't want to give me any results over the phone this time, but insisted we come to Houston to speak to the geneticist in person. On April 20, 2015 we drove down to Houston for the fourth time and walked into the small exam room in the genetics department at Texas Children's Hospital. Within a few minutes we were told that

Lawson's results were consistent with the test results for Calan's whole exome sequencing. The geneticist mentioned that all they knew about the PNPT1 gene is that it causes the mitochondria not to work properly which are the energy producers to all major organ systems. He mentioned that there were no other known cases that have appeared in medical journals other than a pair of siblings in Morocco that had different variations of the mutation than Lawson or Calan had. I remember him telling us that he wouldn't be able to give us information on their life expectancy or prognosis. I carry that sting with me wherever I go and it never leaves me.

We were almost seven years and 15 specialists into our diagnostic journey, and we finally identified that it was a rare genetic mitochondrial disorder with no name and no cure. Relief did not come pouring over me like I thought it would. It was a slow, gradual understanding of what was happening. These were world renown geneticists telling us to go home and give these boys the best quality of life possible, and there was nothing more to be told... no fix, no cure or understanding of what this was. We could have easily let this be our story; gone home, done nothing, accepted it as our fate. This was a pivotal moment for us. Was this a tragedy? Sure. Was this going to be a difficult road ahead? Absolutely. But at this moment, I took it as a sign that our family was meant for more, that our boys deserved to live a life that was full and accessible because they earned every single ounce of mobility through hard work and determination.

We tried to return back to life as usual, but we were different. Life was different. We were now armed with a little bit of information. We knew what they had was mitochondrial-based, so we used that to our advantage. Since we left Texas Children's Hospital without a plan, we created one. We researched mitochondrial-based research, clinics and conferences on our own. One day after work, Jody came up to me and told me he found a symposium that focused on Mitochondrial Medicine and it was in Houston! We felt compelled to attend it so we could learn as much as possible about what we were up against with the boys.

Before Melissa and I attended the United Mitochondrial Disease Foundation (UMDF) conference, we had been talking about remodeling our current home, or trying to build a home for the boys that would be 100 percent accessible. After attending the conference, we knew we needed to research these options much more intently due to what we learned about mitochondrial diseases and how they affect those afflicted. This was a lifelong battle and we needed to do whatever we could to make it possible for the boys to survive as long as possible. It was now all about survival.

We began talking in earnest with remodelers, builders and anyone that would listen to us about what we were looking to accomplish. We had contacted our realtor in late 2014 and had already been looking at homes and properties so we could explore all our options. Our realtor had taken us to one particular property, a fully built home on the outside but completely gutted on the inside. While we really liked what it could offer our family, it seemed to be too big of a project to take on and we continued to look elsewhere. Little did we know God would lead us back to that particular property a year later.

The Mitochondrial conference was incredibly fruitful and we ended up meeting the world renown neurologist that specializes in mitochondrial-based conditions. A year later, she became our boys' primary specialist and opened our minds to prepare for what to actually expect living with a mitochondrial condition, something that was missing from our lives for so long. However, during one of our follow-up appointments with our new Mito Specialist, we were faced with another major decision. She recommended that we move our family closer to Houston so that the boys could be closer to their critical care team to get life sustaining care when needed.

After all that we had been through, we were now being asked to make another massive decision. We had finally found the property we considered to be our dream home, but were running into hurdle after hurdle in trying to obtain it. As has usually been the case for us, one of our biggest hurdles in obtaining the property we found was financial. Now the specialist we waited almost seven years to find was telling us we need to move closer to Houston? Was it a sign that we needed to explore other options? We weren't quite ready to make that decision.

Around this time, I had been doing research to see if there were conferences or trade shows where I could see the different types of equipment available for the boys. I like to know what our options are and to understand what therapists are talking about when recommending equipment for the boys. In my research, I came across a free event called the Abilities Expo and it just happened to be in Houston in August. This is exactly what I had been looking

> *for, as most of the largest equipment suppliers attend the conference to show their newest products, from wheelchairs to service dogs; there is something for everyone. As luck would have it, they were also having a meet and greet with author Tammy Simmons who wrote "The Funding Guide for Children with Disabilities" which Melissa was excited about going to. Melissa, being the most driven woman I know, was determined to pick the brain of the author and see what options she might have in mind for helping us obtain our dream property. Not only did Melissa meet the author, but the author was so impressed with Melissa's enthusiasm and drive, she introduced us to the publisher of the book, Melanie Davis, who lives in the North Houston area and was interested in personally helping us to reach our goal. From this fateful event, a partnership was forged.*

After meeting Melanie and Tammy, it recharged me more than ever. I felt compelled to provide a way for my boys to have a home that was built truly for them. The boys deserved independence. They spend hours each week, years working on a single task and earn every step and movement they make. They deserved a home worthy of this determination. A 100% accessible home. Not 50% or even 80%, but a home where every inch could be accessed. At this point, they had never felt what it was   like to wash their hands at a sink or play in their own backyard due to immense barriers. Over the next few months, Melanie and I came up with a strategy to fundraise to meet our goal of making the home 100% accessible because we knew we wouldn't accept anything less. We had brought in an architect to help us figure out a layout that would make the most sense in providing all the accessible features we needed for the boys to be independent. The cost estimate was more than what we could handle in addition to all the specific pieces of equipment built into the home to help us care for the boys. We came up with a plan to do a large- scale community fundraiser event. We knew the event would need to   be pretty large to fundraise enough to bridge the gap on what we were lacking financially, and the Giving Trees Festival was born. It was an event that helped form community partnerships and celebrate giving the gift of accessibility. We would have over 20 decorated Christmas trees on display at our local conference center during a busy shopping weekend. All decorated trees were donated by local businesses, individuals, schools and civic organizations. It was a sight to see and the giving nature of the event brought me to tears.

> Melissa sought out a non-profit to co-host with and formed a partnership we value to this day. Melissa worked tirelessly from September through December, putting together and pulling off an event I honestly felt was impossible. The event was amazing and something I considered an absolute success, but in the end, we were unable to fundraise enough to purchase the property. Melissa was devastated. She had worked so hard and felt as though she had failed our family. I however, believed it was a sign that perhaps we were destined to move closer to Houston.
>
> We secretly made the decision to move closer to Houston, back to where we both went to college, College Station. Only our close friends and family were made aware of our decision and we began applying for jobs. Through a contact I had made, I began speaking to a new home builder in College Station that was moved by our story and offered to help us more than we had ever been helped before. While Melissa never gave up hope that our dream home in Waco could still become a possibility, I had already moved on and mentally prepared myself for the challenge of uprooting our family to a new city. And that's when it happened...

I have never been good with accepting defeat or failure. I felt responsible for losing out on what I thought was the home of our dreams. It's helped mold me into a wonderful mother and allowed me to keep going through the extremely difficult times that laid ahead of us as a family. In fact, one of the life lessons my mother instilled in me is to never quit something you start. So, I made one last attempt to reach out to the Magnolia Foundation to see if they had a grant program in place to assist us with the many pieces of equipment, we desperately needed to install in the accessible home I couldn't give up on. In preparation of a response, I created a portfolio of all our hard work leading up to this point with newspaper clippings about our family, the community fundraising efforts and the architect plans for the property we wanted the boys to be able bodied in for life. I could smell it. I could touch it. It was just within my reach. In my heart, I knew this was where we needed to be, but it wasn't looking like it was going to happen. Reluctantly for me, we signed on the dotted line to move to College Station, TX to start over. At least our family would be closer to the critical care team in place for our boys in Houston should they relapse or need medical intervention. Two days after we signed a contract to move, my phone rang. It was the Executive Director of the Magnolia Foundation with an interest to meet in person as soon as possible.

We were sitting outside on the steel bench in front of our apartment building. It was cold enough I needed a blanket to wrap around my arms. I could hear the crickets chirping because it was so late at night and so quiet. "I'm sorry, can you repeat that?" I asked. He began to explain that Chip and Joanna Gaines just created the Magnolia Foundation and wanted to help us with our dream of providing an accessible home for our boys. He had showed them the portfolio I sent over with all the efforts that we had done to make this dream a reality. The fundraising, the advocating, the saving, the praying. I remember just staring. I didn't say anything. I was frozen and wanted to remember that this was actually happening. I couldn't really process it. You don't usually get to live out your dream. He then exclaimed that Tim Tebow had also found out about our story and wanted to be part of the project and cover the funding of the renovation costs of the home. Oh, and the best part? That our renovation would be filmed for a special episode of the final season of their hit TV show called "Fixer Upper" on HGTV! I could feel my mouth drop open, and I asked for him to repeat this statement. I literally had to pinch myself because I couldn't believe it. The pent-up relief that I needed to release finally came pouring out and my eyes started to burn. I just kept saying, "I can't believe it!" and "Are you sure?" over and over. Was this really happening?

> *One of the most difficult, but satisfying calls I have ever made was to the builder in College Station the next day. I was fearful of what he would say, but hearing what was happening, he had no problem whatsoever with cancelling the contract and we are forever grateful for his understanding. Knowing the property Melissa had fought so hard to obtain and that I had prayed and hoped for was going to be ours, was absolutely astonishing.*

A few months later, the journey to our dream home commenced, and we started imagining what our home would look like for the first time. We had waited all this time, what's four more months? We met with the design team right away and talked about ramps, barrier-free thresholds, accessible sinks and doorways, hallway width and all the details we only dreamed about before. This was the first time I started to ever get excited about something. It was bigger than us. All the things we thought we would miss seeing our children do were actually a possibility now. We began filming that summer and it was all a blur, remembering only bits and pieces. I'm grateful there was a camera crew because otherwise,

I wouldn't think it was really happening. We had an incredible experience showing what life was really like for us to the outside world. We wanted to show that we were just a family raising two boys that happened to live life on wheels. They love building Lego creations, wrestling with each other and eating popcorn during family movie night.

One of the activities we truly love to do together as a family is be out at the Challenger Little League fields playing baseball. We got to meet Chip and Joanna Gaines and Tim Tebow later that summer and have the boys play a little baseball with them. It truly was a magical day. One of my favorite memories was watching the boys come across home plate and high five Tim Tebow. He was genuinely one of the most kind-hearted individuals we had ever had the pleasure of meeting. Chip and Joanna are just as passionate about their community as they are with everything else they put their hearts into. They were determined to make this home the accessible home of our dreams and more. For the first time in my life, I was able to take my hands off the steering wheel and let someone else drive.

Typically, I try to always stay in control of everything that I'm involved with. I like to know exactly what is happening in all facets of my life. This is the very first time that someone else was making the decisions about something so massive as our home, and I was ok with that! I trusted this was going to turn out perfect and the boys would have everything they needed to access all parts of their home for the very first time. Our excitement was building every single day about our future, and we knew our children would finally have a better quality of life. We would film on and off the next few months into Fall until the big Reveal Day on October 22, 2017. Time stood still this day. I remember not being able to sleep much the night before and waking up knowing our life would change forever, but this time in a good way. We always had to fight so hard for everything for our boys, and this time we were being given the gift of accessibility. We arrived blindfolded at our new home where our future laid ahead of us. I reach my hand out so I could try to get out of the vehicle. A hand grabbed mine and a voice said "Just step forward; there you go! You're here. Today is the big day!" I took my blindfold off and it was Tim Tebow staring right at me with those steel blue eyes. Tim, along with Chip and Joanna, the entire Fixer Upper Crew, and countless bystanders were waiting for us to live this moment out.

All I remember next was the moment they pulled the screen away and I was able to lay my eyes on her for the first time. Pure elation came over me as I looked to my right and saw my two sons and my husband smiling ear to ear, squealing with delight that we were looking at our new home. For the first time, I felt comfort. I had never felt taken care of before. Day to day, we would just try to survive what was thrown at us, trying to make it over the countless hurdles and hardships. Surviving all those denials led us to this moment. We finally had hope staring right back at us in the form of our new home. As we were led all around the home, possibility flashed before me. I saw my son Lawson turn on a faucet all by himself and giggle at the feeling of water flowing over his hands for the first time. I saw the boys flow over entryways with ease and go room to room in an entire house made just for them. Every inch of the home was accessible just like I imagined it would be. I discovered each beautiful room right alongside them seeing the grab bars for transitioning, lowered vanities in the bathrooms, a custom locker room for all their self-care needs and the first backyard they could play in provided by Make-A-Wish. My eyes flashed back to our life where they were toddlers staring out the window of our previous home wishing they could play outside but the stairs leading to the grass prevented them. Now, there were no barriers to play. No obstacles in their way. They finally had an environment that allowed them to be independent and free. It was magical. I was so proud to be their mom and to see this moment happen for them.

The day at the Challenger Little League field and the day of our reveal are days I will never forget. Meeting not only Chip, Joanna and Tim Tebow, but everyone involved in the process of making our dream come true was such an honor. Not once did we feel anything but welcomed and loved. The boys changed some minds and hearts during those days, and it gave me a better understanding and peace that with all we have dealt with, there really

> *was a reason. How can you truly appreciate such a gift if you haven't had to suffer for it? Not only did we receive the gift of a magnificent, fully accessible home, but of independence and new possibilities. The next chapter in our lives is just beginning.*

We named her Hope. Our new home was full of possibility and the hope we had for her never left. What did we learn through this entire process? Patience. Patience. More patience. It took almost seven years and 15 specialists to diagnose our sons. Our diagnostic journey taught us gratitude for each other and the incredible patience during these times. By finding out they both have an incredibly rare and life-threatening mitochondrial condition caused by one little gene mutation that doesn't even have a name or treatment or cure, we were enriched in our journey of continued hope. Years went by in between more heartache and hardships. We fought for everything along our journey while we were fighting against an unknown black abyss of a rare disorder. Not for one medically fragile child, but for two. And guess what? It took years, but they stood. It took years, but they took their first steps assisted with their walkers. It took years, but they spoke their first words. It took years, but they EARNED their mobility. That determination is why we kept going each day to not just survive, but succeed in obtaining better access for our boys. The hope that never left us has now become our home and has allowed us to become the family we were always meant to be.

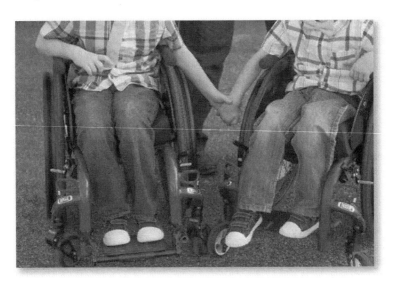

Behind the Story

After their episode aired on HGTV's hit show "Fixer Upper" on January 30, 2018, the Copp Family was blessed once again. Chip Gaines sent out a tweet-seen-round-the-world saying, "To me, this picture is worth a thousand words – a thousand encouragements – a thousand happy moments. BUT, there's more work to do. Let's rally together to pay off the Copp Family's mortgage..." Within 24 hours, the fans showed up for the Copp Family in a BIG way and their mortgage was completely paid off.

Not only did they get the gift of accessibility, but there was one less burden for their family to worry about. Jody and Melissa's desire to help others was formed amid heartache on their arduous journey to find a diagnosis for their boys. After receiving denial letter after denial letter from governmental programs designed to help them, they felt abandoned and helpless. The Copps quickly realized, after receiving several grants from

various local organizations to provide mobility equipment that their health insurance wouldn't cover, foundations and nonprofits are the key to surviving the incredible financial burden that comes with raising a child differently abled. Soon, Jody and Melissa became experts in writing grants for medical support and became highly involved in several community organizations.

Along their journey, community leaders would refer family, friends and clients to them so they could teach people how to advocate, write grants and obtain the necessary support to survive a child's journey to mobility. After settling into their new home, which they call "Hope," the Copps are paying it forward and proudly launched their nonprofit, The *Raising Wheels Foundation* not only to assist other families raising differently abled children but to raise awareness for the need for accessibility. Jody and Melissa share their journey of triumph and the initiatives of the Raising Wheels Foundation at community events, forums, parent support groups, churches and civic group meetings. Their perpetual desire to give back comes from the amazing families they meet along the way which gives an unlimited supply of determination to keep going.

In August 2018, the Copp Family was awarded the prestigious Impact Award by Variety Children's Charity of Texas for their advocacy and awareness work in the differently abled community. A few months later, *Raising Wheels Foundation* launched an Accessibility Grant Program to buy life assist tables for several families in need. In the Spring, they hosted their first annual *Raising Wheels Wash 'N Roll* which is a free community event that focuses on cleaning wheelchairs for the kids in Central Texas while offering fun activities for the whole family. The Copps look forward to many more years of service to their community and beyond through their work with the *Raising Wheels Foundation*.

Life Doesn't End with Quadriplegia

Simon Calcavecchia

At the age of nineteen, I set out on the journey of my life by flying alone to Sydney, Australia. I went there to pursue my dream of playing rugby. I didn't know my experience would dramatically change the rest of my life.

Prior to rugby, I played high school football in Olympia, Washington. I was an overweight lineman with the heart of a running back. Every day I dreamt about running the ball. At 5'7" and weighing 240lbs, few people could stop me when I was running towards the end zone. It made me feel invincible. However, the football coaches at Capital High School were less enthusiastic about giving me an opportunity to score a touchdown. They wanted me on the defensive line. As a result, I was an uninspired player and didn't push myself to excel to become the best player I could be.

At the end of my junior year in high school, a friend of mine told me he wanted to start a rugby team for our school. At the time, I didn't know anything about rugby. It wasn't until he said that anyone could run the ball that he gained my attention. After he told me the basics, I immediately said, "When do we start?" Within two weeks, I was on the practice field with about twenty guys from the football team. It was awesome! My passion for football had been redefined by a new sport, a sport where my talent would shine on the field.

In the first year, we had a lot to learn about being a rugby team. It was going to take someone with a lifetime of knowledge to help a group of clueless high schoolers learn the game. Fortunately, our coach, Pete Sullivan, is Australian and was born with a passion for rugby. He is an incredible coach and role model. Pete also has a talent for bringing out the best in all of us on and off the field. He was the perfect person to lead us into the battlegrounds of life and rugby. Hailing from Australia, Pete knew the game in a way that helped us win over our opponents. He was also the type of guy that inspired us to put everything we had onto the field. When we gathered around him, he spoke from his heart, oftentimes with tears rolling down his cheeks; each tear reinforcing our bond as a team and family.

By our second year, he led us to the Washington State Rugby Championship where we faced our toughest opponent, the Kent Crusaders. They were our biggest rivals in our league. Earlier in the season, they beat us handedly the first time we played. However, the next time we met we played them on our own turf. The game was at Marshall Middle School on a field where we had put blood, sweat, and tears into the soil. It was the place that our rugby team became a family. Homefield advantage also meant that we had an amazing amount of support from our community. I remember half of our high school attending the game. The crowd included the parents of the students and the Capital High School band. They lined the sides of the field with excitement for our most challenging game of the year. It was an incredible feeling having their support. As we warmed up on the field, the band pounded their drums with a triumphant rhythm. When the referee finally blew the whistle, we marched onto the rugby field mentally prepared for battle!

Unfortunately, our team had a rough start. During the first half, we poured our hearts into the game. but the Kent Crusaders humbled us as the score kept going higher and higher in their favor. At halftime, we needed a miracle. Thankfully, we had Pete. I will never forget when he gathered us all around for one of his heartfelt speeches. As we faced what felt like an impossible task, he inspired us to forget the scoreboard and to never give up. After his speech, we fought back with everything we had and played our hearts out to win the Washington State Rugby Championship.

After winning the championship, we gained a lot of confidence in our Budd Bay Barbarian team. We also secured an opportunity to play in the national high school rugby championship in Columbus, Ohio. It was a big opportunity for us, but we still had a lot to prove. Once we arrived, there was no doubt that we were playing against the best of the best. When the tournament started, we beat the first two teams with ease. However, in the following game, we had to battle against a talented team for third place. Sadly, we lost the game by three points. It was a tough loss, but we became a legacy after placing fifth in the nation. With pride, I tell you that our team still holds the highest national ranking in the Budd Bay Barbarian records.

When the season ended, I assumed that my rugby career was over. I loved the game, but I didn't think there was an opportunity to play after graduating from high school. I also knew that I wasn't going to college. At that time, I disliked academics. I barely made it through high school because of my terrible grades. I decided the best thing that I could do was get a job since I knew it wouldn't be long before my mom wanted me out of her house. After talking with my rugby coach, I found even more motivation to get to work. During our conversation, Pete asked me if I wanted to go to Australia to play rugby. With wide eyes and a belly full of excitement, I said, "Hell yes!" I couldn't imagine doing anything more exciting with my life.

Going to Australia seemed like the perfect opportunity to experience my first big adventure. Over the next six months, I saved as much money as I could to pay for my flight and my living costs in Australia. My plan was to stay in Sydney for a full season of rugby.

After arriving in Australia, I headed to Warringah, a small coastal city north of Sydney. It felt like I was living in paradise. For several weeks, I remember waking up with a huge smile on my face. I was in another country, free to do whatever I wanted and it felt incredible.

While I was in Warringah, I shared a house with several rugby players. We all lived in a two-story house within a five-minute walk of some of the most beautiful beaches that I had ever seen. Another bonus was I could literally go out of my back gate and onto the rugby practice field within minutes. It was the perfect location. The house had a brand-new kitchen and freshly carpeted floors but it was challenging living with a bunch of chaotic rugby players. For most of us, it was our first time fleeing the protection of our parental guardians. For me, it was quite a thrill to live on my own. I made the rules, the grocery list, and I chose my bedtime every night. At the time, life was certainly good. It wasn't always fun though. I quickly learned that there was never enough space between my bedroom walls and my roommate's loud interactions. Silence, yeah, that was something I might enjoy at four a.m., and even that wasn't guaranteed. Oh, and one other thing. If you didn't know it yet, teenage guys are more like swines than they are human beings. They are known to leave messes everywhere they go. They will eat your food, and they have zero respect for personal space. Living with the rugby players definitely had its challenges but thankfully most of us quickly became friends.

In order for me to stay in Australia for as long as possible, I had to find a job since I wasn't there to make money playing rugby. I was still too young for that and I would have to put in a lot more work before I could ever consider becoming a professional player. Thankfully, in my time of need, one of the coaches was kind enough to help me find a laborer's job. I started working in construction doing a job I really disliked but I realized it was worth it just because of the freedom it afforded me. I could go out and buy my favorite meat pies whenever I wanted, which earned me the nickname of "Pie-face" by my teammates. I could afford a cellphone plan and, most importantly, I could go have drinks with my teammates after a rugby match

One of the lovely things about Australia is that the drinking age begins at nineteen. Drinking was a big part of rugby life. It was also one of the best ways to bond with my teammates. Surprisingly, the responsibility of being an adult made me feel good where previously I was scared of the responsibility. However, I was loving my independence in Australia. It wasn't long before I felt like I could live there forever.

Once I started getting comfortable with my new living quarters, I had to get serious about my rugby training. We began practice by doing intensive cardio drills. Most of them were new to me but I quickly learned the different routines. I remember the conditioning at the end of each practice was brutal. We would take jogging tours through the town, followed by running through the soft white sands of the local beaches and after that, we ran up hundreds of stairs. It was the kind of running that felt like my heart was going to burst out of my chest. It didn't feel good until it was over.

In Australia, I was the only American player on the team, so that meant the coaches usually referred to me as the "Yank". At first, I wasn't sure how to feel about it, but I eventually gained pride in my nickname, along with being called Pie-face. Albeit, I still had to prove to my new teammates that I could play rugby with the best of them.

Moving quickly through the start of the season, we had our first practice game. Playing in a game was exciting, especially when playing in Australia for the first time. I had a lot to prove. These kids had been playing since they could pick up the ball. I was just a novice to the game. I was definitely fresh meat in their eyes. The only way I could change that was by getting on the field and showing them what I could do. The problem was that there were hundreds of kids on my team. In Olympia, I was used to playing with thirty or forty guys. If we were lucky, we might have made two full teams. In Australia, they had five different teams for one club. It was intimidating at first, but I had an advantage. I was hungry for success. I wanted to be the best player I could possibly be.

In my first game, disappointingly, I started out on the third-grade squad. My goal was to get promoted to their first or second grade team, although I still had to earn the coaches respect. Yes, they were giving me a chance, but in their minds, I was still just a "Yank" from America and at that time, I'm fairly sure that America held last place in international rugby. That sure didn't help my cause but I refused to let it stop me. During the first practice game of the season, I played well but I didn't make any significant plays. However, during the second game my team kicked the ball deep into our opponent's territory. After the ball was caught, I ran towards my opponent like a human locomotive and collided into him with a thunderous force. The impact caused the rugby ball to fly into the air as his body sprawled out onto the grassy field. When the ball hit the ground, I was in the perfect position to pick it up and run the ball into the end zone. As you can imagine, it was a big play. It was just what I needed to finally gain the respect of my coaches. In the very next game, they promoted me the second-grade squad. It was time to celebrate!

After the rugby matches finished, most of the fellas liked to go out on the town. We would walk from bar to bar until we could hardly walk at all. it was nice to have them finally warming up to me. Everything seemed to be going the way I dreamed.

A week before my third game of the season, I remember talking with my rugby friend who was a Kiwi. A Kiwi is what the Aussie's called a New Zealander. He was a super cool dude who I connected with instantly. He was also the number one tight-head prop on my team. Tight-head props are like linemen in football which meant that he was a big guy. I remember that he wanted to help me get even better at my position. Trying to help me improve, he gave me some advice for the scrum (a scrum is like a huddle in football). In the scrum, players group together and slam into each other to gain possession of the ball. It is also the most dangerous part of the game. While we were chatting, my friend told me that if I get my head a little over to the side when I go into the scrum, then my opponent would have a disadvantage. I listened to every word he said until I felt like I could visualize the technique working in a game. I also remember trying the technique out in practice when we were using the padded dummies. I wanted to use his advice in my first game as a second-grade team member.

With only one week before the next game, I still had to keep proving to the coaches that I could play at this level of rugby. The team we were playing against was much stronger than the previous week. I am sure they would dominate any team in the U.S. at the collegiate level but this league was beyond the collegiate level. For my first game on the second-grade, we headed to a subdistrict in Sydney. I was both nervous and excited. I was playing with the big boys now. I knew these games would not be as easy or as fun as the lower level games but they would mean a lot more to me. Unfortunately, I had no idea how much the next thirty minutes would change my life forever.

As the game started, the whistle blew loudly as two dozen men ran onto the field to compete against each other. After the ball was kicked into the air, my heart pounded as we flew down the stretch to tackle our opponents. On the next play, the referee's whistle blew loudly as he spotted a penalty on the field calling for a scrum. The moment I had been waiting for was finally here. After lining up for the scrum, the ref yelled, "Engage!" We slammed together like I had done a thousand times before but this time my vision went black. Without knowing it, the scrum had collapsed all around me. After a few minutes of being unconscious, I woke up with doctors surrounding me.

As soon as I opened my eyes, I remember laying on the ground with my face up and my arms across my chest. It was as if I had just woken up during the middle of my funeral. I remember the doctor asked me if I could move my arms. In my mind I thought I was perfectly fine but when I tried to move them nothing happened. It was terrifying when my arms laid motionless on top of my chest. I knew that my life had been instantly changed. As the medical crew loaded me into the ambulance, I asked them to raise my arm to let my team know that I was okay, when in reality, I was far from okay. I can't imagine how my teammates felt as they watched my paralyzed body being carted off into the ambulance.

Once the gurney was locked down in the ambulance, I heard the doors shut as the sirens screamed in a foreign tone. As we sped to the hospital, the shock from my injury began to fade and the feeling of pain crept into my neck. I remember breaking down behind the closed doors as I hysterically begged for the medics to give me morphine. I had reached the point where I no longer had the strength to be strong for my team. As time slowed down, I felt an overwhelming sense of panic take over my mind until I burst into tears.

After drowning my pain and my fears with opioids, I fell asleep on the ride to the hospital. Shortly after arriving, the doctors operated on my neck. It was horrible. I woke up the next day with tubes down my throat. I was unable to move or even communicate. It was excruciating to go through my traumatic injury and then deal with the aftermath of surgery. It felt like torture as I helplessly laid on the hospital bed with tears rolling down my eyes in frustration. I was trapped in a nightmare.

After the first operation, the doctors noticed that something else had to be repaired on my spinal column. They sent me back in for another emergency surgery where the surgeon took a piece of bone from my hip and secured it to my spine with a plate and screws. I had to go through the torture all over again. When I woke up this time, I was thankful to open my eyes to the sight of my mother standing at the side of my hospital bed. It was a relief to wake up to a familiar face when I felt so vulnerable.

During my hospital stay, I almost the whole rugby team came to visit me. In my short time living in Australia, I made a lot of friends who showed me an incredible amount of support. I will never forget my rugby family and how they helped me get through the hardest time of my life. With my supportive friends and family, I spent the next six weeks in the Prince of Wales Hospital in Sydney before the doctors felt it was safe for me to travel home.

When I arrived in Seattle, I was transferred by ambulance to the University of Washington Medical Center spinal cord unit. It was called Eight-North since it was on the eighth floor in the northern wing. It was home for the next two months. Thankfully, I had even more support when I came home. It was tough! I knew my injury had been really hard on a lot of my friends. It was rough just to talk to them on the phone in Australia. Now, I had to see their faces. When I did see them again, I think my positive attitude helped my friends realize that even though this traumatic injury had occurred, I would still be the guy they loved before my injury.

The next two months in the hospital flew by but I was ready to go home and start living my life again. I was tired of the hospital rules, the food and not being near my friends. True to my nature, I remember coming home from the hospital and going straight out to my friend's party. I really was the same person. The only thing that had changed was my body. It felt so good to be surrounded by my friends and be outside of the hospital. For a few hours, it felt like nothing had changed.

Becoming a quadriplegic, meant that my life had been completely altered. When I broke my neck, I lost about ninety percent of my body's feeling and function. I was paralyzed from the chest down. My fingers and triceps were paralyzed. I also had very little feeling in my arms. As you can imagine, all these limitations made me dependent on the help of others. Every day, I needed help getting dressed, bathing, restroom functions and getting in and out of bed. Even my wheelchair accessible van had to be driven by someone else. Now, after sixteen years, I can't imagine living my life without the help of my caregivers.

It was going to take time to adapt to my new life. At first, I played a lot of video games. It took my mind off most of the new challenges I faced. Also, I no longer had to worry about finding a job. Most of my needs were being met but my sense of purpose was on a downward spiral. At   a certain point, I decided that going to college was the best way to enrich my life. I enrolled in some of the local community college courses and life as a college student began. After a few years at the community college, I decided to transfer to the Evergreen State College. I spent the next several years there. Eventually, I graduated in 2009 with a Bachelor of Arts and a focus in Psychology. It took seven years to accomplish my goal, but I did it.

After graduating, I had a hard time finding work and I was discouraged by the Social Security program. I also noticed that I became more and more depressed. I had lost my sense of purpose. My depression went from rarely appearing to staying for months at a time. Not feeling like myself, I knew I had to change something. I decided to seek out a counselor. During our sessions, I realized that I was missing out on important things in my life. I was lacking purpose, I was serving myself too much, and I wasn't building any new friendships. The counselor and I decided that the best solution for me was to start volunteering in the community. Just the idea of volunteering had an immediate impact on my mood. I was finally excited about something. I started serving at the local food co-op, the children's museum and the local theater. I noticed that my depression was vanishing from my life. I was beginning to feel like me again. In fact, I was better than me. I was becoming empowered by giving back to my community.

For the first time in a long while, I was beginning to feel inspired. I decided that with this inspiration, I would try to empower others by creating a YouTube Channel to share my message. I started by making videos of me experiencing various adventures. I wanted to show people that even though there were more challenges in my way, I could still chase my dreams. I called my YouTube series, *Life Doesn't End with Quadriplegia*. Most of the adventures consisted of doing things that were on my bucket list. Some of those experiences included driving a monster truck, flying a plane over Seattle, creating art, going tubing down a river, and even making my first glitter beard. However, my greatest accomplishment as a Youtuber came when I was looking for my own inspiration. To find new motivation, I frequently visited YouTube to check out what other people with quadriplegia were doing with their lives.

Luckily, I came across a guy named, Genesis Del Bosque.

When I first became injured, I accepted that my physical lifestyle was over, but Genesis was a quadriplegic bodybuilder and his biceps were bigger than most people's heads. He was the first guy I had seen with my level of injury who was working out. When I saw Genesis, I realized that I had been making excuses for the past ten years. It was time to start working out.

Excited by the possibilities, I immediately started looking on Craigslist to find equipment that would work with my functionality. Luckily, I found a pull-down machine that allowed me to attach different types of equipment to it. With some determination, I slowly discovered techniques that allowed me to work out every muscle that I still had functioning. Then, I decided that the coolest thing I could create with my new passion was to document my progress. I wanted to create the most inspiring video that I had ever produced. For over two years, I took a photo once a month of my muscle transformation. I didn't make any huge gains in that time, but my body was definitely transforming. People were starting to notice that my muscles were popping out a little more than usual.

It was so rewarding when I shared my YouTube video on the internet. Overnight, one hundred thousand people watched my YouTube transformation video and I received hundreds of comments from people who were inspired to stop making excuses. It felt incredible to share my journey with people all over the world. It also felt amazing to have the muscles that I dreamed about when I was in high school. However, the coolest part had to be when I was able to return to something that I truly love.

During the time I was working out, I had my sight on achieving something I thought was nearly impossible. The game was called "Murderball," also known as wheelchair rugby. It is one of the most badass sports around. From the post-apocalyptic looking wheelchairs, to smashing people out of them, I had to get on that court and see if I could play rugby again. Once I made the decision, I looked up the website for the wheelchair rugby team called the Seattle Slam. The name couldn't be more fitting. They met once a week in Tukwila, Washington.

I remember the first day of practice. It was tough; everyone was faster than me. I definitely felt more like a roadblock than a teammate as players flew around me on the court. It didn't help that the rules were complex and confusing, either. I realized it would take a decade to master the strategies of wheelchair rugby. However, I still felt compelled to come back every week. After ten years, I found the passion I had lost when I broke my neck. Of course, there was more to the sport than just slamming into each other with our wheelchairs. I also inherited a community of people who knew my experience. It was incredible to connect with other people who were fighting against the same challenges I was dealing with.

It also felt amazing to share the knowledge I had gained during my ten-year journey with quadriplegia. After the first practice, I knew I was where I was supposed to be.

With my life feeling full, I continued to grow in many new ways. One of my favorite experiences was when I decided to be a participant in the *Procession of the Species* in downtown Olympia, Washington. One of the members encouraged me to take part by creating a float for the parade. Excited for the opportunity, we quickly started designing ideas of different creatures. If you haven't noticed yet, I am the type of guy who tends to think big. At first, I wanted to create a three-headed purple dragon, but I didn't understand the meaning behind the celebration of the *Procession of the Species*. The purpose was to celebrate the beauty of the animal kingdom.

After meeting the creator of the Procession, I decided that it was best to use a different type of dragon, a komodo dragon. When I started thinking about it, I had grandiose ideas of mounting a giant float onto my wheelchair and driving it through the streets, but I'd never done anything like that before. Plus, I only had five weeks to get my float ready and build a team of people to help me make it happen. It was going to take a lot of volunteers to bring my vision to life. I told everyone I knew about my project, and I shared my idea with excitement and passion with anyone who would listen. If they got excited about it, then I knew they were the right person to join my team. During the next five weeks, I built a team of fifty different people. They spent a combined effort of five hundred hours helping me create my vision. It was an exhilarating project that created a family out of the most dedicated team members.

One of those team members ended up being a friend that would help change my life forever. His name is Art, a talented artist that embodies his name to the fullest extent. When he first showed up, he was reserved and quiet, but he quickly became an essential team member. With his dedication, our friendship evolved into a brotherhood. After five weeks of determination, our komodo family marched through the streets with a float the size of a bus mounted onto my wheelchair. It has to be one of the top five coolest things I have ever done. Not only that, by accomplishing my goal, I gained a tremendous amount of confidence in my ability to be a leader. With that confidence, I now know that I can manifest my dreams.

As my friendship with Art continued to grow, we came up with all kinds of new projects to work on together. Most of them were small projects. That was until after two years of getting to know him, then he finally drew a cartoon doodle that made me realize that he was the perfect person to help me manifest another dream. Creating our first children's book.

In ten years of volunteering with kids, not once did I read a book to them that had a character using a wheelchair. However, I wanted that to change. I also thought it would be really cool to combine my passion for art projects with my passion for hanging out with kids. When I saw Art draw a cartoon character, I knew that he was the perfect guy to work with. I said, "Dude, have you ever thought about illustrating a children's book?" I told him that I had been dreaming about writing one for years. He said, "No, I haven't, but let's make it happen!" We both were excited about our new project as we bounced all kinds of ideas off of each other. It was really fun coming up with different concepts for the book. As we worked on it together, I knew I wanted the main character to use a wheelchair. I also knew I wanted the characters to be animals. I thought a wiener dog would be the perfect fit since they are the most common animals using wheelchairs. Once I figured that part out, I knew I had to name him Frank. I couldn't resist the opportunity to make a hot dog joke. The next assignment was to come up with Frank's best buddy. In my life, I constantly rely on the help of others. This character had to represent all the people in my life who have helped me be more independent.

At first, I thought a fox would be kind of cool, but then I thought it would be even cooler if the character could ride on Frank's back. A fox would definitely be too big for that. I had to come up with an animal that was a little smaller, so a bird seemed like it would be fitting since a small bird would have no problem riding on Frank's back. The tough part, however, was figuring out his name. We played around with some different ideas until Art suggested that we call him Mustard. When I first heard it, I wasn't sure if the name was too ridiculous. I needed a night to sleep on it. When I woke up the next morning, I told Art that his idea was brilliant. We called our book series, *The Adventures of Frank and Mustard*.

With Art, the Illustrator

Now, we needed a story for our first book, and I had the perfect idea. Just six months before we started production. I went to the VanDusen Botanical Gardens in Victoria, B.C. A friend was taking care of me for the weekend. We were there during the fall. It was a typical, wet and rainy day in the Pacific Northwest, but I wasn't going to let that stop me from seeing the beautiful views. I was also excited about doing some off-roading in my wheelchair. It was one of my favorite things to do. Once I made it onto the trails, I fearlessly flew down them spitting up dirt in every direction. I think I even caught some air off one of the jumps. My reckless off-road driving led me into some major trouble. I got stuck in some serious mud. It was something I had dealt with in the past, but this time it was particularly bad. Unfortunately, there was some rubber matting on top of the mud that made the situation even worse as it became wound up in my tires. It was so bad that I couldn't even move my wheelchair. Sadly, I knew there was no hope of getting out of this situation on my own.

After yelling for help, my friend came and tried to get me out of the mud, but there was nothing she could do to free me from it. After trying for thirty minutes, we decided that we needed help. Thankfully, she found a few staff members wandering around the park. When they came back, they brought some long wooden boards to help dislodge me from the mud. Once they were underneath my wheelchair, we all worked together to get me out of it. At the time, I had no idea that getting stuck in the mud would lead to one of the best things to ever happen to me!

On May 1, 2016, after a year of hard work we finally accomplished our goal; we had written a unique children's book about a dog in a wheelchair and were holding the first published copy of *The Adventures of Frank and Mustard: Stuck in the Mud*. With fifteen hundred books in hand, the real work was just beginning. We had no idea how to sell them. After some research, we found success at local bazaars. Some were fantastic, but most of them were mediocre. It was challenging to find the best events. Luckily, we only lost money at a couple of them, although I knew there had to be a better way. I started looking into festivals that drew in thousands of people instead of dealing with bazaars that only brought in a few hundred. They were much more expensive, but it felt like the only way to truly grow the business. It was definitely paying off as my monthly sales improved dramatically. I could see my vision coming to life. For me, this wasn't just a career opportunity, it was a way to pursue my dreams and follow my passion of being a children's book author.

The very best outcome from the whole experience was when I realized the benefit of sharing my story to children in school assemblies regarding disability awareness and acceptance. I knew I needed guidance and knowledge in learning how to hold the attention of an assembly of grade school children. The first thing I sought was a mentor so I reached out to a principal who I met during my time volunteering at an elementary school. He offered many good ideas which would help keep the attention of my audience. He suggested that I use several different mediums including videos and interactive activities. He was also the perfect connection for getting into a lot of local schools. As I continued to develop my presentation, I relayed my life experience. My goal is to create more disability awareness, to educate, empower, and inspire students. My purpose is to show what can be accomplished with a positive mindset.

Even though I have experienced difficult and challenging times, I refuse to let a negative attitude define me. I have found strength in accepting what I cannot change, and I continue to fight to make life worth living. At first, I thought this was just a good way to tell kids about my book, but it has become something far more meaningful. I have been able to tell my story in a way that will have a positive impact on future generations. I can only hope that the work I am doing is making the world a better place.

My plan for the future is to continue pursuing my passions and following my dreams. In the last fifteen years, I have accomplished more than I ever believed possible. Much of that is due to having the right mindset and the support of the people around me, especially my mom. (Thank you for everything you have done for me. My life would not be the same without you, Mom.) Over the next fifteen years, I promise to forge ahead working towards my goals

Simon's biggest supporter

of Simon's biggest supporter becoming a national-level speaker and a nationally-recognized children's book author. I will do everything in my power to manifest my dreams. Now, to all of you people reading my story, go out there and pursue your own adventures! You are amazing just the way you are!

Behind the Story

Today Simon is busy speaking at school assemblies with his message of perseverance, growth mindset and never giving up on your dreams. He mainly addresses elementary school students because he's a children's book author, but Simon presents to all ages. He makes appearances up and down the West Coast, but is willing to travel anywhere in the country that would like to hear his message.

The YouTube videos Simon began before his book writing (and which he continues to create) are found by searching: *Life Doesn't End with Quadriplegia*. There is also a YouTube channel where you can watch *Frank and Mustard Stories* and hear the music composed by Simon to go with them. Use key words: *Frank and Mustard*.

The *Frank and Mustard Books* are available at *www.FrankandMustard. com* including a blog which features book signing and speaking events. On Facebook, you can also learn about Simon's events and messages by following the page: *The Adventures of Frank and Mustard*. You can do the same with Amazon. The messages shared through these platforms are meant to inspire optimism and strength when facing life's challenges. By telling these stories, Simon hopes children will recognize they can choose to see their challenges as opportunities for growth. His books emphasize the power to create love, joy and strength in response to adversity. Simon's ambition is to become a nationally recognized author and motivational speaker who empowers students to overcome their challenges no matter the obstacle.

Amazing Grace
...How Sweet the Sound

Erin Kiltz

I identified with Forest Gump when he said, "I don't remember being born, I don't recall what I got for my first Christmas, and I don't know when I went on my first outdoor picnic..." but I do remember looking at Gracie for the first time and thinking she was the most beautiful baby girl I had ever seen!

Reverse the clock to 1991, when life in West University of Houston, Texas was making my head spin. John, my husband of almost 8 years and I felt the need to pray about a long-term place to raise our family. By circumstances only God could have orchestrated, our family landed on 16 acres in Hockley, Texas. We had two beautiful children, a girl and a boy, Emily, almost four and Riley, almost two. John and I felt our family was complete but convinced God was leading us out to a slower life in the country to invest in our family. Lo and behold, we were more than surprised to find out during the week of packing up our city home, we were pregnant! "Wow! I thought we were done, but obviously God wasn't!"

However, soon after unpacking all our boxes, it became obvious with each trip to the bathroom I was miscarrying our "surprise" baby. I began to grieve in a way that was so foreign to me. I had always thought miscarriage was no big deal until it was me. Through early morning prayer and Bible study, God comforted us. And yet the loss sparked in us a desire for a fourth child. Knowing only by God's grace would we be able to have another;

John and I began to pray daily for another child. Two months later, we found out we were pregnant. I felt a greater responsibility carrying our fourth child. We decided to pray fervently about a name that would be fitting for him or her. We were convinced we were going to have a girl. I had been studying Rebekah in the Old Testament and desired our girl to have a servant's heart as Rebekah did. I asked John one morning as he entered the kitchen, "What do you think about Rebekah Grace?" "I love it!" he replied, and that was it. We were having a girl; Rebekah Grace Kiltz would be her name, but we would call her Gracie.

Gracie was born May 17th, 1992. In the early evening, our friend and pediatrician, Dr. Lange, entered the hospital room and quickly blurted out, "Three out of four doctors think Gracie has Down syndrome." I can still feel today the shock that bounced off of John's body with that startling news. I was trying to quickly reflect back to my biology class and recall what Down syndrome was and how it would affect Gracie's future and ours.

Prior to Gracie being born, we had prayed for God to reveal to us a fitting life verse, which He did: 2 Corinthians 12:9, "My grace is sufficient for you, for my power is made perfect in your weakness." God reminded me compassionately of this verse at the news. We had no idea she would be weak or that she would be anything but perfect.

Little did I know the emotional roller coaster was just beginning. The hands and feet of Christ showed up at our doorstep through 5-course meals, our 16-acre lawn being mowed and help with Emily and Riley as well as constant encouragement through prayer. How beautiful is the body of Christ! It is amazing how God designed us to, "suffer when one part suffers and rejoice when one part rejoices." There was plenty of tears and laughter over the next year and constant therapy. We were so thankful for our Gracie girl. Every night it became the tradition to sing to her "Amazing Grace how sweet the sound..." and to this day, she thinks it's all about her.

Gracie as a happy toddler

Gracie had just turned one when my best girlfriend Jamie and I had big plans of going to the Roundtop Antique Fair for the weekend with our toddlers. Thursday morning, as I was changing Gracie's diaper, I noticed little red broken blood vessels below the skin, which at the time appeared to be Roseola. For fear Gracie may be contagious, I made a last-minute appointment at a "doc in a box" clinic where I met a sharp Asian doctor who explained the red-looking rash was not Roseola but something called Petechiae – it happens when your platelets (blood clotting) are low or malfunctioning. She proposed we run a complete blood count and minutes later she returned with concern and recommended that Gracie see the hematology/oncology team of doctors at Texas Children's Hospital. To say the least, my weekend plans with my best friend were canceled.

Mother called and wanted Gracie to meet her at a fundraiser for the Down Home Ranch in Elgin, Texas. I thought, *I'll keep Gracie in a stroller and she should be fine.* I searched for directions to the fundraiser in the shuffle of papers on the junk counter. As I located it, I noticed on the back of the invite a beautiful photo of a little girl with Down syndrome and a plea, "Please pray for Sarah, she has Leukemia and just had a platelet infusion."

Chills came over my whole body when I saw platelets and Leukemia in the same sentence. The whole way to Elgin, I prayed, "Please Lord, allow me to meet this family if they may be able to shed some light on low platelets." As my mother and I stood in line to purchase tickets, I turned around and recognized this beautiful little 2-year-old baby girl in a stroller as Sarah, the little girl on the flyer. I said, "Excuse me, I know you don't know me, but I know about Sarah and have prayed for her." I introduced my mother and Gracie. I showed Sarah's mom Gracie's Petechiae and told her that we were being referred to Texas Children's Hospital. Sarah's mom shared how Sarah was misdiagnosed for months and then, through a chromosomal study, was diagnosed with one of the most aggressive forms of AML (Acute Megakaryocytic Leukemia). She encouraged me to demand a chromosomal study when we met with the oncologist.

As we drove home, I felt like God had shown me the writing on the wall. I was at peace, but it was difficult to believe that this was most likely going to be Gracie's future. On Monday, Gracie and I headed into Texas Children's Hospital to have blood work done and to be examined. Dr. Murali was Gracie's doctor and could not have been kinder, but he was not concerned. He told me she most likely had a platelet disorder and they would treat it with steroids, which was exactly what the doctors had told Sarah's parents. *Oh gosh, here goes what is going to sound like "crazy mom" talk.* "Dr. Murali, I know you don't know me from Adam, but something happened this weekend that I don't believe was just coincidental but providential."

I told him about Sarah and about meeting her and hearing of her story and how the Leukemia surfaced through a Trisomy 7 discovered in a chromosomal study. He thought it was my fear speaking but continued to respectfully listen. I said I didn't want to leave without a promise from him that he would do a chromosomal study on her blood. He thought it was pointless but with my continued persistence, conceded. Two weeks later, Dr. Murali called and, since he didn't seem concerned on the phone, I headed to Texas Children's Hospital for a follow-up appointment with all three children in tow. He entered the room and greeted Emily, Riley, and Gracie. He laughed, observing them bouncing off the walls. He asked, "How is Gracie doing?" "Great," I said, but then he proceeded to tell me how he was completely dumbfounded by the findings. Down to the chromosome, it was exactly the same kind of Leukemia that the little girl Sarah had.

My first thought was, *Why in the heck did he not ask for John to be a part of this meeting?* And secondly, *God had completely prepared me for this.*

Life as we knew it would never be the same. Everything comfortable and secure had been pulled out from underneath us. Our new home for the next year was a 10 x 12 room at Texas Children's Hospital. Being a designer, it was my goal to make our room and Gracie's environment beautiful in every way. I brought an area rug, lamp, pictures, Gracie's floral sheets, a candle, flowers, a cd player, and a cappuccino machine. I rearranged the furniture, and it became our little home away from home. Over the next year, our friends and family rallied and showered us with unprecedented support, delicious meals, care for Emily and Riley, and most importantly, constant prayer.

John and I survived separately as he primarily took care of Emily and Riley, but then sometimes we would trade out care for Gracie so that I could see Emily and Ryan. It was a year of making a lot of lemonade out of what seemed like the sourest of lemons. God provided the sweetest of sugar and as a family, we bonded for life. He met us in our darkness and guided us every step of the way. After Gracie's induction of chemotherapy, we realized that Hockley, Texas was not close enough to the hospital, so we relocated to the medical center area. We stayed in a garage apartment of a friend of a friend's who had just completed this building project. They didn't even know us but offered up their newly built garage apartment during Gracie's treatment. For the most part, this was John, Emily, and Riley's home since Gracie and I were in the hospital the majority of the time. The doctors encouraged us to pull Emily and Riley from school because Gracie had never experienced chicken pox or other childhood illnesses and could no longer be vaccinated while she was immunosuppressed. Thankfully, a group of friends in the area offered to homeschool them.

My mother faithfully drove down to Texas Children's Hospital most Thursday nights to care for Gracie for the weekend so that we could spend time as a family. We received countless notes of encouragement from strangers that I feasted on, as they were laced with scriptures that fed my soul. These are just a few examples of God's many graces shown to us daily in the midst of the harsh world of childhood cancer.

Well, ten months of a 14-month protocol of treatment had been completed and surprisingly went by faster than I expected. As a family, we decided to return to Hockley for the last four months of treatment. The day we moved home, my neighbor and dear friend Val asked me a question she had not dared to ask, "Erin, what is Gracie's prognosis?" I said with great confidence, "About 50/50, but I can't imagine what could go wrong now as she has skated through treatment and immediately responded to chemotherapy." She had been in remission since induction which was a 6-week treatment. Her doctors were also confident that she was good to go in every respect.

Just when I thought we were back in Hockley, home free, the greatest of all curve balls was thrown our way. Yes, we had moved home, and Gracie had been running around our pool, sitting, splashing her feet, and enjoying home sweet home after ten solid months of hospital existence. It was June 4th, 1995 and the Rockets were in the playoffs. John and his best friend, Buck, were finally back in Hockley together on the couch viewing the game.

Gracie found herself a cozy spot in between her daddy and Buck as they cheered on the Rockets. When I picked Gracie up to put her to bed, I immediately noticed she was running a fever. Infection was constantly the number one threat throughout treatment and was always what ushered Gracie and me back to the hospital. This was a drill we had repeated ten other times since Gracie's protocol had begun. It usually followed a round of chemotherapy when her immune system was so low from the effects of the treatment, and she was susceptible to infection. Once an infection was found, ten days of "big gun" antibiotics were administered only to be prepped for the next round of chemotherapy. Tonight was different because we were finally home, 40 minutes from the medical center. I noticed her fever was rising quickly which prompted a call to the oncologist. She said that the hospital would be prepared for Gracie's arrival, and she would be pre-admitted. I encouraged John to stay with Riley since he was already asleep, and Emily was in Austin with grandparents. Gracie and I knew the drill and would head for the hospital.

As we arrived through the ER at midnight, I asked the valet to stay with Gracie while I fetched a mask, as I was instructed to never enter the emergency room without a mask due to the severity of Gracie's immunosuppression. I wanted to guard her against any germs she may encounter in the ER. I was challenged by the triage of nurses for requesting a mask as they assured me the ER wasn't busy. I politely insisted on a mask for Gracie explaining that I was following her oncologist's orders. My persistence probably set up the evening for the perfect storm because this nurse immediately sized me up as "high maintenance." She ushered Gracie and me into a back room and did an initial blood reading. If I had been told what it was, I would have known she was in trouble, but, in every way, this was an off night. Little did I know that June 5th would be the game changer for the rest of Gracie's life.

Four hours later, a nurse who would escort us to our room awakened me. What I didn't know was that it is protocol for ER patients to have their blood pressure taken every 30 minutes, and this had not been followed. Feeling disoriented, I glanced at the time and was shocked it was 4:00 a.m. *What had taken so long for us to be admitted?* As we walked towards the elevator, I noticed Gracie was shaking, which I computed as chill from the fever. As we passed the nurse's station, I commented, "Gracie seems chilled, could they please get her a blanket?" The nurses on the cancer floor knew Gracie like one of their own children, as she had been treated on this floor for almost a year. "No, she isn't," they replied; then the nurse hit a code red button (which means a patient is in acute distress of some type). My initial response was, "Who is in trouble?" never thinking for a moment it was Gracie. With the push of that code red button, I felt as though I knew for the first time what an out-of-body experience was. I felt helpless, like I was watching things from afar. Doctors and nurses began appearing from doors I didn't even know existed and the medical team went into full action. After a few minutes, a nurse turned to me and said, "You need to call John, we don't know if Gracie will make it." I thought, *you must be mistaken, she was running around our pool today!* I picked up the hospital phone and calmly told John he needed to hurry... Gracie was in trouble.

I will never forget the loud popping sound as the nurses opened the blood pressure medication and began pushing medication into Gracie's central line. I was trying to comfort Gracie as she began to bleed from the nose and mouth. She was fighting the oxygen mask as a drowning victim does, so they immediately intubated her. Curtis, one of the nurses who had been close to our family throughout Gracie's treatment, encouraged me to give the medical team more space. Curtis took me across the hall to a family room and pulled me down to our knees where he began to pray. This was all surreal, yet I knew God held Gracie in the palm of His hand. It was my job to trust.

Twenty minutes passed until I walked back across the hall to her room. Curtis stuck his head in the room to check on Gracie and discovered her heartbeat was back after flatlining for 20 minutes. "What, I don't understand?" and then the team appeared with Gracie on a gurney rolling her down the hallway of the hospital towards ICU. John and Riley arrived, and somehow word had gotten out quickly that Gracie was in critical condition because friends began to surface. One of my friends, Mary, was posted outside of the ICU waiting room with Riley and tried to entertain him at 5:00 a.m. with markers and paper. John and I were placed in the family room of ICU, which we later realized was kept reserved for the family with a "dying child."

Gracie's surgeon entered the uncomfortably small, cold room and began to quickly explain Gracie's situation. He had done an ultrasound on her distended belly and, through the ultrasound, had confirmed a hole in her duodenum. It was a matter of life and death how quickly he could get in there to repair it. There was no time for the Operating Room... he would have to do surgery in her ICU bed. "Do what you need to do," John said, "but beforehand, can we lay hands on you and pray for you?" With that, he said, "Yes, but hurry!"

Off he went for what seemed like an eternity. During this emergency surgery, friends gathered around us in the family room and began to sing and pray. At one point, an unexplained gust of wind came through this 8x10 foot room which caused a pause in prayer. Everyone raised their heads, looked at each other, and then continued to pray. About an hour and a half later, the surgeon returned perplexed and shaking his head. He first explained to us that he was a Christian and prayed over every one of his patients before operating. He further assured us that he never would have put Gracie's life any more at risk if he wasn't convinced, based on his findings through the ultrasound, that he needed to repair the life-threatening hole in her bowel. However, after opening up her abdomen examining three times for any loss of integrity, he came up short. We assured him he did the right thing and we didn't fault him. Obviously, God had performed a miracle, and we praised Him for that.

My parents arrived and began doing what they do best. They were there, asking good questions, comforting, and visiting with our friends. They also brought provisions of water, snacks, etc. for the refreshment of our network of support. An hour later, the head of ICU came in and asked everyone to leave. He told us that Gracie would be dead by noon and we needed to prepare to say goodbye. *After Gracie had survived 20* minutes of cardiac arrest due to sepsis (a triple bacterial infection which had permeated her entire blood stream), and undergone major abdominal surgery, she is going to die???

Although numb, we shared the news with our family and friends; then proceeded to check on Riley and Mary, who was still entertaining him hours later. As far as Riley was concerned (age five at the time), he thought we were back in the hospital due to Gracie's fever. When he saw us, he immediately wanted to share a story about a picture he had drawn for me. I really didn't know if I could emotionally conjure up the wherewithal to listen. He began to explain, "This is a picture of Gracie climbing a mountain. The first face is mad because the mountain is so big, so she climbs a little further. The second face is sad, as she doesn't think she can make it, but she climbs a little further. And the third face is happy, as she can see the top of the mountain and knows she can make it." John and I were stunned and wondered, *Is this God's way of telling us Gracie wasn't going to die?* We didn't know but told Riley it was the most beautiful drawing he had ever drawn for mommy and daddy and one day it would hang in our home. Of course, Mary took it upon herself to quickly frame it, and it hung in her ICU room the duration of Gracie's stay there. The next two weeks were touch and go with the doctor's expectation that death was imminent. They would not recognize any of the miracles that happened along the way but said there was no reason Gracie should be alive! It's always been a mystery to me that the majority of our doctors witness the intricacies of our bodies at work under a microscope, and the miracles of life and death on a daily basis, but for the most part chalk it up to science.

Two weeks later, Gracie opened her eyes, but something was very different. At first, I thought it was the influence of drugs slowly wearing off. After inquiring with the neurologist, however, he informed me that the drugs had worn off a couple of days ago. My heart jumped. Frantically, I said, "Then why can't she track keys or respond to any commands?" "Doesn't she have Down syndrome?" he replied snidely. I thought I might be put in prison for punting a doctor through a window; instead, I demanded an EEG as soon as possible. I remember going down into the basement of the hospital, which seemed like a dungeon, with my less-than-responsive daughter, while hearing the loud clanging of medical equipment being used in the area.

The Neurologist ran the test which revealed that during the septic shock, which had led to her heart flatlining for 20 minutes, Gracie had incurred a severe brain injury that caused gross damage to her entire brain. Her prognosis, according to the doctor, was that she would never walk, talk, eat, know anyone or smile again. To me, this was worse than death. But I remembered thinking when we began this fight for Gracie's life against Leukemia that there were two outcomes I needed to consider: God would either heal her through treatment or take her home. This third outcome I never could have imagined, and it felt like a curve ball from nowhere that I couldn't begin to catch. In fact, it felt like the ball hit me right in the head and knocked me out cold. Our reality left me disoriented. From that day forward, I humbled myself before God from whom I felt distant. I couldn't imagine that God's perfect plan for Gracie's life or our family's was a severe brain injury.

Before this defining event, I had read *A Path Through Suffering* by Elisabeth Elliot. She and her husband, Jim, were ministering to the Quecha Native American tribe when Jim was speared to death. Her mantra as she grieved was, "With acceptance lieth peace." Without acceptance, I knew I couldn't move on. So many friends with good intentions said, "If you and John just believe, Gracie will get up and walk!" If I ever wanted to believe or put my hope in that idea, it was then. As we began to process what was happening. I kept coming back to Psalm 62:5-8, "Put your hope in God alone..." If I put my hope in what I hope to happen and it doesn't come to pass, where does that leave me and my faith in God? John processed his grief through journaling daily, which could be published as a beautiful record of an honest grieving father.

The next month we were finally discharged from the hospital with 24-hour medications, tubes everywhere, and one session with a nurse teaching me how to administer feeds and medicine through a newly placed G-button within Gracie's belly. We were given no manual on how to care for a severely brain injured child, and still to this day, when I think back to our reality, I cry. I remember thinking, "Will I ever laugh at a movie again.... even want to watch a movie again?" My concern was that our response to this catastrophic event as parents would greatly affect Emily and Riley's faith and future. So, our prayers were simple S.O.S prayers of daily survival. I remember kneeling down at the edge of our bed and desperately praying, "Lord, your word says in Romans 8:28 that you cause all things to work together for the good of those who love you and are called according to your purposes... show me anything good that can come from Gracie's brain injury???"

The next morning, I remember awakening an hour later than usual, causing me to panic, as I knew Gracie usually opened her eyes around 7 a.m. I ran into her room to find Emily and Riley in bed with Gracie singing to her their vacation bible songs and loving on her. Immediately, I thought, *thank you God... Emily and Riley will be different as a result of loving and serving a sibling with a severe brain injury.* I felt God had shown me the resilience of Emily and Riley as they were still celebrating their sister despite her altered state, and it was time for me to move on. I didn't pretend that processing our new Gracie would be quick or complete within a year. I just knew I needed to trust God for the grace needed for today.

I remember one night specifically, as I was putting Emily and Riley to bed, they both shared how much they missed Gracie's smile. With that, they began to pray every night for God to bring back their sister's smile. I would leave their room crying, as once again, I felt the crisis of belief and faith, and cried out to God for our heart's desire. I shared Emily and Riley's prayers with John and told him I thought we needed to sit down with Emily and Riley to tell them the doctor's prognosis, that Gracie would never be able to smile again. He very wisely asked, "Do you think we should tell our children what they can and can't pray for?" I said, "Of course not, but I don't want their faith to be thrown out the window when that doesn't happen!" He assured me God would work it out. Well, six months later (me of little faith), Gracie's smile returned bigger than ever. Every day her smile is a constant reminder that God can choose to do the impossible. I don't believe we can ever presume miracles, but the return of her smile definitely encouraged me to pray for them! Thank God for the faith and hearts' cry of Emily and Riley!

God surrounded us with so many friends, as well as our extended family and as ill-equipped as we were, we began to walk this "road less traveled." Specifically, He provided the Anderson Family, our closest friends, the opportunity to build a house next door. This provision allowed us, as a family, to heal and have the support we needed. We built a new future alongside our best friends. They poured into our family daily. We lived in true "community" as few people get the privilege of experiencing for the next 12 years. We homeschooled four years together, constantly consulted each other regarding parenting challenges, grilled-out countless meals and shared them on our screened-in porch. The Andersons constantly committed to learning and helping to execute therapy for Gracie's rehabilitation. The Anderson's living next door was the most tangible gift God gave us post-Gracie's brain injury because I knew I wasn't alone and the Andersons made that clear on a daily basis.

Years later, about the time Emily and Riley entered college, they thought to ask if we had ever considered counseling as a family after Gracie's brain injury. We never did. I don't know if that was a result of living 40 miles from the city or just being somewhat numb for a while. But what we did do was talk honestly with our children which was very difficult. At ages five and seven, the questions were equal to freshman Theology 101 like, "Does God still love Gracie? Then why would He allow something so bad to happen to her?" Our answers were a clear, "Yes, God loves Gracie," but all while we too wrestled with how a brain injury could be filtered through God's sovereign hand of love. Instead of therapy, we bought two pairs of

$100 running shoes and began to train for a marathon. These shoes lasted for about four months of "running therapy." Running distances gave John and me time to think, pray, cry and process our pain.

The most significant part of our healing came through starting a ministry to the bone marrow transplant unit of Texas Children's Hospital. Many lawyers advised us to sue the hospital for medical malpractice (the triage of nurses was certainly in violation), but we knew God had clearly impressed upon our hearts to begin a ministry to encourage families walking a similar road. We had witnessed over the year of Gracie's treatment the contrast between the overflowing support we experienced and the void of support so many others experienced because of not being in their hometown, not being plugged into a church, and the exit of family and friends at the devastating reality of childhood cancer. We desired to return to the hospital and give back the loving support we had received from our friends and family to these hurting families. *His Grace Foundation* is now 22 years old and has paid forward healing dividends to so many hearts, including our family's. Val Anderson, my neighbor who walked with me through the messy, awkward years of adjusting to a new Gracie, is now the Executive Director. She received the torch from me as Founder/Executive Director 15 years ago when John took a new job in the Austin area.

Gracie's therapies continued three times a week, formally through a therapy center in Houston and at home every day. Our family, along with the Andersons, became Gracie's greatest therapists. We had no idea what we were doing; we just prayed for wisdom and God led us through uncharted waters. Between the Anderson's three girls (Abby, Hillary and Olivia) and our two (Emily and Riley), Gracie was constantly stimulated, not to mention Val and Buck, and John and I. Abby, Hillary, Olivia, and Riley all played the piano, so music therapy was intact daily. During the summer, Gracie was in the pool at least once a day, so aquatic therapy happened. Emily was destined to be a nurse, so she constantly helped with all medical procedures and feedings. All the children read her books, which is still one of her favorite activities. Riley also played hoops with her for hours, not to forget the great vestibular therapy happening organically through every ones' love and use of the trampoline.

It just so happened that one of Houston's finest therapeutic horseback riding programs was basically in our back yard, over the fence 400 yards away. As God planned it, Gracie was in the middle of all activities and we adapted the environment to make it work for her. We all enjoyed doing it for the joy it gave her. I'll never forget one of Emily's comments when she was pre-pubescent and emotional. She said, "Mom, I never have time to think about myself or my worries when I'm serving Gracie."

As I mentioned, John took a job in Austin which led our family to Georgetown, just north of Austin, Texas. Emily was beginning her junior year of high school, Riley his freshman year, and Gracie the sixth grade. As a result of this move, we became aware of many services for Gracie we had no knowledge of while living in Hockley. She had been put on a Medicaid waiver waiting list by someone, which may have been her social worker at the hospital, for which I am forever grateful. Some parents of children with special needs still have no idea this program exists and are never informed that these services are based on the needs of the child and not the family's income. If you are reading this and do not know about Class or HCS Medicaid waiver program, please Google and sign up for services. It may take up to 12 years for your number to come up, but it is one service which helps provide support for a child and the family for a lifetime. It has been a game-changer for our family, especially when both Emily and Riley left for college and I needed physical help lifting Gracie. Class has provided therapies and assistance within our home and many other services that have added to Gracie's overall quality of life.

Gracie continued to thrive and was embraced, especially by a program at Georgetown High School called Peer Buddies. Peer Buddies is an approved elective where typical students choose to come into the Special Ed classes and help their peers with special needs to meet daily goals. It was Gracie's senior year that this group of individuals collectively decided to nominate Gracie, as well as another young man with Down syndrome, for Homecoming Queen and King. They won 2010 Homecoming Queen and King by a landslide at Georgetown's 5A High School. This made national news and blessed all of their friends. For John and me, it was a complete paradigm shift from anything we experienced in high school. When the student body was asked, "Why did you vote for Gracie for homecoming queen?" They responded, "Gracie can't do anything on her own, but she can light up a room with her smile. Every day when I see her in the halls, her smile encourages me!" They were completely unaware of her journey and the miracle of her smile! So, the smile the neurologist said would never return had now earned her Homecoming Queen of Georgetown High School! We can complain about so many things our youth are not getting, however, they do get many things our generation didn't, like realizing the value their peers with special needs bring to the world. This was beautifully evidenced by their homecoming choice of Queen and King.

Gracie winning Homecoming Queen

One week after Gracie's homecoming victory, I sat in her "graduating ARD" and asked, "So what's next for Gracie and her friends?" They just looked at me like, *where have you been?* "For Gracie," they answered, "nothing is next, and for some of her friends, there are few options." The reality is, as a society we have made monumental progress and spend millions of dollars meeting the needs of our children with disabilities in the form of early identification, therapy, and the best of education, but that all comes to a dead end when our children age out of the school system at age 21. So, we are addressing only 1/3 of these individual's life span. We need to recognize that a large percentage of these individuals, cognitively speaking, are "children for life" and they need to be given the appropriate support. This is one population that cannot take advantage of the system, but for whatever reason, our government is not making provisions for those who cannot independently care for themselves.

The black hole post-graduation was enough information to launch any mom on a mission. I was convinced there had to be some post-high school vocational community within the Austin area. Sadly, my search fell short, and most of the time I left what are called "day-habs" in tears. The thought of Gracie attending one of these places turned my stomach, so I prayed, "Lord, lead me to a beautiful place, a life-giving place that will celebrate every individual for who you created them to be."

Through a Google search, I discovered the Brookwood Community (BWC) in Brookshire, Texas, just west of Houston. It was everything and more I ever dreamed of in a community for Gracie. It was God-centered, celebrating every "Citizen's" God-given gifts. It was entrepreneurial in that everything they made and grew was sold in a beautiful gift and garden center, and it happened to be home and workplace to 220 "Citizens" with special needs. It is truly a slice of heaven on earth and the founder, Yvonne Streit (almost 90), gives all the glory to God! The Brookwood Community also has 47 production greenhouses, a five-star café, a fine arts gallery and a 10,000 sq. ft. gift shop. It was obvious that the Brookwood Community had set the bar of excellence within the industry and it became my goal to establish Brookwood in Georgetown. Under the tutelage of the Executive Director Vivian Shudde, daughter of founder Yvonne Streit, I began a pilot program that emulated the BWC.

Citizens loving their work

After about six months, Brookwood in Georgetown became the first and only expansion in 30 years of BWC's history. We are honored to steward their name and feel the weight of upholding their excellent reputation. Brookwood in Georgetown, better known as BiG, started small with eight Citizens in free-church space. Now we have 75 Citizens with 30 in a waiting pool. Our Citizens are thriving like never before and changing the way our world views this population. Everything our Citizens make is beautiful and is sold in our retail store, café and/or greenhouse. We are already in need of program expansion, and once that is done, we will build a full residential community. A beautiful thing has happened, and it has all taken place as a result of one life: Gracie Kiltz. The prayer I prayed way back, "Lord, show me anything good that can come out of a brain injured child" has been answered as God faithfully continues to show   us good upon good and all for His glory through Gracie's tragedy. By the way, Gracie has a wonderful life and has blessed and taught so many of us beyond what any education could ever have provided. Yes, Gracie has kept our eyes off of self and meeting her needs has reminded us of the things that really matter in life. She has been the anchor of our family!

A beautiful Citizen in the green house at BiG

When her 25th birthday was approaching, John and I, knowing she would not marry, decided to have a wedding-style birthday. So we invited all of her co-workers from BiG and the many family and friends that supported us over the years. 325 people showed up, and it was the best dance party ever! Gracie was honored, but it was our way of thanking all who prayed and came alongside us as a family as we fought for her life. It will be a night we remember forever!

I conclude with this: As a human being, I would have never chosen Gracie or her road. But knowing Gracie, what her birth, illness and brain injury has accomplished, I would choose her again and again. Has the journey been tough? Yes, beyond imagination. Is it still tough? Yes, but in different ways. I am fully confident in who God created Gracie to be and in His loving sovereignty over every detail. He continues to surprise me again and again with "hidden treasures found in the darkness" as Isaiah 45:3 speaks. It is a privilege to be her mom in spite of the challenges and to watch all the ways in which God works in and through her. He radiates His love and mercy personally to me through her smile and sparkly eyes and continues to draw me closer to Him. For that, I will always sing… "Amazing Grace how sweet the sound!"

Behind the Story

Erin was given a book titled, "Let me Grieve, but not Forever" by a considerate person anticipating the family of a Citizen at BiG might need it one day. It sat by Erin's bedtable for two years when, on September 8, 2018, it became a blessing to Erin and her family. On that day, Gracie departed to Heaven from sepsis due to a twisted colon.

Thursday afternoon, September 6th, at 2:00 p.m. Gracie was taken to the ER where the doctor didn't physically examine her, disregarded the evidence of shock on her hands. It was clear to Erin looking back on the experience that Gracie was not given priority because of being special needs. The doctor did a CT scan of her abdomen and the obstruction was overlooked, so Gracie was sent home.

Erin recalls how they couldn't get Gracie comfortable, even after giving her multiple doses of Tylenol with codeine. Gracie's breathing became labored, and they knew she needed to return to the ER immediately, which was 1:30 a.m. on Friday morning. Upon seeing her, the ER doctor wanted to do a CT scan of the chest, convinced Gracie had a pulmonary embolism. John, Gracie's dad, asked for another CT of her abdomen, which the doctor refused since one had been done the afternoon before. In response to this rejection, Erin and John asked for another radiologist to at least read the scan of her abdomen again. The doctor said, "Oh no, we don't second guess another physician's interpretation."

Forty-five minutes later, the ER doctor came back scratching his head while Gracie's belly distended further. John and Erin asked if Gracie could be transferred to ICU but were told she wasn't stable enough to move. So, Erin asked for ICU to be brought to Gracie. When they finally arrived, the medical staff knew immediately what was going on, that Gracie was suffering from Compartment Syndrome which is when pressure builds and presses on internal organs. She would need to be opened to relieve that compression. The only possible way for her to survive was for a surgeon to go in and find the source of the sepsis. A foot of twisted bowel that had become gangrene was discovered during the operation. The surgeon felt Gracie could recover but would need to have her abdomen open for three days for the swelling and infection to be removed.

They packed gauze on her open belly starting at 10 a.m. September 7 until 1:15 a.m. September 8th when Gracie departed.

Erin observes, "God, in His sovereignty, chose to take Gracie home, but the whole reason BiG exists is to elevate and give dignity and value to the lives of our children with special needs. After experiencing what happened to Gracie right before her death, we can see the need to continue that mission into the medical field." Erin explains that when they first arrived to the ER, not one doctor touched her. There was evidence of shock on her hands. Erin asked if it could be an allergic reaction and was told, "No, an allergic reaction would come with breathing problems." Beyond giving that answer, no attention was given to the blotchy patches.

Once the ER doctor who was treating her during the second visit realized how much trouble Gracie was in, he had her intubated and then came out to talk with the family about a DNR (do not resuscitate). In just ten minutes time, Gracie had to be revived twice and the doctor began to make a case for the DNR. The doctor persuaded, "If we have to do compressions, I will break every bone in her chest." Erin told him, "Bones heal!!!" Then the doctor made another attempt, bringing up "the cancer." Erin asked, "What cancer?!" He said "The Leukemia." Erin informed him that Gracie had been in remission for twenty-three years and was the healthiest child in their family.

As it became obvious Gracie wouldn't survive, the Kiltz family gathered around, singing Amazing Grace and praying to know that it was God's will for Gracie to depart. At 1:15 a.m. there was a loud, solitary clap of thunder. Erin says it was so loud, she thought a huge piece of equipment had turned over above them. No other thunder was heard that night. Gracie's death brings Erin back to that moment twenty-three years before when she was in the hospital being told that Gracie had flatlined for 20 minutes. She had been praying in the 8x10 foot room set up for parents of a dying child when a wind rushed through from nowhere, bringing with it Gracie's complete healing. Erin observes, "Gracie had so much more against her then, yet survived. She was gone for 20 minutes but lived for 23 more years. This time, overlooking a simple twist of the bowels brought death." Erin realizes how God has protected her so many times. She knows too well God gives, and takes away.

Erin has been asked if she is angry, and her answer is, "No, that's not my temperament." Have her feelings been hurt? "Yes!" she replies, "There's so many parents who don't delight in having a child with special needs. I delighted in Gracie, and enjoyed her every day, so her early departure is something I can't understand. Being able to usher Gracie through life felt like a sacred assignment. It was a privilege serving and advocating for her. Every time we went out, she was a little magnet. She was the living paradigm shift of what BiG is all about; but this paradigm shift started in our family, where we loved Gracie and saw God's purpose through her life. I saw such a presence of God's Spirit as I fed her, bathed her, dressed her, and when she departed, I felt the presence of the Lord leave with her."

Nine hundred people attended Gracie's funeral. Erin prayed that God would anoint the service and since then people have constantly reached out to her saying how life-changing it was for them. Even those with no belief came to the funeral and witnessed the impact of Gracie's life.

Erin has a long-term goal to build a full residential community on 150 acres, not just for those with intellectual challenges and physical disabilities, but also for those with deafness and visual impairment. It will have an element of sustainability including a wedding venue and chapel, as well as "Retirement with a Purpose" where people who want to retire but still volunteer can live in little cottages and be part of a vibrant, purposeful community. The 150-acre community will be called, *Grace Place*. Learn more at: *www.brookwoodingeorgetown.org*

Erin holding the last piece of pottery Gracie made before her departure

With God, All Things Are Possible

Lynette Connell Jones

On October 1, 1999, the "thought for the day" on my desk calendar at work, said, *"Don't let the need for perfection paralyze you."* I had no idea how that phrase would come to mind in the days, weeks, months and years ahead.

Things that are seemingly insignificant at the time can change everything; including shaping one's purpose in life. That is what happened to me that same October day in 1999.

At 2:20 in the afternoon, I was driving to a live broadcast when I reached across the passenger seat in my SUV for a split second, reaching for the directions to my destination. (It's funny, how important one second of our life can be). As I did so, the tires of my new vehicle went off the road. I can still hear the crashing sounds from the metal of my vehicle as it rolled over and over six times. Thrown from my car, all I could think to do was sing, "Jesus loves me."

I was raised in Harlingen, Texas, about 45 miles from South Padre Island. My childhood was not what many would call typical, or maybe sadly, in our culture today, it might actually be considered "typical." Although my parents loved me, my mother was a chronic alcoholic and my dad was busy working, and also had his own problems with alcohol. I loved to sing and that became an escape for me, but I also began hanging out with the wrong crowd and subsequently, at the age of sixteen, began a relationship with an abusive boyfriend.

Everything seemed to be spiraling downward, and I wasn't doing well in school. My mother's alcoholism was growing worse, and my dad had been diagnosed with Parkinson's disease. He was now going into a deep depression. In the midst of all of this, my brother was about to go to college, so my dad decided to move us lock–stock and barrel to Killeen, in Central Texas, where he had many family members. At this same time, my mother continued going to treatment centers, so many that I couldn't count. We all got sick of that; so in some ways, moving to Killeen seemed like it would be a fresh start.

The change to living in Killeen turned out to be gut-wrenching for me, and what we thought would be a "fresh start" for my mom only got worse. Mom hired cab companies to bring her booze. She always found ways to get and hide it. My dad had just given up, and mom got to such a low point that my aunt took her to Starlight Village Hospital in Kerrville, Texas. They knew this was it; her last time to detox.

Again, the singing was an outlet for me, and I also began hanging around with the "right" crowd. Was there any hope, any silver lining, for a girl like me? Hold on to your hats, because then came the deep-seated knowledge in my heart that God had a plan for my life. Let me take a moment to say, "We have an amazing God. Even with an imperfect life – not so great choices – no great role models in my life at the time– God gave me assurance in my heart. He loves me and has a plan for my life!" Not only that, but God had taken me out of situations I shouldn't have been in. He didn't stop there; He also came and told my mom that she would be alright. After 20 years of alcoholism, during my junior year in high school, my mom got sober!

Now, it was time for me to go to college. I didn't have a clue of what I wanted to do. After auditioning at different colleges, Southwest Texas State offered me a small scholarship. (It's now – Texas State University in San Marcos). I majored in vocal performance, and while there I sang in several operas, including the role of Musetta in Puccini's opera, "La Bohme."

In 1987, I left college to help my mom and dad. My mom had a triple bypass in Houston, and because of medications given to her, had to go back to detox. During this time, my elderly dad's Parkinson's was progressing.

After my mom recovered, I went back to college and then in 1988, just 30 hours short of my degree, I met a Killeen man, and we were married. Both of my parents were doing well and life was wonderful. My dad had learned to accept his Parkinson's and was still able to walk me down the aisle.

Life was truly wonderful. Throughout my marriage, I performed in the Vive Les Arts Theater in Killeen, which was a highlight of my life. I loved singing and enjoyed the lead roles I played in "Oklahoma," "Hello Dolly," "Lend Me a Tenor" and many more!

Then there are those hilarious times in my life, when at 32.5 weeks pregnant in 1995, I was singing at a funeral and as I hit the high note in the "Lord's Prayer," my water broke! I finished the song, but the only available car to take me to the hospital was the hearse. Not only that, but the funeral director had to drive me, as everyone else was in the funeral. The look on the face of the nurses who were prepared for any emergency was complete shock and disbelief. What was going on? The funeral director explained to them that a woman in his hearse was having a baby and they asked, "Is she dead?" This recollection is much funnier now than at that moment!

Kyle was born seven and a half weeks early, and he was in the hospital for two and a half weeks. There are consequences to our actions. A few years before Kyle was born, my mom found out that she had throat cancer from smoking. As a result, she had a laryngectomy which meant she had to speak using a voice prosthesis (buzzer). As I was in labor, mom leaned over me and counted my contractions with her buzzer.

Again, our amazing God is able to bring good out of bad situations. There's so much strength that I learned watching her relationship with God while going through the alcoholism, cigarettes and heart disease, followed by throat cancer. It was strength I would desperately need in four short years.

After 20 years of hatred for the demon grip of alcoholism that held her; my mom became the most incredible mother and example for me. God is able to do that which seems impossible. He brought good and love out of the evil demon of alcoholism.

Because of the voice prosthesis, doctors told my mom she would lose her personality and most of her friends. (She lost friends, but definitely not her personality!) One might say, her personality was feistier than before as she became president of the Laryngectomy Society and frequently spoke to those who also had throat cancer. She wanted to make a difference in the lives of others. What is impossible for men is always possible with God!

During the declining health of both parents, I had a premature baby with complications. Kyle's lungs weren't fully developed, and he had respiratory syncytial virus (RSV) which meant he was in and out of the hospital. He couldn't breastfeed as he couldn't latch on. Because of this, he didn't get all the initial antibodies that were needed and had many allergies. Kyle's weight went down to 4lbs, 6oz.

After bringing Kyle home, we found that he was allergic to all of the formulas and responded to them with projectile vomiting. He was in and out of the hospital at the same time my parents were in and out of the hospital, sometimes in different hospitals and in different cities. I was back and forth, all over the place, spiritually, mentally and physically.

My mom's cancer had moved to her lungs when Kyle was about eight months old. During this same time, my elderly father's Parkinson's began to worsen. As a result, we had to make the decision to place dad into a nursing facility where they could give him his medication and assist with his mini-strokes.

A bright spot was Kyle's first birthday on August 3; however, clouds again moved in as my mother died just a month later, September 17, 1996. When we told my dad that mother had passed, he had a stroke that same day as he had not been able to go and see her and the clouds over us became darker. He died a month later, on October 23.

I eventually separated from and divorced my husband. I didn't want to be in Killeen anymore since my parents were gone, and I needed space from my ex-husband after the divorce. Since I had been in marketing for a radio station, I moved to Waco, Texas where I took a job with Clear Channel Radio, which broadcasts five radio stations. I needed the move. So, I packed up my little son and myself and bought a beautiful old house that was built in the 1930's.

After my parents died, I got caught up in materialism. Boy was I into it! I had new furniture, new clothes, new shoes, etc. All these worldly things were important to me at the time, but I was so lost. Now, please understand, nice house, nice furniture, and nice clothes are not wrong in and of themselves, but they had become the priority for me. I hadn't found a church home in years. God kept knocking on the door to my heart. I knew He was right there for me, but the stress of everyday life, the overwhelming job, my young son, taking him to meet his father on weekends, everything seemed to take precedence over and above God and yet, I knew...

At 6:30 in the morning, I was taking my young son to the daycare and not picking him up until 6:00 in the evening. This job was really too much. I was in way over my head. On Saturdays, I had live broadcasts, so I'd meet his father halfway, and he would take Kyle for the weekend. My son spent every night sleeping in bed with me because he was too afraid to sleep in his own room without his daddy there.

I remember early one morning sitting on the back porch of my beautiful new home. I had all I ever thought I wanted right up to a good looking brand new 4-wheel drive Suburban with fancy tires. A few moments passed. It was about 5:00 a.m., when I cried out to God: "I'm lost and alone!" I didn't know a single soul, just the people at my job. I had moved away from everyone and everything.

My morning started off as every other morning. I dropped my son off at daycare and went to my office as usual...just another seemingly ordinary pressured day in my routine of life. Little did I know that "usual" and "ordinary" would not be words in my daily life within a few hours.

October 1, 1999, I pondered the "Thought for the Day" on my calendar at work: *"Don't let the need for perfection paralyze you."* I left work to go to a live broadcast and at 2:30 that afternoon, I reached over on the passenger seat of my SUV for one split-second to retrieve the directions to my destination.

There are 60 seconds in a minute, 3,600 seconds in an hour, 86,400 seconds in a day: One second – what is the value of one second? In one tiny, minute second my entire world came crashing down – literally! In one second, the accident happened. As I bent over to reach for the directions lying on the passenger seat, the tires of my new Suburban went off the road! My hand was on the bottom of the steering wheel as I suddenly lay thrown, twisted and contorted across the passenger seat, which caused me to over-correct. The violent crashing sounds of the metal sharply penetrated my ears as my vehicle rolled over six times.

Although I had my seatbelt on, I was thrown violently from the SUV. I could hear the fierce smashing and destruction of the metal as I was hurled from the car to the ground, and all I could think to do was sing: "Jesus Loves Me." Jesus loves me this I know! I remember feeling a total peace and warmth from where I landed. Had I not been thrown from my car, despite having my seatbelt on (which was a life-saving-miracle), the Suburban would have crushed me.

As I was being loaded into the ambulance, I was calmly giving the first responders all the contact information they needed. I didn't think anything was wrong because I couldn't feel anything. However, that was about to drastically change and so would the rest of my life. But, God...so many times that has been the "distinct" phrase that comes to mind...God created me and you; God has a purpose for each and every life. God had a purpose for my life, and I could have easily died, But, God...

Once inside the ambulance, all went dark. My lungs collapsed. At 5:20 that afternoon, they told my family that I had broken my neck at C 6-7 and would probably be paralyzed from the chest down. Because my lungs were collapsed, I was on a ventilator as well as a feeding tube. I was in traction and on a striker bed, which goes back and forth, and side to side, so you don't get pressure sores.

I couldn't see my son! I was 33 and Kyle was four years old. We had only lived in Waco for two months when the accident happened. I had no friends – no church – only people at work. The husband of a co-worker went to the school to get Kyle and bring him to the hospital as my family from Killeen had not yet arrived. My ex-husband was in Corpus Christi, Texas and had to drive back from there. I had no one – or so I thought. But, God was there patiently waiting, watching, providing wisdom, all in His grace and mercy and love.

The vertebrae of my neck were lying side by side because the neck had broken. It wasn't severed, but there was a contusion. The doctors had to put my spine back together, because the vertebra were on top of each other. They put a plate from C 5, C 6, and C 7, on the back and the front.

The nurses kept trying to wean me off of the ventilator, which resulted in eight bronchoscopies because the lungs would collapse, and they had to use a machine to inflate them again. While I was on the ventilator, I couldn't talk. I could only blink once for yes and twice for no. I remember during the last bronchoscopy, I was praying they wouldn't have to do it again, because it's a horrible procedure. During this last bronchoscopy, I was under anesthesia, when suddenly I was standing there on the side of a stream, and Jesus was on the other side. I was a little girl. He put his hand out, and my small hand reached up to grab his hand, just touching the palm. Jesus led me on stepping stones, one by one by one, over to the other side. After that experience, my oxygenation went to 99%, and I didn't need to have any more procedures.

The doctors discovered that my vocal folds were paralyzed and as they were trying to wean me off the feeding tube, whenever I would eat something, it went straight into my lungs. That is why the lungs were filling with fluid. My vocal folds being paralyzed also meant my vocal cords were not functional. I was told I probably would never sing again! My mechanism, my outlet was gone! But, God...

I had to learn a different way to swallow. Praise God for therapists! I had to start with everything pureed. For 57 days I remained on a feeding tube; although, they had weaned me off the breathing tube.

Eventually, I was moved from the hospital in Waco to TIRR (The Institute for Rehabilitation and Research) in Houston, Texas, which is a world-renowned spinal cord injury hospital. I was there until January, 28, 2000.

Finally, after three weeks (which seemed much longer), my son was brought to see me. Kyle didn't recognize me. He cried. So did I. Kyle was

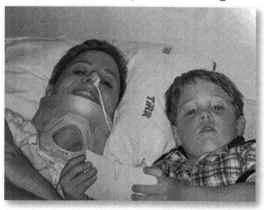

brought a few more times; finally my ex-husband would stand there with Kyle and set him on the floor, where he would walk around a little bit. Eventually, he was crawling up on the bed. He would sit on top of me, lay on the pillow, and we'd watch cartoons.

When they weaned me off the ventilator, he would sit and feed me. Kyle would help me do my therapies, and the very first thing I wanted to do was teach him to crawl up to my lap so he could ride with me on my wheelchair. They taught him how to climb in and how to push the wheelchair, even though he couldn't see over it.

My family was in Killeen and I was in Houston, so they got an apartment which made it easier to visit me. My hands were paralyzed, so they strapped utensils to them using an adaptive hand splint to teach me how to use them. One day Kyle wanted me to color with him, and I had to tell him:

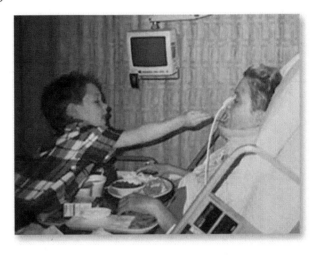

"I can't, my hands don't work." Kyle answered, "Yes, you can Mommy!" He placed the crayon in the sleeve of my adaptive strap and moved my hand back and forth on the page. He was pleased with our masterpiece. During this time, I also had low blood pressure, and my feet had to be elevated or I would faint. Kyle was there with me through all the things I had to learn.

When I had to go in for another procedure, I remember coming out of the anesthesia thanking the doctors for playing the movie during the operation. They asked, "What movie?" I answered, "The movie on the ceiling." I was watching cheerful, chubby cherubs which were jumping from cloud to cloud, teasing the stately, beautiful angels with long wings. It was peaceful, but, also a comedy as the little angels were mischievously tormenting the more majestic angels. The doctors told me they didn't play movies; there were lights above, but no pictures. I felt this was God's sign to me that I was progressing, and He was leading me through the next steps.

At 33 years of age, I again received some news that was hard to swallow in more ways than one! Because of the nature of my paralysis, I was going to need constant care. My parents had died and I was divorced, so it was essential that they place me in a nursing home and they were looking for one in Killeen for me. I was devastated. I thought I'd be in the retirement home side with my own apartment. Because my body now required so much assistance, I would need to be on the nursing home side. I prayed for strength and wisdom to know and do God's will, even if it wasn't what I wanted. I read and clung to Philippians 4:13: *"I can do all things through Christ who strengthens me."* Through every trial, everything that had happened, this was my go-to verse; God had led me through all these things so far just like the stepping stones: one by one by one.

I had a young son and couldn't see how it would be possible to still be a mother, caring for her child, while living in a nursing home. Lying there at night, with no one around, unable to get up even to make a phone call, I tried to figure out what to do next. I had been through many losses in my life: my parents' death, divorce, and all the physical disabilities since the accident, including the ventilator when I was unable to speak. But this, with my young son, the prospect of living my life in a nursing home – the feeling of loss was more acute than ever, and it cut like a deep knife!

Again, I clung to Christ in prayer. Soon after praying and pondering this difficult situation, a social worker arrived to give me the news that because the accident had happened on the job, I qualified for 24-hour nursing care. This meant I could live in my own place! My family immediately went to work setting up an apartment which was completely accessible. When I was able to go home to the apartment, it was prepared with my own furniture, a hospital bed, a roll-in shower and a sink that my wheelchair could pull up to where I could strap on the devices to brush my teeth and put on make-up. I was finally gaining some independence and there was also a room for my son. I was exuberant!

Kyle could come after school and visit me. His father had a car dealership and Kyle loved to play "car lot" with his matchbox cars lined up in a row, joyfully reciting their prices, sometimes to the tune of "One Million Dollars!" Kyle would take me for walks and push the wheelchair. He would make picnic lunches, and we'd sit under the tree eating the craziest of things! Life was getting better. As a mother, being able to have Kyle with me was so important.

Then, the Monday after Mother's Day, darkness again entered my life as I was served papers seeking sole custody of Kyle. The thought of that loss was totally unacceptable. My motivation to get better after the accident was almost centered entirely on being part of Kyle's life. I was Kyle's mother, and I knew I had to do everything I could to fight that custody battle. I called my attorney, and we started working through the details. First, I needed to learn to drive. In June of 2000, I went to a second rehab at TIRR to learn more skills for independence. I really needed to learn to drive as soon as possible. I couldn't hold myself up, so they velcroid my chest to the seat. I learned to drive with handheld brake and gas. I also had a knob on the steering wheel which I turned with one hand. Soon, I was able to operate a van on my own and pick up Kyle, which helped with my custody battle.

There were lessons for Kyle and me both to learn. I had to learn to take him and pick him up from school. And, I had to learn to teach Kyle many things: to wash all parts of his body, to stand on a stepping stool to do his laundry, and to microwave meals. I'd get the little boxes of cereal for him to eat on his own. Even though I had nurses there, I wanted it to be him and me doing these things together. There are so many jokes about me picking him up from daycare...we had some good times! The daycare would bring Kyle out to the car and strap him in; then when we'd get home, it was our time to play. I called the attorney to tell her what I had learned to do and remember her saying that there's not a judge in this world that would take that child away from me.

When I went to the second rehab, I wanted to see the ENT doctor that told me my cords were paralyzed, and I couldn't sing. He told me he understood I wanted my vocal cords to work, but not to get my hopes up. I asked him to test them. He put a camera down my throat and asked me to say "ah." When I did, he lit up, saying, "Your vocal cords are healed!" Up to that point, I had light speech and wasn't very loud, so I just assumed my cords were still paralyzed. But I sensed they were getting stronger, and that was the reason I asked him to check if they might have regained some function.

The doctor told me they were restored, and I started slowly singing again...which was awful at first. I knew that I was to sing for the Lord, not to sing opera, but to sing for God. So, I started a journey of singing and speaking everywhere. I spoke to a lot of MOPS (Mothers' of Preschoolers), groups and churches – any group that needed inspiring. My message was especially centered on what we will do for our children, and what they will do for us. As a mother, my son was a big part of my motivation, and because of him, I never allowed myself to be sad.

In 2001, just a few years after the accident, Kyle and I had our accessible home built in Harker Heights, Texas. With an accessible stove, oven and pull-out dishwasher, we had our version of normal life. I still had 24/7 nursing, but everything was accessible for me. My bathroom had a roll-in shower and accessible sinks. There were sidewalks all around the house so that I could go everywhere outside with Kyle. We lived on a cul-de-sac and Kyle would ride his bike around it while I kept up in my wheelchair. Our life was "normal" for us. There was a core of good friends, the stability of loving family members, plus everything I needed for a sense of some independence was provided. I had the van and our new home. Worker's comp helped me with the van and paid for all of the modifications I needed for my vehicle as well as modifications for my home.

I had sold my house in Waco, that we had only lived in for two months. With selling my house, everything I owned went into storage for two years. Clothes, shoes, personal items – all were waiting in storage. Sweats were my only clothing for a short time and then my nurses were creatively ingenious, dressing and undressing me with what I called "costume changes!" In the past I had worn the most fashionable high heels; now, I was just thankful I had someone to help put on my shoes. But, at the same time, I was humbled and so broken that all I could do was look up. Everything I thought was important: clothes, shoes, house, car...material things...were all gone. I had to look up – to the light away from the dark. I had to look for a new life, and with God, all things are possible!

Look to the Light

I awoke in the middle of the night, and walked to the edge of the cliff. Stopped, looked up and glanced at the stars shining bright...

Then I was drawn back, to the deep, dark, dismal canyon far below.

*Tears running down my face, I was compelled to take a step closer to the dark......
When I heard a voice from on high, speak calmly to me,*

"When you are in the dark - look to the Light." To my knees I dropped with head lifted up – The light from above - shining down on me.

No matter the problem – no matter the case When in the dark – look up to the Light

When in the dark – When in the dark – Look Up to the Light!

-Joan Box

As I go to hospitals where people are newly paralyzed, I now comprehend their feelings. The sadness is real – I didn't understand it when I first visited those newly paralyzed. God covered my heart, and I was protected through most of those feelings. These people have lost so much, and they don't know what they will do next. One man was a plastic surgeon, and his hands were paralyzed. How could he support his family? There are so many difficult questions.

Looking back, it was partly naivete that kept me from feeling a lot of the concern and, at times, it seemed as if I was just floating along with the protection given me. (Of course, I know now it was the hand of God staying with me.) Now I realize the experience of being paralyzed is something people can only take one day at a time, often, just one hour at a time. There is a helpless feeling of being in a bed where people are talking down to you and talking over you. It feels as if you've lost your voice, lost control over your decisions, over everything! I had a lot of different emotions. As a mom, my son was that driving force to make me want to be able to do as much as I could – more than was thought possible.

Now, God says to pray in specifics, so after my accident first happened, I was praying for a man of God with a good back to come into my life! Well, that is pretty specific, one might say! I dated around and tried to find that special relationship and decided it wasn't coming. But, God....

I kept saying that same prayer. I was at a stop light and heard, "He is coming!" Well, let me tell you, I was waving at every driver that went   by that day! Then online I found someone I thought I wanted to have   a relationship with, but what he was looking for was someone to be a speaker for his ministry called, "Christian Courage." We were talking back and forth, and he said he'd like to meet me.

Terry and I met for dinner in Temple, Texas. We kept missing each other until we finally got parked in the same area. My sense of direction is awful, and I couldn't find the meeting place. As he was walking towards the car, got to the car, and sat inside with me, I just knew Terry was the one, and I believe he knew it too. There was a certain way we looked at one another... we just knew...I think it surprised him. Terry wasn't looking for another wife with physical challenges, as he had just watched his first wife suffer through cancer.

I joined his Christian Courage Ministry sharing our testimonies through speaking and singing. Terry would meet me at my car to help me in and out. There were hugs, and I was just dying inside, because I knew! He was

always so encouraging about my voice, my singing, my gifts – and how I should be singing for the Lord. Terry was a cheerleader for all the gifts and purpose I felt in my life. Sometimes he would come by to just talk, but I knew he wasn't coming by "just to talk." Whenever I would hit rough patches on the road, in this, my newest journey in life, he'd always call, pray with me and get me through.

I met Terry in August of 2011, joined his Christian Courage Ministry, and then in September of 2012, we started dating. I knew all along that it was more. We were married August 31, 2013 and my son, Kyle, walked me down the aisle. Oh, and going back to when Kyle would come to see me after school and play with his match box cars...he now operates two used car dealerships!

Whenever I haven't been able to get into certain places, Terry picks me up and takes me there. He has a strong back and is a man of God. Terry is exactly who I had been praying for all that time. Remember that specific prayer! We're an incredible team, and we do everything together. We are involved in another ministry, "Racers for Christ." Terry raced sprint cars, and so wherever there's sprint car racing, we go pray with all the drivers. If there's an accident, we go to the hospital with the drivers. Some want to pray, some want knuckles, and some just want to wave.

Joni Erickson Tada is a well-known Christian quadriplegic who paints with her teeth. I was blessed to sing with her at one of her banquets for the nonprofit she started called, "Wheels for the World." Now, Terry and I are ministers for her nonprofit. We collect manual wheelchairs in Texas and send them off to a prison where they refurbish the chairs for children with disabilities in third world countries. Physical therapists travel with these chairs and rebuild them for people in impoverished conditions. Seeing a child with no mobility sitting on a cardboard mat being given their own chair where they can wheel around is unbelievable. I always go back to the message I read on October 1, 1999, the day of my accident, *"Don't let the need for perfection paralyze you."*

When I first had the accident, I wondered what I'd be able to do with Kyle. I knew I couldn't pick him up, play ball with him or do things little boys love. In 2005, I went on my first Eels on Wheels scuba diving trip to Belize, and from there went on to Aruba, Bonaire, Honduras and Grand Cayman. Kyle

learned to scuba dive alongside me and started going with me as my dive buddy. He was ten the first year he went. Then, we started going to New Mexico where I learned to snow ski, and he would snow board. We have enjoyed many outdoor activities together.

One day my friend, Liz, called me; she had found a saddle online. It's built with a leather back on it, and straps that go completely around to hold someone in the saddle. The saddle was in a pawn shop and was made for  a quadriplegic. I bought the saddle, took it home, and noticed that the man who made the saddle had his name on the back of it. So, I called him asking for info regarding the saddle. After all, it is not every day one finds a saddle made for a quadriplegic! The man who made the saddle was a roper and had an accident driving a truck. He wanted to ride again, so he learned to construct saddles. He makes custom saddles and asked for the other name on the saddle. This particular saddle was made for a thirteen-year-old boy, and the boy was 5'3" and weighed 110. I said "I'm 5'3" and weigh 120 pounds. He said the saddle needs to fit correctly or one will get pressure sores.

Now, here is the rest of the "saddle story": my son saddled the horse at my wedding, and I was led off on a beautiful paint horse! We went to Jamaica for our honeymoon and experienced sailing. This past weekend, we took our family to Lake LBJ where Kyle and Terry put me on a tube, with them sitting on either side of me while we were pulled behind the boat. These are things people often think they will never do, and it just goes to show that disabilities don't have to stop you from experiencing everything in life to the fullest. Of course, there is one "Catch 22" – God needs to be # 1 in your life and in control, and boy has He been in control of my life!

Everything I have done and will ever do, is because God strengthens me. (Philippians 4:13) I am completely dependent on Him each and every day just to move, to get out of bed, and to be watched over should my blood pressure be too low or too high, causing catastrophic damage to my body. God has always provided for me. I still have 24-hour nursing. Someone is always here. These are blessings that are insurmountable. Everything that is good in my life is based on the trust and faith that God is going to take care of me, and He is in control. I don't know where I would be without Him.

Being dependent on God, and praising him every day, is a gift that I am able to share with those who have experienced disabilities, heartache, hardships and discouragement. God has been with me through it all, and He will never leave me!   Some may wonder about the purpose of such a horrific accident and loss of mobility, seeing it only as a tragedy, but it is the way I have come to draw closer to God, to know He lives and, most importantly, to know His will for me. *"Always pray, continuously, give thanks in all circumstances: for this is God's will for you in Jesus Christ." -1 Thessalonians 5:16*

Behind the Story

Lynette's husband, Terry, dreamed of forming an organization to help people realize that life is a wonderful journey, and it takes Christian Courage to be the messenger God intends us to become. His late wife, Suzanne, fought cancer for 14 years and is the inspiration for this message. Despite the adversity of battling cancer, she lived with hope and exuded positivity. Terry became the founder and partner of Christian Courage Inc. which is the ideal platform for Lynette to share her music and message! Because her vocal cords were restored, Lynette feels called to encourage people to have hope and believe that, with God, all things are possible.

Christian Courage is an organization that seeks to recognize and proclaim acts of courage by the faithful. They highlight stories of courage for the glory of God and hopefully inspire courage in those who need it most.

Terry says, "We see courage in others; sometimes we are courageous ourselves. We want to recognize the courage that comes from faith in Christ." He adds, "Christian Courage is humble strength; it is how we show the Holy Spirit that is within us."

Terry and Lynette speak and sing all over the nation to anyone who needs the message they bring and are available for bookings. They can be contacted through: *www.ChristianCourage.org.*

A Wheelie Perspective

Cami Barney

When asked to contribute to this book, my initial reaction was, "Why me? My family life is so very normal. We are a mom, a dad, and a little boy. We like to make pancakes for breakfast; we go to work and school; we love the park and the pool. We go to the zoo, and have story time at the library, sit in traffic, and deal with toddler temper tantrums before bed. We have a garden in the backyard, and bikes in our garage." Everything about our lives seems so normal to me, except that we do it all on wheels. However, had someone shown me a picture of my life five years ago and told me I would describe it as normal, I would have looked at them like they had three heads. So maybe we aren't so "normal" after all.

Our journey began almost five years ago, with our initial positive pregnancy test. I immediately started planning for my baby. First, I figured out his due date. Then when he would start kindergarten. Then the year he would graduate from high school...and so on. We talked about family bike rides, Nate (my husband) coaching his soccer and T-ball, and we argued if he would be allowed to wrestle or not. He would, of course, be a mommy's boy, and I would teach him to be the perfect gentleman: always open doors for ladies, give grandmothers kisses on the cheeks, and so on.

I spent the first 20 weeks getting to know my little baby. On slow nights, I would sneak into the back of the ER where I worked as a nurse with the ultrasound machine and catch little glimpses of him swimming around in there, kicking up a storm. *Oh my goodness, that little fetus was ADORABLE!* I talked to him, sang to him, and planned his life for him.

I went to my 20-week ultrasound the week after Thanksgiving. It was December 3, and the Holiday season was in full swing. Christmas happiness was in the air, and I was ready to get up-close and personal pics of the little guy, excited that Nate could finally get a piece of the ultrasound action. We waited with anticipation as the tech got everything set up and started looking around with the equipment. She was very quiet. I was smiling so big and showing off my little baby to Nate. But then the ultrasound tech stood up and said she was going to get the doctor because there were some things she wasn't sure about. The room was dark, and Josh Groban was singing "Silent Night" over some invisible sound system. A few minutes later, the doctor walked in. He started looking, and then starting talking, telling me to "look at this, it shouldn't be like that" and "this right here isn't normal" and "here are your options."

I felt like I was in a vacuum, or a tunnel, or a black hole, or one of those rides at the fair that spins you around and around where you stick to the wall, and you can climb up and down the wall because right then gravity was confusing, and you wanted to throw up but you had heard that if you threw up you would choke on it and die, because kids tell horrible stories like that. Nothing made sense.

I held back my sobs somewhat effectively until the doctor left. I felt abandoned, confused, guilty, and alone. Alone because the baby I had gotten to know and come to love was no longer there. He was gone, replaced by a new baby that I didn't know anything about besides his brain was all wrong, and maybe his foot too, and his spine, and HE WAS ALL WRONG.

Our baby's diagnosis came back myelomeningocele, or Spina Bifida, which means he had a giant hole in his spine where skin and bone should have been. He also had an Arnold Chiari malformation, which means his brain stem was being pulled down into his spinal cord, as well as hydrocephalus, which is too much fluid around his brain.

We were devastated and in shock for several days before we decided to call a high-risk OB from our church and ask him for advice. He told us not to wait around for the second opinion and gave us a list of six specialty programs in the US to contact that deal with this diagnosis. After looking at the programs, we decided to start with the one at the Children's Hospital of Colorado in Denver. We called the following Monday afternoon and they immediately scheduled us for a full day of tests and consultations for that Friday.

On Thursday, December 12, Nate and I flew to Denver. Friday (the 13th) we had a fetal MRI, a fetal echocardiogram, an ultrasound, and a meeting with a geneticist. Immediately following our tests, a large team of doctors met to discuss our case. After about 40 minutes of discussion, we were invited in to meet with the team. Our team included the head of the program and pediatric surgeon, a maternal fetal specialist, a neonatologist, a pediatric neurosurgeon, a pediatric neurologist, a pediatrician, an OB/GYN, a geneticist, a radiologist, a fetal cardiologist, and an orthopedic surgeon.

They decided that we met the criteria for an intra-uterine, or open fetal surgery on the spine. On Friday, December 20, 2013, less than three weeks after our diagnosis and at 25 weeks gestation, they made a horizontal incision on my skin from hipbone to hipbone, and then a vertical incision on my uterus. They then exposed our baby's back and corrected the open neural tube defect by placing a patch over the hole. He was out for approximately 38 minutes. Then they replaced the amniotic fluid that was lost with normal saline and stitched everything back up. Everything went well, and I remained on bedrest both in the hospital and the Ronald McDonald House across the street for the next nine weeks.

The weeks between receiving our diagnosis and meeting our baby were incredibly difficult: emotionally, mentally, and, because of the surgery and pregnancy, even physically. Pregnant moms and dads like to plan, to imagine an exciting and happy future with their children. With a prenatal diagnosis, there is so much that is unknown. Our biggest and ever-present question was, "Will he walk?" But there were so many other unanswered questions as well. *Will he survive the surgery? Will he make it to delivery? Will he be able to breathe on his own? Will he get an infection? Will his brain and his ability to think and reason be compromised? Will he be able to live independently?* and so on. And the ONLY answer to every question was, "Time will tell."

Our baby was born on a cold February morning. We named him Calvin, and after all we had been through over the last few months, after all the unanswered questions, he was our perfect answer. All of our worries seemed unimportant as we held him in our arms and watched him breathe, and eat, and wake up, and take in the world. We realized how little most of our questions mattered anyway. Someone told us a few weeks in, "Maybe he'll walk, maybe he won't. Either way, it doesn't matter, walking has no bearing on someone's ability to be happy." Holding our sweet little baby, we realized that was true, and actually, we didn't much mind that he would probably never walk, because our hearts were so full of love for our little miracle, there wasn't really room for fear or doubt at that time.

Calvin was in the NICU for about a month, and it is still one of the most special times for our family. I remember sitting in the cozy little hospital room, watching the snow fall outside our window, feeling like the only three people in the whole world. We got to know our little boy, and began our life as a family there. It helped that Calvin did so well in the NICU, just learning how to eat and growing. His lungs and heart and brain all did great, and finally after over three months away from home, we were discharged and drove away with a new baby.

We had only been home a few days when our new-baby euphoria started to fade. Calvin started having concerning symptoms and at six weeks old had an emergency surgery to place a VP shunt that would drain fluid from his brain to his abdomen. I remember driving home from the hospital after the surgery for a change of clothes and bawling my eyes out, praying loudly, asking God how much he expected me to take, and telling Him that I couldn't handle much more.

Calvin was discharged after two days in the hospital. When we took him home, he cried and cried – when we moved him, touched him, tried to feed him, all the time. It was awful. He was in pain and there was nothing we could do about it.

The second night home he started breathing funny. We watched him for a while and then decided to take him to the ER. When we got there, he had fallen asleep, so we decided to not check in and just go home.

We watched him all night and at 8:00 am the next morning, we got too nervous and took him back. After six hours in the ER, it was deemed that his breathing was totally normal, typical of premature infants, and we took him home.

The next two days I watched him and watched him. He kept breathing different, eating different, crying different, acting different. We tried to convince ourselves that, like the ER doctor said, that was all normal. We attributed it to post-operative pain, to him being more alert now that the pressure on his brain was gone, to normal baby fussiness.

I got more and more worried until I was no longer functioning like a normal person. I couldn't think, couldn't focus, couldn't talk, couldn't eat or sleep, couldn't even look at Nate. All I could do was watch Calvin's breaths. Every motion I went through was to make sure he was still alive.

He had an appointment with his pediatrician soon, and I could hardly wait to hear another confirmation that, yes, this was all normal. Then on a Wednesday morning in April, one week after his shunt was placed, as I was holding him in my arms, Calvin went limp, turned blue, and stopped breathing.

When I looked down and saw that my sweet little baby was blue, my heart stopped. Immediately I thought back to the last blue baby I had coded at work. I remembered that baby's face, his eyes wide open staring blankly into space. I imagined my hands holding that little boy, doing chest compressions. I remembered the team doing CPR.

I knew what I was supposed to do, but my body couldn't do it. I let out what, if anyone had heard, they would have described as a blood-curdling scream. But no one heard, because I was home alone with him. I screamed out his name, told him to wake up. I kept screaming. He kept not moving.

I ran down the hall and somewhere along the way remembered that I should do rescue breaths and call 911. I was shaking too badly to do either. I put my mouth on his face and attempted to breath for him, but I knew I didn't do it right at all. I ran down the stairs and out the front door. As I ran across the street to my neighbor's house, I tried to call 911.

But I couldn't get past the home screen on my phone – I couldn't remember how to place a call. I kept looking at the calculator app and trying to remember how to press the right numbers.

When I reached my neighbors door, I pounded and screamed. Nothing happened. They weren't home. At this point, something inside me clicked. I was all alone, and I needed to be in control.

I was finally able to call 911. I was not, however, able to talk in a normal voice. After waiting on hold for what was probably seconds, but seemed like an eternity, a lady answered, "911, is your emergency medical, (something, something)?" I told her medical, my baby is blue, please send someone NOW! "Calm down ma'am! I can't understand a word you are saying. What's your location?"

That made me mad enough to remember to give another rescue breath. This time Calvin gasped a little and startled. He looked at me, and his eyes were so wide. He started to go from blue to grey and was trying with everything he had to breathe. I ran back to my house and tried to answer their questions in between my screams to Calvin.

"Does he have any medical history? Is he responding appropriately?" What???!!! Again, this jolted me back to reality and I was able to give another breath, which is good, because not once did the lady actually tell me to breathe for my baby. He began breathing irregularly, and went from grey to white.

At this point my neighbor drove by on her way home. She ran up to us, and I threw her the phone – I couldn't handle the 911 lady any more. I gave him a few more rescue breaths and he started to come to. Finally, a fire truck came around the corner. They immediately put Calvin on oxygen and he started to improve. He was still pretty limp in my arms, but he was breathing.

My neighbor called Nate and minutes later we were both in the emergency room – the emergency room where I worked – once again. They began to run some tests, and took the oxygen off to get a swab of his nose. This time Nate was holding him when he stopped breathing, and, once again, started to turn blue. The doctor watched him. And watched. And watched. Finally, I asked him if he would maybe like for me to give my baby some rescue breaths.

"I want to see what he does," was his reply. He turned blue, and went limp. They called a code on my baby. People came running. Nurses, respiratory therapists, pharmacists... My co-workers. My friends. They worked on my baby until he was intubated and stable. They hugged me and gave me tissues. They stood next to me while everything was happening, comforting me, saying just the right things (Not like the 911 lady).

Calvin had a CT and an MRI checking his brain and his shunt. They showed that while the shunt had relieved pressure on the top of his brain, the Arnold Chiari Malformation was still causing pressure on the bottom of his brain, the brain stem, which controls the body's ability to breathe.

Calvin had rocked in the NICU. He started out strong and improved from there. We were there for a month but really only had bad news a few times. We had many friends in the NICU who got bad news a lot. Nate and I talked about how awful that was for them, and I told him I didn't know how we would handle bad news because really, we only got good news. We felt so blessed because we had the best baby in the whole NICU, and in the whole world.

And yet, the NICU was hard. People would tell me how strong I was – but I didn't feel strong. I cried a lot. I even thought, "Why Calvin? Why me?" There were days and nights that I thought things like, "This is the hardest thing I've ever had to do," and "This is the worst day of my life."

Perspective – and time – changes everything.

While in the NICU, we were able to hold our baby just about whenever we wanted. We were able to feed our baby when he was hungry, except once, right before his surgery. We were able to hear our baby when he cried, and watch him as he breathed. We were able to touch our baby. But the biggest thing – and the thing I didn't appreciate at the time – was that we always knew we would bring him home. It wasn't a matter of *if*, only a matter of *when*. After months of not knowing what our future would hold, it was finally easy there to imagine our lives with Calvin, easy to look forward to the future. I would imagine laying on my soft carpet at home, with the windows open, basking in the sun with him. We imagined going on walks, reading him books, watching him grow... We even looked forward to the normal new parent things – midnight feedings, diaper changes, taking him on car rides when we couldn't get him to stop crying. I thought that that experience was the hardest thing I would ever have to do.

But the pediatric intensive care unit (PICU) was a whole different world. We couldn't hold our baby. We had to watch him cry, but we couldn't hear it because there was a tube down his throat blocking the sound. But

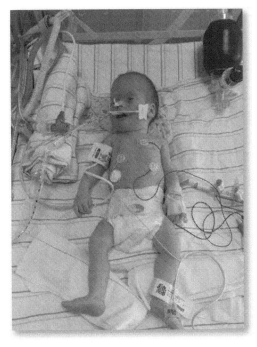

he needed that tube, because he couldn't breathe by himself anymore. And we couldn't comfort him, because if he moved, it would put pressure on his brain stem, and he would stop breathing, even with the tube.

The first day was one of the hardest. We still weren't sure exactly what was going on, or why Calvin wasn't breathing, so he had a second MRI in the morning. When he got back, we stopped his sedation and waited for him to wake up. He started to stir around 5:00 pm, and I was able to hold him for about 10 minutes. The last time I'd held him was over 24 hours before, and he had stopped breathing. I was terrified, but grateful to hold my little man again. Then the doctor decided to take out his tube and see how he did. He didn't do well. We watched him struggle for an hour- a very long hour. He stopped breathing five times in the hour. The doctor told us, "He doesn't have the drive to breathe."

I left the room sobbing. I couldn't watch my baby struggle anymore. The doctor tried to put his tube back in, but his throat was too swollen and she couldn't. Nate watched them bag our baby while the emergency room doctor – the one that sent us home a few days earlier and told us his breathing was normal – raced upstairs. He was able to replace the tube and Calvin turned pink again, the shade I've termed "baby pink," the color babies should always be.

Calvin didn't do well that night. He started producing thick green mucous in his lungs as a result of all the intubations. His kidneys stopped producing urine. He had a period where he stopped breathing – even with the tube in him.

That night my best friend who was a NICU nurse came and took care of Calvin for us while Nate and I went home to eat, shower and change clothes. While there, I asked Nate if he wanted to play the best-case/worst-case game with me. He asked if I thought I really wanted to do that. I told him that we are both thinking it, we might as well talk about it.

Best Case:

Calvin wakes up, pulls his tube out (because he's breathing on his own and knows he doesn't need it), and is in his crib waiting for us when we get upstairs. He stands up and tells us he loves us and wants to sleep in our bed with us, please?

We had a good time coming up with our best-case scenario. When we finished, we were quiet. Neither one of us wanted to finish the game.

Calvin spent three weeks in the PICU on life support. During that time, he had a decompression surgery, where the neurosurgeon removed part of his skull and top two vertebrae. Eventually the pressure on his brain stem was relieved enough that he was able to come off the vent. We went home Mother's Day weekend, and it seemed like half the PICU came with us. Our home was now filled with oxygen tanks and concentrators, pulse ox machines and probes, nasal cannulas, boxes and boxes of equipment and so many bottles of medication. We had been in the hospital almost full time since the week before Christmas, and the whole time had wanted nothing more than to be home with our baby. Now that we were home – almost five months later – we missed the safety of the hospital. I often tell parents of sick kids in the hospital that are desperate to get home, "The only thing worse than a super sick kid in the hospital is a super sick kid at home." It seemed like the doctors had done everything they could do to keep him alive, and now it was our turn. Actually, just my turn, because Nate had to go back to work. Though he was able to breathe enough to get off the vent, Calvin still stopped breathing A LOT. He was on oxygen full time and a pulse ox monitor, so I knew pretty quickly whenever he stopped breathing and was able to "remind" him to breathe by gently shaking him, and occasionally giving rescue breaths. We moved across the country a few weeks after being discharged and began seeing all new doctors. Calvin's new pulmonologist was shocked that he hadn't been given a tracheostomy (permanent breathing tube), and looking back, he really did need one, but our method had worked so far, so he let us continue without the trach and vent for the time being. He told me during one appointment, "You call me as soon as you're too tired to do this anymore. I will put the trach in the next morning."

I was tempted to call him so many times. Calvin didn't go for more than 20 minutes without taking a pause in breathing that required intervention for months. Nate had just started his first year of medical residency and was working 80-100 hours a week. We had just moved across the country where we had no family, no friends, and actually didn't know a single person. I was so, so tired. There were nights when I would scream into my pillow after waking up dozens of times to help my baby breathe. I would ask God time and again, "Why can't you just let my baby breathe!? It's NOT too much to ask, I know it isn't!" I fell into a fog and for the rest of Calvin's first year, barely functioning above survival. Calvin had a total of seven surgeries that first year, in three different states and five different hospitals. We spent weeks and weeks in the hospital. We were deprived of sleep and of hope. But right around Calvin's first birthday, things started to change.

Calvin's brain began to heal. He could go longer and longer without oxygen, and around his second birthday started only needing it when he slept. He started sleeping for longer stretches, and eventually became a great sleeper, sleeping through the night by age two and 12-14 hour stretches by age three. We made friends in our new home, and everyone that met Calvin immediately loved him. Sleep, being home, and being surrounded by

loving friends helped Calvin heal and grow. When he was eight months old, his uncle and a neighbor made Calvin a Bumbo wheelchair. Though he wasn't able to sit up, roll over, or crawl, he could propel himself forward in his little chair, and Calvin began to explore his world.

We immediately realized what a huge blessing this little Bumbo wheelchair was. We watched Calvin learn and explore, become independent and curious. Right before his first birthday, he was fitted for his first real wheelchair, a bright orange Ti- lite twist. We were

SO excited for Calvin. This was an AMAZING (and super expensive and high-tech) chair. It would mean independence, no more stroller, now he would have a say in where he went and what he did. Perspective is a funny thing. A year and a half after learning our son might need a wheelchair, and hoping and praying that wouldn't be the case, we were ecstatic about the fact that he was about to get his first big wheelchair.

When he was 16 months, we went on our first official outing on wheels. It was to an art museum, somewhere I thought was a safe bet for accessibility. I remember being overwhelmed and surprised at how hard it was emotionally. Calvin had been using his little Bumbo wheelchair for over six months, and I thought I was used to how he looked in a wheelchair. But a Bumbo wheelchair is cute and little and original, and almost looks like a toy. A *real* wheelchair is definitely a piece of medical equipment, and there's no question that we are telling the world, "My son cannot walk. And this is forever."

I thought I would already be used to the stares. Calvin had been on oxygen for over a year and people stared, and asked questions about his health all the time. It was always centered around his breathing though. I never said, "Yes he has trouble breathing, oh, and by the way, he's also paralyzed." I was always able to give the strangers hope, "Nope, the oxygen isn't forever, it's just temporary; he's getting better every day!" But the wheelchair provided no such hope for those that didn't understand. So many people, really a surprising number, asked, "Will he ever walk?" I used to answer, "Well, we just don't know, medicine is advancing; he's still growing," on and on, just to make things less awkward, and to make the strangers feel better, giving them hope that this sweet, happy little boy wouldn't spend his whole life in a wheelchair.

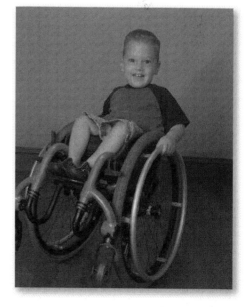

But then I realized how truly wonderful and amazing Calvin's wheelchair is. I know a wonderful

14-year old girl who also lives her life on wheels, and she recently spoke to a group of young people and said, "What people assume to be my greatest trial is actually my greatest blessing." It's hard to understand how life on wheels can be such a blessing until you live it. I see how happy he is in his wheelchair, and how much freedom it gives him. I see how it opens doors to let people into our lives. I've learned about a delightful, secret world full of people living on wheels. I observe strangers watch Calvin, and they can't help but smile at the happy little kid wheeling around like crazy, popping wheelies and spinning circles so fast that *I* want to puke. And now when people ask, "Will he ever walk?" I happily and confidently say, "Nope! He's paralyzed for life. And look at how amazing he does on his wheels! Isn't this world we live in so great!?"

Behind the Story

Calvin has grown into a happy and active little boy. He loves sports and participates in wheelchair racing and tennis. He loves going to the skatepark and wheelchair motocross. He recently got to meet his hero, Aaron "Wheelz" Fotheringham at an adaptive sports event, and loves coming up with plans to do his own wheelchair stunts. He also enjoys going bowling and to the driving range with his dad.

Calvin is kind to everyone, and very patient, traits that have come with the territory of doctor appointments, therapies and travelling to specialists. He is confident and independent in his wheelchair, and though he is sometimes sad that he can't do some of the things his friends can do, he never complains. Questions have been raised by Calvin lately, wondering why others walk and he doesn't. Cami sees this as his next big struggle. She says his health has stabilized, but the emotional part of growing up is on the horizon. Cami shares, "This is a hard balance we are learning how to deal with. I'm trying to acknowledge his feelings, but I am concerned he will take on what I feel about it, so I'm not going to be sad about the situation, even though it's so hard to watch him struggle. I know he will follow my emotional lead, so my strategy is to stay positive."

Calvin is starting kindergarten soon, and is very excited to learn new things. He also just became a big brother to Weston and is so proud. Cami says, "I was worried because he's been an only child for five years and has had more attention than is probably normal, but he has taken to sharing everything so well and is never jealous." She also shares how patient Calvin is for his age, with a calm demeanor. "He is sympathetic towards others. I think being in a wheelchair has made his personality welcoming and friendly."

The Barney Family

The Best I Can

David Farber

I was a stubborn, shy little kid. I wanted nothing more than to be alone in the small woods behind our townhouse in Park Forest, Illinois. At age four, I caught my first garter snake. From that moment on, I was hooked on critters, especially those other people were afraid of. My parents seldom reacted to my fascination for bugs, birds, mammals and reptiles because, at that age, I was more into a just-watching-the-critters stage than the bringing-them-home advancement. Also, my parents were too busy fighting with each other. I suppose some of my desire to spend time alone in the woods came from wanting to escape the fighting. Both my parents were chain-smokers, and I probably enjoyed the fresh air as much as I enjoyed the critters. I hated the stench of cigarette smoke, and I still hate it to this day.

When I was five, they separated. My father tried to explain what was going on, but I really had no concept of what it all meant. A year later, they divorced. Had I been older, I probably would have seen it coming. Back then, in the late fifties, custody of children was almost always awarded to mothers. My mother, two sisters, and I moved to a small apartment in Chicago near Morse and Ridge. Unfortunately, my mother was not equipped financially or emotionally to handle me and my two sisters, ages three and eight, so by the time I was eight, my sisters and I ended up in different foster homes. I don't remember much about my feelings at that time except being relieved the fighting was finally over. I was glad to be away from my mother and sisters, but all I knew about a foster home was

I would be living with complete strangers and wouldn't really feel like I belonged there.

My first home in Chicago was a good one. My foster father was a Chicago cop, which I thought was pretty cool. My foster mother was a chain-smoker, so instantly a wall of dislike was thrown up between us which kept me from getting close to her. What I really wanted was a brother that I could play with, but in that first home, I only had a younger foster sister who was allergic to animals. As a result, I was allowed no pets except for a small tank of fish. Once, I brought home a baby alligator a friend from school had given me, and tried to put it in the fish tank. Since it had no fur, my foster sister wasn't allergic to it; still they wouldn't let me keep it. After barely a year in that home, I told the counselor at the Children's Bureau that if he didn't find me a new home, I was going to leave. He believed me, and by the grace of God, he found me a new home in Skokie, Illinois.

I thought I was the luckiest kid in the world. Mike and Clara Burg were the greatest parents I could have asked for. Clara made me feel like this was really my home. I grew to love her very quickly and deeply. I loved Mike also, but in a more distant way, since he was a chain-smoker. At nine years

old, I was able to appreciate what they were doing for me. They taught me the value of hard work and that I should always do the best I could. They also encouraged my individualism along with my love for animals of all kinds. Soon I had a menagerie: garter snakes, frogs, ground squirrels, hamsters... the works.

Except for the hamster, my pets were all ones I had caught myself. But when I was in seventh grade, I saw a really neat three-foot-long Columbian rainbow boa at a pet store. I had never approached

Clara or Mike before about getting a boa of any kind – actually, I had never even really thought about it. I came home from school and asked Clara, "How come you won't let me get a boa?" I think I caught her off guard because she responded, "I never said you couldn't get a boa." "Then can I?" I said. Shortly after, that three-foot- long Columbian rainbow boa which I named Hercules became the first of many pet boas and pythons.

If God has always been watching over me, as I'm sure He has, I guess I have unintentionally kept Him on His proverbial toes. From my earliest days, my fascination for critters of all kinds has led me into woods to get scratched up, stung and bitten. This fascination bloomed into a study of the venomous snakes of the world. By my junior year in college, I was sharing an apartment in Chicago with my friend, Karl, and I had a fairly good collection of venomous snakes. Among them were four species of cobras, a number of old-world vipers and a growing collection of North American rattlesnakes. This hobby was not in itself dangerous. What made it dangerous was the fact that I enjoyed handling these creatures without tongs, hooks or gloves. Cobras, water moccasins, rattlesnakes- it didn't matter. *What's the worst that can happen?* I figured. Well, I could get bitten and possibly die, but somehow, this thought never bothered me. I enjoyed using my knowledge of the snakes' behavior and my skill and speed to keep from getting bitten.

I miscalculated only once, in the summer between my junior and senior years in college. I had just gotten a small Malayan pit viper from a supplier in Thailand, a cousin to our water moccasin. He arrived with a bad shed, so after soaking him in warm water, I proceeded to peel off the dried unshed skin. For some reason, this was the one time I wore gloves for safety, and I didn't feel him slipping through my grip. He bit right through the glove and got me at the base of my right thumb. I swore at him and locked him back in his special fish tank. Then I picked up my surgical dissecting kit and went into the bathroom.

I called out to Karl to let him know what happened and asked him to bring me my manual on poisonous snakes of the world, the one used by U.S. amphibious forces. Again, because I had been studying venomous snakes for seven years already, I was able to remain completely calm in this new and somewhat dangerous situation. It seemed that this kind of thing was becoming second nature to me. In the book are LD50 charts which calculate how much venom from any given species it takes to reach a lethal dosage, killing 50 percent of the mice injected. With this information, I calculated my body weight metrically and the amount of venom it would take to reach the LD50 level for that body weight, compared to how much venom might have been injected given the size and approximate age of the snake. Then I compared that to the venom production charts in the book. I have always had a high natural resistance to bites, infections, and pretty much any sickness, partly due to my healthy lifestyle. I have never smoked, and I tend to not go anywhere there is smoking. I also never drank anything other than milk, water and a couple of fruit juices, so I wasn't too worried about the bite; after all, I had been reading and studying about this sort of thing for about seven years. As I saw it, this was just a test of my knowledge, and the pain wasn't so bad it kept me from concentrating. I had already applied a tourniquet a little above the bite, just tight enough to slow the circulation, but not so tight as to cut off the circulation. I made measured incisions into and just above the bite. I then applied a suction bulb to each incision. I had to be careful because of the location. If I cut too deeply, I might sever a tendon or nerve and lose the use of my thumb permanently.

One property of that type of venom is that it also acts as an anticoagulant. This should have made my job easier since I'd always had a strong clotting factor and because the incisions had to be very shallow due to the location. Even with the venom acting on my blood, the bleeding from the incisions kept stopping, making my job that much harder. Eventually, I had to make a total of eighteen shallow incisions, each a pair of incisions a little farther up the arm just ahead of the swelling. After about forty minutes, I figured that was about all the venom I could get out. I was exhausted. Making those incisions into my own arm took more out of me than the effects of the venom. After I cleaned up everything, Karl and I went out to grab some dinner...Chinese food from a place by our apartment to satisfy the Malayan viper in me.

The next day, my arm was swollen to about the size of my leg and the guys at work hounded me until I relented and went to see a specialist at Northwestern Memorial Hospital in Chicago. He examined my hand and arm, said I had done a good job, gave me a tetanus booster, and charged me fifty bucks. Within a week or so, the swelling had gone down, and the arm showed no aftereffects except for a little soreness. The only unfortunate outcome of the whole incident was that, two weeks later, the snake died, probably from some illness it had when I received it. Then again, maybe

I have bad blood. I don't know anyone else who has ever been bitten by a venomous snake and the snake died.

I don't know if I'm accident-prone or just a klutz. Back in 1977, while working on a large steam safety valve at Allied, I did something wrong and the valve blew. I was hit in the middle of the chest with 350 pounds of steam per square inch at 425 degrees. I suffered second and third-degree burns from my waist up to the base of my ears. I had thrown my right arm up to protect my face, so the underside of the arm was also burned. My shirt looked like it had gone through a paper shredder with me still in it. The skin on my chest was split open, and there were blisters the size of my fist just dripping off me.

My body must have gone into immediate shock because I felt almost no pain...*yet*. Everybody in the shop was in a panic, but somehow, I remained calm. I think my martial arts training had a lot to do with being able to remain calm in this situation. Mentally, I was able to control much of the pain, but the rest had to do with the fact that my body was already in shock and the full effects of the burn had not yet hit me. Some of the ability to take charge of this situation came from always having to rely on myself, growing up in foster homes, and also the lack of God in my life. I had to learn to depend on myself at a very early age because I didn't know that there was anybody else that I could rely on. Of course, now I know that the Lord has been and is always with me. He is the one who gave me the strength to endure the kind of pain I was going to go through when that steam hit me, especially after the shock wore off.

I was just glad it was me and not one of the other guys who normally tested the valves at that station. Most of them are of a smaller build than me and would have been seriously hurt. I told them to bring cold, wet clothes. Then, when they were driving me to the hospital closest to work, they made a wrong turn, and the pain finally got to me. I almost ripped the dashboard off the van. As soon as I walked into the emergency room, they started asking me questions. I told them I would gladly answer all their questions later and ripped open the electric doors to the treatment room. The doctors there saw the problem immediately, got me onto a table and started covering me with ice. My heart was racing, and I was hyperventilating. Somehow, I was still completely coherent. By this time, the pain was too intense for me to control mentally. I told the doctors I was going into shock because I couldn't catch my breath. They gave me an intramuscular shot of morphine, but it had no effect. Finally, after trying but failing to control the pain, they gave me an intravenous shot, and that did the trick. Finally, my breathing slowed down enough to answer all their questions.

They placed me in a room where I was in complete isolation. Nobody was allowed in to see me without a cap, gown, gloves and mask. With burns that severe, there was great danger of infection. Having a degree in biology, in a pre-med sequence, helped me to know just what my body needed. Immediately, I instructed the nurses to keep a pitcher of orange juice at my bedside at all times to replenish body fluids and for extra vitamin C. When the doctor came in, he told the nurse the same thing, then as he turned around, another nurse came in with the orange juice. When he asked who ordered it, she said I did. That night, when the male nurse came in with a shot, I asked him what it was. He said it was for the pain. When I told him I did not want it, he said, "I think you should take it." I told him to take it and get the heck out. I have never believed in painkillers because I believe that if you mask the pain with drugs, your body doesn't realize it's been injured and does nothing to heal itself.

The next day, the doctors were discussing whether or not to debride. Debriding is the removal of all the burned skin. Back then, this was still a debated topic because it leaves the area vulnerable to massive infection. I told them to go ahead and debride the whole area because I was extremely resistant to infections. After the painful process was finished, the burned areas were covered with a thick layer of silver sulfa diazine burn ointment.

The accident happened on Tuesday morning. I checked out of the hospital on Saturday morning. Allied Valve had a large emergency repair job, so instead of going home, I went in to machine valves until late into the night. Every day for the next two weeks, I went back to the hospital for whirlpool treatment, after which new dressings were applied. By the end of three weeks, there was no trace of me being burned, except that I no longer had a tan, and I was a lot more nervous – and cautious – around the big steam valves. If given a chance, the human body has remarkable healing abilities. Now, I realize God had been watching over me even when I tried to blow myself up.

In my junior year of college, I bought my first motorcycle. Money was tight and I couldn't afford a good car. The motorcycle got great gas mileage, and

I felt freedom on the bike. Also, since the bike was more maneuverable than a car, I would be able to avoid any accident, or so I reasoned. I didn't figure on somebody else running me over seven years later. My mother, however, hated the things, and would not even let me talk about getting one when I lived at home, even after starting college. I should have listened to her. Mothers know best, of course.

I was twenty-eight-years old when I finally, fully woke from a three-month coma. It took me a while before I was able to comprehend what my doctors, friends and parents were telling me. I had been in a horrific accident on the way to the health club, the one time in seven years of riding I had forgotten my helmet. I found out that a teenage driver had made an illegal left turn coming from the opposite direction. She had cut off a few cars and met me in the intersection of Route 68 and Hicks in Palatine, IL.

This life-altering event happened September 8, 1981. The injuries were a broken back, T10 and T11 fracture dislocation resulting in a Brown-Sequard lesion of the spine which affected only my right leg. Most of my ribs were broken, causing my lungs to collapse. My collarbone on the right side was broken. I had a fractured C6 vertebra in the neck, a shattered right cheekbone and the entire right occipital bone in my skull was crushed, causing a cranial-cerebral trauma that paralyzed the entire left side of my body. The cranial nerve damage completely deafened my right ear and rendered my right eye non-functional. Other than that, I didn't even get hurt.

> Odds against surviving the first night: less than 10 to 1
> Weeks in a deep coma: 7
> Weeks in a semi-coma: 6
> Total weeks in the hospital: 50

After the accident, I was rushed to Northwest Community Hospital in Palatine, Illinois. Though I had survived the first night, doctors told my parents I would not live more than two or three days. By the second week, they were calling me "Miracle Boy." Then they told my parents that I would not likely come out of the coma, and that if I did, I would probably be a vegetable. (I know that I'm more than a little nutty, but nuts are a fruit, not a vegetable.)

I have no memory of the time spent in the deep coma and only fragmented memories of drifting in and out of the semi-coma. I remember the needle, a morphine shot hitting my leg, and then I was out for a while longer. Once I woke to my father, Daniel Farber, trying to shave me. And at other times, I remember calling for the nurse because I couldn't breathe. My lungs were filling with fluids and needed to be suctioned. This is a frightening ordeal because it not only sucks excess fluids out through the tracheotomy of your throat, it also sucks out all the air. I felt like I was drowning.

Near the end of November, I was more or less out of the coma, though still having hallucinations from the brain trauma and the morphine. Darn! My ten-year high school reunion was the day after Thanksgiving, but it looked like I would miss it. My biggest worry back then was just surviving. I had been a physical fitness buff, mountain hiker/climber, weightlifter, martial artist, swimmer, scuba diver, and anything else that nature offered me. Now I had to learn to live with the use of only one functional eye, one functional ear, and the use of only my right arm. I had been pretty much a loner and agnostic almost all my life. Now I was forced to accept help for almost everything, from caregivers to people in general, but I still had to try to do it myself.

In mid-December, I was transferred to Lutheran General Hospital's rehabilitation unit in Des Plaines, Illinois. This hospital was much closer to my parents' home and they could visit every day, but I hated its cruel doctors and nurses. I was in agony. Almost everything was broken from the waist up, and all I wanted was to lie in bed and be left alone. Because of the broken back, they had fused my spine from T8-T12 with a chunk of bone taken from my pelvis. They also implanted Herrington rods from T8-L1 to stabilize the spine until the fusion could heal. I had to wear a specially made back brace whenever they sat me up at more than a thirty-degree angle. Unfortunately, they measured me incorrectly for the brace, so when I was in a sitting position, it would cut into my lower gut. As a result, I was even more miserable, but the doctors thought I was just whining.

Since I was left-handed and my entire left side was paralyzed from the cranial cerebral trauma, I could no longer write. The therapist decided I must learn to write with my right hand. I still was not cognizant of the extent of my injuries, but kept thinking that one of these days I would wake up and my left arm would be fine. Nonetheless, the insistent therapist kept putting this big pen in my hand and telling me to make a capital "A" and a lowercase "a," which is not the way to teach an adult with a bad temper how to write. Frustrated, I kept crushing the pens, and it made me even more determined not to write with my right hand. It took a long time before I realized that everyone was doing what they thought was best for me.

In April 1982, I was sent to Bethany Terrace Nursing Home for three weeks, until the Rehabilitation Institute of Chicago had my bed ready. By this time, I was no longer wearing the steel brace that had been causing me so much trouble; instead, I had to wear a heavy elastic body binder to help support my back. One morning, the aide forgot to put the binder on, and a couple of hours later, I doubled over in agony. When they got me down for a rest, I saw the binder sitting on the dresser. Now I understood why my back was in such bad shape. At the same time, I also realized that the binder was doing all the work, and that's why my back wasn't getting any stronger. I never wore the binder again. After a few days of slowly diminishing pain, I have never had any real back pain again – at least, not debilitating pain.

At the nursing home, I befriended Jan Pagen, a woman about my own age who fell from a horse and broke her neck the day before starting nursing school. She was a quadriplegic, but because the break was C-6, low cervical, she had partial use of both arms but not her hands. After being babied by her parents for ten years, she decided to go back to school and get her master's degree in sociology. Talking to her did me a world of good. An able-bodied individual may know theoretically what you are going through, but they don't really understand. Jan knew and understood because she had gone through it all. On her door was a poem that I fell in love with. When it was finally time to transfer to the Rehabilitation Institute, I didn't want to trust the poem to my memory, so the day before I was to leave, I sat in front of Jan's door for over six hours with a pencil and paper determined to legibly write down this poem. Well, I did it! And that incident showed me that if you are trying to re-teach a literate person to write, give them something worth writing not just an uppercase "B" and a lowercase "b." A couple years later, Jan left the nursing home to move out West and gave me the copy of the poem that was on her door:

Tomorrow Is a Dream that Leads Me Onward....

Tomorrow is a path I've yet to choose; it's a chance I've yet to take,
a friend I've yet to make, it's all the talent I've yet to use.

Tomorrow is a dream that leads me onward,
always just a step ahead of me....

It's the joy I've yet to know, the love I've yet to show,
for it's the person I have yet to be.

-Karen Ravn

*(Karen Ravn, I don't know if you are still alive, but God bless you for having
the sensitive heart to write this poem.)*

The Rehabilitation Institute of Chicago has a reputation for being the best in the world, and I quickly found out why. At Lutheran General, all I wanted was to be left alone. Their rehab floor is geared more for elderly and stroke victims. I don't think they were ready to handle someone with injuries as extensive as mine. Plus, there was only one other patient on the rehab floor anywhere near my own age to whom I felt I could talk.

At the Rehabilitation Institute, there are patients of all ages, some with injuries that made mine seem like a minor scrape. What's more, they were all trying their hardest, and that gave me the will to fight and improve. Within a few weeks, they were chasing me around to get me to lie down and rest so I wouldn't get pressure sores.

One day my next-door neighbor, Diane, and her parents came to Chicago to visit me, and we walked – and rolled – to Water Tower Place for lunch. After lunch, Diane's parents went into the Walgreens store while Diane and I waited outside on the busy corner of Michigan and Chicago Ave. I was in a RIC electric wheelchair that was equipped with a cup holder and a drinking cup. As Diane and I chatted, a woman walked up to us and gently dropped a quarter into the empty cup. We just stared at her, trying to keep from bursting out laughing. The lady looked at us and said, "Isn't that what it's for?" "Nope," I answered, "it's just for drinking." She turned about every shade of red imaginable. Later, I related the story to my doctors. After they stopped laughing long enough to catch their breaths, they said I should have told her, "Folding money only, please." Lady, if you are still out there, thank you and bless you for the kind heart and many good laughs at a time when I did not find much to laugh about.

When I was first discharged from the hospital, I had frequent periods of sometimes very deep suicidal depression. *Why did this have to happen to me? What am I going to do for the rest of my life?* Luckily, I no longer had my fascination for poisonous snakes. It would have been so easy to stick my hand into one of my cobra cages and painlessly end it all. Thinking back, I probably couldn't have ended my life that way because my reflexes for avoiding snake bite had become so honed that I don't think I would have allowed myself to be bitten. Also, my zest for life was still strong. I would have to look on this as one more challenge to overcome to prove to myself that I could, and I had a secret weapon – my own anger. This anger gave me the desire to fight off depression and the will to get better.

The healthcare professionals kept telling me that I must only look forward and not dwell on the past. They say you can't live in the past, but I had to rely on my memories of that past to fuel my future hopes, especially when I had not yet learned to trust and rely on God. On my living room wall is a large photograph of a moose I had photographed on my last trip to Glacier National Park. Because this trip was still clear in my memory, I was able to use my imagination to lose myself in that picture. When I did this, I could turn my anger at the world back towards myself by thinking, *what have you done to yourself?* Then I'd remember the beauty of the area in the photo and I would think, *it's so beautiful; I've got to get back there.*

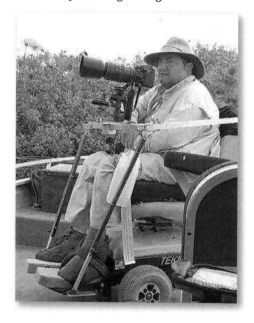

And that gave me the strength and willpower to fight through the depressions and keep going.

Almost a full year after my discharge from the hospital, I finally had the courage to pick up a camera again. I kept asking myself, *what if I can't do it anymore?* Then one day, when my Amazon parrot, Beethoven, was outside with me, I decided to try to photograph him. I'd been away from photography for almost two years, and now I had the disability to cope with. It took me a long time to set up the shots, checking and rechecking all the camera settings, but much to my surprise and delight, the shots came out better than I had hoped.

At first, I tried not to use the tripod. I wanted to prove to myself that I could still take a photograph even using only one hand. I was okay as long as I used a high-speed film and no lens longer than 200 mm, but soon, I was able to use a heavy 300 mm, then a 500 mm. When I got a new 1,000 mm lens, I was forced to use a tripod. Unfortunately, unless I planned to stay in a single position, I could not manage a tripod by myself. The configuration of my wheelchair made it too difficult, even when I had help.

I toyed with different ideas for a device that could be attached to my wheelchair and onto which the camera could be mounted. I held brainstorming sessions with friends. During one session, my friend Murray Fisher said, "What about an infant car carrier seat?" Bingo! A light went off in my head. I saw the handle of the carrier seat, and I envisioned a roll-bar device attached to my chair that would flip over me. I took my idea to Mr. Tool, a machine shop in Schaumburg, and Orin, their engineer, helped me design a utility frame for the wheelchair that would hold up my camera and the large lenses. Now I could use my long lenses.

The next problem that arose was this: when my one functioning hand was stretched out to focus the lens on a bird, by the time I got to the shutter release button on the camera, the bird was in the next tree. I needed a system to fire the camera so that my hand never had to leave the focusing ring. First, I purchased from Nikon an extended cable release for the motor drive. But the release came with two jacks on the end that had to be touched together to fire the camera. With only one hand, that was as hard as reaching for the shutter-release button. I soon came up with the idea to take the jacks off and wire the cable release to a glove so that all I had to do to fire the camera was touch my ring finger to the palm of my hand.

Another problem: I needed the glove to be loose, so I could get it off and put it on myself, but the looseness caused the contact to fail at times. Plus, when you have the use of only one hand to operate the camera, drive the wheelchair, and everything else, it's hard having that one hand wired to the camera.

My next bright idea was to take the contacts off the glove. I wired them to the outside of a clothespin with a C-shaped copper wire going from one to almost touching the other contact. This I held in my mouth. When

I wanted a photograph, I simply bit down on this clothespin. It worked fairly well, though sometimes I'd end up pulling on the clothespin and firing the camera whenever I turned my head. Also, I enjoyed sitting for hours by the Fox River near my home trying to photograph the winter ducks; in those temperatures, my tongue got awfully cold.

So, it was back to the drawing board. I thought about the sip–and–puff systems that quadriplegics use to drive their wheelchairs, so I contacted wheelchair manufacturer Everest Jennings to inquire about it. I was informed that the system cost about $11,000, which was about $10,900 more than my meager budget. I was thinking of constructing a system that would work by blowing into a tube that would shoot a ping pong ball up to hit a simple switch that would activate the shutter of the camera. That's when I remembered that my friend Murray builds pipe organs and player pianos as a hobby. Player pianos work by changing air pressure to electrical impulses. I called him, and he looked in his parts catalog and found what I needed, a simple microswitch that hooks up to the cable release. I attached a tube to it, and when I sip into the tube, that completes the needed circuit. The whole thing fits into a small three-dollar electrical box I purchased from Radio Shack.

The rest was sometimes easy, but more often frustrating. A natural-born lefty, I taught myself to cut mats, build frames and do color printing up to sixteen–by–twenty inches in a darkroom built to my own design – using only my right hand. The "quality control engineer" that still resides in me continually forces me to try and improve my work.

My invention days depended upon many caregivers. Most of my first ten live-in caregivers turned out to be drunks and thieves who preyed upon people who could no longer fend for themselves. I was paralyzed from the neck down except for my right arm. There wasn't much I could do except sit and stare out the window. Though the doctors had called me the Miracle Boy, I pretty much thought my life was over. But that's when I met Susan Fern Lopez, a selfless, giving, strongly religious woman. Sue sacrificed a great deal to take care of me, and I grew to love her very deeply. She was my friend and companion for nineteen years until her death from ovarian cancer in 2001. She gave me back my life and so much more.

How could two entirely different people, almost total opposites, survive together for nearly two decades? One thing we had in common was a love for travel. Sue had never done any traveling before she met me except for one trip to Florida, but she loved to drive and look at nature. In this respect, we were perfectly matched. Even better, Sue enjoyed listening to classical music which is the only kind I listen to. Over the years, we took many two-, three-, and four-day trips for various photographic sessions, and we tried to take a major two-week trip every other year or as often as finances would allow.

February 28, 1997, I was ready to tackle a photographic opportunity I never thought I would have. Sue and I had driven to Clearwater, Florida with my 1,000 mm Nikon lens mounted to my specially modified air pressure-triggered Nikon F3 camera. With the camera firmly attached to the specially designed utility frame on my electric wheelchair, I set out to try my luck and skill at photographing a nesting pair of bald eagles. The nest was on six acres of private property in the middle of a sprawling residential community. It was an unusually low nest, only about twenty-five feet up in a live red pine and about thirty-five feet away from a somewhat busy road. The bald eagle usually builds its nest seventy to eighty feet up in a dead tree, far away from civilization.

Sue and I got there about nine o'clock in the morning, a little later than I would have liked because we got slightly lost. I found a good spot to set up about 150 feet from the nest tree; at that distance the angle upward to the nest was negligible. By the time we got there, the female eagle was already out hunting, and the male was standing watch in a dead tree a hundred feet or so away from the nest but right next to the road. I got some great shots of him up in the tree with a beautifully clear azure blue sky behind him. After an hour of watching him, I started a conversation with a passerby who had also stopped to watch. He was interested in my unique camera setup, but we talked mostly about the eagles. I asked him what it was like to live so close to a nesting pair, and he told me how everyone who lives around the area loves to walk by and just watch these magnificent birds.

At last, the female returned to the nest, with a fish or an eel in her talons. In the deep nest, all I could see was the top of her white head going back and forth, pausing only to tear another bite off her catch as she fed the eaglets. When she finished, she settled down to rest, and all that was visible was the top of her unmoving head. After a while, the male flew in and landed on the branch only inches above the rim of the nest. This was a much better angle for me to photograph him. For a change, the sun was to my back, perfect for photography.

Now instead of just a clear blue sky behind him, I had pinecones and pine boughs added to the picture. He was busy preening himself and looking around. When he finished preening, he started calling. I got some great profile shots with his beak wide open. Then all of a sudden, he bent down and screeched at the female. I don't know what he said to her, but she stood right up in front and slightly below him. This was a situation I could only have dreamed about! I had been hoping to get some shots of the pair side by side.

I had six exposures left on that roll of film and they were quickly gone. I tried to reload the camera as fast as I could, but of course, when you're excited and in a hurry, everything seems to take twice as long. I was afraid the male would fly off now that the female was up. I finally got the camera loaded – it seemed like ten minutes, but I'm sure that it was less than a minute. I looked through the viewfinder only to see the female retreat into the nest out of my view. I think I said a few choice words, but before I even realized it, the female stood up with a chunk of red meat in her beak and was having a tug of war with one of the eaglets. That fresh roll of film (thirty-six exposures) lasted less than fifty seconds. I reloaded and was able to shoot off two more rolls during the feeding sequence, a total of 108 photographs. Even though I was having a hard time focusing my eyes through the tears of joy at actually being able to witness and photograph this incredibly beautiful event, I got some great shots – so close that you could see the pupils of their eyes.

Towards the end of 1997, after editing and printing some of the slides many times, I picked out a dozen of the best slides and sent them to *Birders World* magazine. They immediately published one of the feeding sequence shots in their readers' photo gallery in the January/February 1998 edition. I didn't get paid for it, but the feeling of accomplishment was reward enough.

Over the years, I have asked myself, *why did I have this accident? Was it truly just an accident that nobody, not even God, had any control of?* I don't think so. God gave man control over himself, but He still knows and controls everything that happens or is going to happen. Back in February 2004, I was having one of my usual restless nights, so I was reading the Bible. I'm pretty sure it was somewhere in 1 Kings that something clicked inside of me, and all of a sudden, I felt I knew exactly why I had the accident. When I woke the next morning, I thanked God for the accident and for my surviving. My accident was not a punishment; it was a wakeup call. God knew my lifestyle was fatalistic, leading me toward disaster. I'd been handling the deadliest snakes in the world without any precautions, climbing or hiking in the mountains by myself using no safety equipment, riding motorcycles, doing just about anything that was dangerous. Sooner or later, I would have either gotten bitten fatally, or crashed, or fallen alone and died.

That by itself was no big deal, except I would have died without ever knowing or accepting God's grace by the sacrifice of His only son, Jesus Christ, for our salvation. God does not want this to happen. He does not want to lose even one soul. I had never done anything so morally wrong that I could not still be saved by simply accepting Christ into my life.

The more I think about it, the more I realize that even if I could, I would not change anything about the accident except the pain I caused others. I definitely would like to have spared my parents and friends the worry and anguish they went through sitting beside my bed those first three months. Even before I found God and accepted Christ, I don't think I would have changed anything because of all the wonderful new friends I have made since my accident. Plus, I have a whole new outlook now. Before the accident, I worked fifty to sixty or more hours a week, many of which were out of town. My photography was basically a hobby, even though I had plans to build a darkroom in the home I bought when I was twenty-five years old. I may never have gotten around to it because money was always a problem. Looking back, I would probably still be working my life away – that is, if I were still alive. I would never have met Sue and had nineteen years of her love and learned how to love in return. There's just so much I never would have experienced and so many people that I hold very dear to me now, who I would never have met.

I don't thank God for everything as often as I should because it's not second nature for me yet, but whenever I think about it, which is quite often, I thank God for everything, especially my accident. I needed this second chance to learn what life is really all about. It's not just about biology. Although we do live in a body that is flesh and blood, it's a spiritual life not to be squandered away without God's grace. Over the years, I have learned to embrace this life. It's the life that was gifted to me by the Lord, to live for His glory.

Behind the Story

When Sue was alive, David was able to go on many photographic travel adventures using his wheelchair photography inventions. One of his favorite places is the Sonoran Desert in Arizona to photograph anything and everything, especially scenery: the beautiful desert with saguaro cactus, and the backdrop of sunsets and birds. He always went when everything was in full bloom. David says, "It's a magical, haunting place. I love the desert, probably because it's where all the rattlesnakes are!"

David took five trips to Alaska after Susan passed. He went twice to Chilkat Valley fulfilling his dream to photograph eagles. When all of Alaska is frozen solid, there's one three-mile stretch of the river that stays thawed because of the underground water rising up. As the salmon are spawning in late fall, the Eagles fly over 100,000 square miles to feed there. It was established as a National Bald Eagle Preserve in the early 1980's. David heard about this while still in the hospital and always dreamed of going, as a birds of prey and eagle fanatic.

Photographing the eagles in the Chilkat Valley

Twice he went to photograph grizzly bears in the Katmai National Park at the base of the Aleutian Islands. Another of the five excursions to Alaska was a dream trip, renting a vehicle and driving to Denali National Park and then traveling on down to the Kenia Fjords. One of David's Alaska trips was filmed showing how a bus was converted so he could photograph out the windows as they drove through the gorgeous scenery. Hopefully, it will be made into a documentary soon.

Mt. McKinley in the background during one of David's trips to Alaska

Ready to go in a float plane in Alaska

After the Alaska trips, David went on a safari to Botswana Africa in 2010 to photograph everything that moved: giraffes, zebras, a lion pride and a female leopard. All of these adventures are described in detail inside his published memoir, *As Best I Can*.

David jokes, "Today, I'm twiddling my thumbs, but only one twiddles." His most recent photography trip was 45 miles north of Duluth, MN, where it was a balmy 13 below zero. "It was just perfect!" says David who lives 50 miles N.W. of Chicago, where it is often much colder.

His destination, Sax Zim Bog, Minnesota, is a magnet for arctic owls. David is checking off his list as he celebrates capturing some great shots of both ends of the owl spectrum: the Gray Owl, the largest owl in North America, and the Boreal Owl, which is the smallest at just six inches tall. He spent a full weekend, from Friday afternoon until Monday morning, on the owl photography safari.

This story in *RAISING WHEELS* is a compilation of excerpts from David Farber's full book, *As Best I Can*, chronicling his journey from a life-changing motorcycle accident to fulfilling his dreams and goals, never letting his challenges prevent their achievement. David's life is a testament that with humor and undaunted determination, nothing is impossible, even if it means doing "the best we can" because there *IS* fulfillment in knowing we've done our best!

David's book and prints of his photography from all of his travels, including note cards, are available at: *www.NaturallyFarberPhotos.com*.

When God Shows Up

Evonne Fraga

In 1996, Robert and I had been married a few years when I gave birth to a beautiful baby named Christopher. He was healthy, strong, rough and tough – the quintessential boy. He loved Power Rangers and the story of David and Goliath. He wanted to be a shepherd and take care of sheep like David. He was funny and smart. Chris knew Jesus as our Healer and Savior, and talked to Him daily. He never forgot his prayers at night, and after saying his, he would remind us to say ours. He talked to God as a friend, the way we all should talk to Him. He was also very thankful. From his toys on up to his dad's UPS truck, he expressed gratitude – for the clouds... for everything!

Christopher on his fourth birthday

As Christopher neared his fifth birthday, we started noticing he was having trouble with his vision, such as a wandering eye. He began struggling with gait and dragging his right foot. Also, his speech was becoming slurred. So in July of 2001, we took him to the doctor, two weeks before he turned five. Christopher was diagnosed with an inoperable tumor on his brain

stem and given a 20% chance of surviving. We were numb. The news was unreal because he was still just a baby, the center of our world. How could this be happening?

We were sent to Cook Children's in Ft. Worth, TX where the doctors outlined a plan to treat Christopher with radiation and chemo in hopes of shrinking the tumor. He took it all in stride, showing no fear. He also became wise beyond his years when he was sick. Through the whole trial, Chris always talked about Jesus. He was dealing with his illness so much better than we were. It amazed me how well he handled everything, including the radiation and losing his hair, which made him a little self-conscious. Ironically, with all he had to go through, Christopher seemed to be more concerned about us.

After all the treatment, I never imagined Christopher would die. I prayed and prayed for a miracle because we couldn't imagine our lives without him. But five months later, Nov 23, 2001, he passed. It was unbearable. We were lost, and I felt I wanted to die; I couldn't be here without him. It took a toll on both Robert and me. For a time, we weren't sure our marriage would survive. We didn't grieve

together. At one point, Robert would be ok and I wouldn't, then it would reverse. We weren't going through it together. Robert was very angry... angry at the world and angry at God. I felt angry too because for me it was so unfair. Chris was just a child, and my beautiful boy was taken from me. I felt broken and alone, but I held onto my faith. At the time, it was all I had. We prayed that God would somehow bring us out of this darkness.

In the midst of the turmoil, our family was amazing. My mom kept reminding me of God's promises in the Bible. She let me cry, scream, be angry, but always encouraged me to lean on the Lord. At one point, Robert and I were talking about Chris when Robert got upset with me and asked, "How can you still have faith in God?" "Because Christopher did," I replied. "I know when my baby left me, he was met with a familiar face and I know I want to reach where he is. I know God gave Christopher to us, and He is the only one who could take him. I know that God loves him more than we do."

At that point, Robert broke down, but he didn't let himself feel the hurt. For a long time, he was just so mad, but eventually, he found a small church he was comfortable in. The amazing thing for me was that after two long years of ups and downs, we were finally able to get back to each other. To top it all off, Robert found his way back to Christ and was baptized, and it changed his life. I felt the Lord had been waiting to heal our hearts, but we had to be ready to receive it.

Eventually, things got better between Robert and me. At the time, my two stepchildren were living with us, and we went back to attending their school activities, our work, and our normal day-to-day living. Then, two and a half years after Christopher's passing, we talked about having another child. It was emotional and we were afraid, but we felt it was God's will. We tried not to think too much about it; if it happened, it happened. After almost five years passed, we were still unable to get pregnant. I went to the doctor and had tests. He recommended invitro, but we decided not to do that. If it was God's plan, it would happen. So, we continued as we were. During those days, I often felt empty and lonely, and sometimes it hurt me to see moms with their kids. I had that twinge of: *Why wasn't I able to have that?* But, we did our best to put it behind us.

Then mid-May of 2008, I was not feeling well and thought I had a stomach bug. A friend told me to take a pregnancy test, but I refused. I'd taken so many tests the past years with disappointment, I had no interest in taking another one. My friend ran out anyway to buy a pregnancy test and had me meet her in the restroom. I was waiting for the negative sign... but it was positive! I immediately took another test just to make sure.

My doctor was amazing and knew our situation. He was very kind, saying he was in this with us, and assured us it would be great. I had just turned 38, and the baby was due February 11. We were ecstatic, and the whole family was over the moon, as well; it was such a blessing. I was feeling good and taking care of myself. When we found out we were having a boy, we decided to name him "Santiago" after his grandfather.

On the night of October 25, I rolled over in my sleep and my water broke. We went into a panic, and Robert rushed me to the hospital. When I arrived, I was given medications to stop labor and the baby received steroids to help his lungs. I was terrified. This was too soon and we didn't understand how this could be happening. My doctor wasn't on call, but the nurse there was the same one who helped deliver Christopher in 1996, and she remembered that he had passed in 2001. She was so kind, understood our fear, and took great care of me. She called my doctor as he was getting ready for church, and a few hours later he walked in and I just lost it. He held my hand and assured me that ruptured membranes can heal. He wanted me on full bed rest to see if we could make it to 32 weeks – we were only at 24 weeks.

I thought, *I can do this; everything will be fine.* But after three days in the hospital, I was about to lose my mind. I thought I could just hang out and watch Oprah, but it was unbearable. Thankfully, I had a great support network: people who visited, family, and church members. Though it was harder than I thought it would be, I knew this is what I had to do to be able to hold my baby.

The days passed with vital signs, ultrasounds, and baby's heartbeat checks during which I'd have a panicked moment until they found that beautiful pulse. I prayed I could hold on long enough for him to be safe. Four weeks later, I woke up depressed with Christopher on my mind. Robert called and, sensing my need, said he was on his way. The nurse came in and asked if I was ok, and I began to cry with tears cascading down my cheeks. Seven years ago that very day, Christopher had gone to heaven. The nurse was kind as we talked about Chris and the time we had with him. After, I thanked her for letting me talk about him, then she helped me get up to go to the restroom. When I arose, there was amniotic fluid on the bedsheet and I began to panic. They called labor and delivery to check on me, and again, it was the same nurse who helped deliver Christopher. Somehow, she was there each time I was in distress.

The nurse phoned the on-call doctor who was on his way, but they couldn't reach my doctor. When the on-call doctor arrived, I was starting to feel contractions. They told me they were preparing me for a C-section.

My panic rose out of control and I thought to myself, *This can't happen today.* I can't lose another child on this day! A few minutes later, I could hear Robert calling my name as he came down the hall. He held me close, told me he loved me, and we prayed. Santiago was born November 23, 2008, seven years to the day after Christopher's passing. My water had broken at 24 weeks and I delivered at 28 weeks. He was 12 weeks early.

The doctors took him as soon as he was delivered. When I got back to my room, all my family was there crying. I knew they were thinking the same thing I was, *It's the same day as Christopher's passing.* I continued to think, *I just can't lose another baby today. He has to be ok!* The suspense was unbearable and I cried out to God continually to please save my baby. The NICU doctor came in to let us know that Santiago was in bad shape. He pulled Robert aside to see the baby. Robert said, "No, I'll wait until Evonne and I can go together." The doctor urged, "You need to come see him now!" So, my two older sisters went with Robert to see Santiago for the first time. They took a few pictures for me so I could see him as well. He was so sick, and the pictures broke my heart into a million pieces.

For a long time, I was angry at myself. All I had to do was hold on until 32 weeks, but I failed Santiago. I didn't protect him, and now he's hurting. I was given pain medications and instructed to rest and sleep. But, how could I sleep? All I could think was: *What if Santiago died while I'm sleeping?* I closed my eyes and asked God to help me endure whatever was coming next.

The next day, I was wheeled into the NICU and Robert helped me stand up so I could see this little baby fighting for his life. I just wanted to hold him,

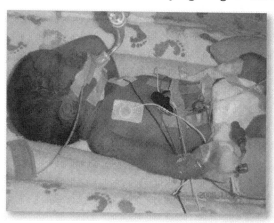

but of course, I couldn't. It was heartbreaking. Robert was good and did his best to encourage me, but I know he was just as afraid as I was. A few days later they released me, but I stayed in the NICU as long as I was allowed. Robert and I would go home to sleep at night and come back the very next day. It was torture leaving at night, and I'd call twice during the evening to see if Santiago was ok. We'd stay all day until they'd tell us it was time for us to go.

When Santiago was a week old the hospital called us early in the morning. We were already going out the door as they informed us that Santiago's right lung had collapsed. We were urged to get there right away because they didn't think he had enough lung tissue to survive. We were preparing for the worst, but he held on and made it through that day. When Robert and I got home that night, I fell to my knees and Robert did his best to console me. He begged God to send His angels to protect Santiago and to help us. He was suffering and we needed help. Then I thought of a verse I have on Christopher's headstone, Proverbs 3:5-6, "Trust in the Lord with all thine heart; and lean not unto thine own understanding. In all thy ways acknowledge him, and he shall direct thy paths." We knew we had to give Santiago over to God as we had with Christopher. We knew that He loved us and loved our boys. Even in this, we had to trust in Him. I went to bed that night and felt I had been in a fight. My body was exhausted and hurting. Early the next morning, we went to the hospital to find that Santiago had held on that night and was doing a little better. We remained hopeful. He gradually improved, and four days later he was taken off the ventilator and put on a CPAP. Then, two days later, he was breathing room air! We were amazed. On December 8, I finally held him for the first time. Santiago was so small and fragile; I wanted to hold him forever. It seemed we had cleared this huge hurdle.

The NICU doctor noticed that Santiago's head was growing at a rapid rate. He tried several lumbar punctures to relieve the pressure, but he continued to have swelling. They did an MRI, and it showed a grade three and grade four brain hemorrhage. When I saw the scan, I was devastated. We were transferred to Cook Children's in Ft. Worth, the same hospital where we had been with Christopher. When we walked in, I felt like I couldn't breathe – all those memories of Chris. But, I knew it's where Santiago needed to be. We spent several weeks in the NICU where they monitored him closely. Having to travel between Ft. Worth and Waco where we lived was hard for Robert. Thankfully, I have family in Ft. Worth who opened their home to let us stay. They were great! Actually, they are the same family I stayed with during Christopher's time there. My family was amazing supporting me through all of this.

It seemed like we were there forever. Seeing Santiago was hard because, for us, it wasn't supposed to be this way. The doctors told me I would go through grief for the child I was supposed to have. To make matters worse, we still didn't know what disabilities Santiago might have from these issues. I remember at one point a doctor walked in, looked at Santiago's chart, and examined him. During the examination, I recall him shaking his head saying "It's a shame!" *What*?! I thought. This is my baby. I couldn't even speak. That day really hurt me and set me back.

Santiago was really sick, and we knew it was bad. On Christmas Eve, they placed a temporary shunt close to the hairline of Santiago's head, so they could relieve the pressure on his brain. Also, they brought in a pediatric eye specialist. Santiago was diagnosed with retinopathy of prematurity, stage three, which means his retinas weren't completely detached, but there was a high probability he would be blind. What's more, it was decided Santiago needed a ventricular peritoneal (VP) shunt to treat his hydrocephalus. (A VP valve is placed just behind the ear and is connected to a long tube, so when the fluid in the head reaches a certain level, it drains out through the tube into his abdomen where the body absorbs it back.) The procedure was done successfully on January the 10th. Santiago started to get stronger and was soon taken off oxygen altogether.

We were finally able to bring Santiago home the end of January 2009 with a list of follow-up appointments though. There was a high probability Santiago wouldn't do well with the amount of damage to his brain, but we came home to Waco happy to have our baby boy, although we weren't sure what his future would have in store.

He did well those first few months and got the hang of drinking his bottle. They told us he had to drink at least 2oz at each feeding, but it was difficult for him to learn to use the bottle. We found he was weaker on his right side. His mouth and tongue struggled making feeding hard. But as the months went on, he became really good at eating and turned into quite the chunky baby. He was adorable, and we were so happy. We had to drive back to Ft. Worth once a week for the first two months because that's how closely Santiago needed to be monitored. The doctors wanted to know right away if the retinas detached. Each time they would examine him, inform us that he was stable, and reschedule us for the next week. We did that for a few months until the doctor said that we were out of the woods, but we'd have to wait to discover what he would actually be able to see when he gets older.

He ended up needing glasses at nine months, but the glasses made him even more adorable. Despite our initial struggles, we were blissfully happy. We had our baby and he was beautiful. He wasn't what we expected, but he was everything. Everything about him was a blessing. After the first year, we noticed that Santiago was having a hard time sitting up or rolling over. Also, it was difficult for him to hold his head up whenever he was on his tummy. We kept working with him and went for our follow-up visits. It was just before he turned two years old that he was finally diagnosed with quadriplegic cerebral palsy. At the time, there was so much unknown with CP. There was also such a broad range of complications, from mild cases to severe cases, and we didn't know what he had. Santiago began physical and occupational therapy where he continued to do well. Thankfully, we had no problems with his VP shunt. We heard stories of other families needing revisions and surgeries when something malfunctions with it, but we were blessed that he was doing fine.

Santiago with a picture of his brother, Christopher

When Santiago turned three, we started him in half-day preschool. This is also when he got his first wheelchair. I think that's when it hit us that Santiago was going to be different, and our lives were going to be dramatically different from other parents. We wanted to give him every opportunity possible, to be able to reach his potential whatever that might be. Starting school was hard at first, but he liked it. As Santiago has grown older, we do see where he is delayed. He's had trouble reading and struggles with math. But the amazing thing is that Santiago is really smart; it's only in academics that he's slower. He can sit and talk to you about nine innings of Texas Ranger baseball and give the play by play. We were told it's going to be up to the teachers to find the ways he will learn because it won't be like everyone else.

Santiago started trying to communicate earlier than I thought he would, and he quickly learned signs such as *please, thank you*, and *more*. The neurologist was pleased with Santiago's abilities. Too often, he told us they see parents who find out their kids have a disability and may not do well, so they take the baby home, put him in the crib, take him out to feed or change, and put him back. On the other hand, you have the parents who say, "I'm going to give my child 110% to help him be successful!" That's what we wanted for Santiago. He constantly had someone in his face reading to him, singing to him, giving him love all the time, and I think that's made a big difference.

Santiago is 10 years old now, and many of his issues are in his legs. They're very spastic. When you try to stand him up, his legs scissor really bad, so it's hard for him to take steps. He has Botox injections and physical therapy. In 2016, he had a baclofen pump put in, which is a muscle relaxer, providing him a constant flow of medication to give his legs and his right arm some relief from the spasticity.

When Santiago was born, Robert and I were both working, and we had two insurance coverages. When Santiago was four, however, Robert was injured at work. In 1996, he suffered ruptured discs and his back was never the same. His employer at UPS thought he'd never come back, but, being stubborn, he returned. Robert worked there many more years, but after getting hurt again, he finally said, "I can't do it anymore." When he filed for disability, I decided to file for Medicaid for Santiago as well. The

system made us jump through so many hoops, it's unbelievable! I needed help; I wouldn't be wasting my time and theirs if I didn't. It was very frustrating because they wanted to know everything. I even had a discussion with a representative who went so far as to ask if we have any burial plots. When I told him that I had two, he wanted to know how much they were worth. I said, "I'm not sure." Then he got snarky with me, asking, "You purchased these plots and don't know how much you paid for them?!" "They were bought when my son died," I replied. "I don't remember how much I paid for them." It's terrible the way the system makes it so hard for kids that need help.

At one point, I called to find out Santiago's claim status: Where are we? What's going on? The woman stated that they were still trying to determine if he's medically disabled. I was exasperated, "He's in a wheelchair; how much more disabled does he have to be?!" She said there's a process he needed to go through including a review.

We finally got the Medicaid and it was a big help covering a lot of Santiago's expenses. When Robert got his disability two years later, they cut off Santiago's Medicaid which had covered a lot more. It took four years to get it, but they cut it off quick, fast, and in a hurry. Thankfully, the company I work for is fantastic, and we've always been able to make sure he has what he needs, even if we have to fight for it.

I want Santiago to have every opportunity. If Botox gives him relief and helps him work on getting stronger, that's what we're going to do. If having the pump put in will give him a better life, that's what we're going to do. If we can get his spasticity under control and work on strengthening his legs so that he may walk one day, even if with a walker, it's what we're going to do. We want to make sure Santiago has that chance and we'll do whatever we must or fight whoever we must to make sure he gets what he needs.

For his part, Santiago takes everything in stride. He's at a point where he's beginning to see that he's different, and I think he has a little bit of difficulty there. But overall, he's happy, that's all he knows; that's all we want him to know right now. Santiago has a lot ahead of him, but for right now, he's good. It's been quite a journey, but by God's grace, we're still here. We've got precious memories of Christopher, and now we see little pieces of him in Santiago – it's beautiful.

Even for me, it seems so unreal that we have been through all this. There can be so much fear so I live by Isaiah 41:10, "So do not fear, for I am with you; do not be dismayed, for I am your God. I will strengthen you and help you; I will uphold you with my righteous right hand." In the chaos of it all, this scripture always gives me peace because I know His hand is in all of this. I know His hand is on Santiago. The biggest hope I have is through Christopher and the way he knew Jesus. I know when he left me, he wasn't afraid because he knew where he was going and who would be there when he arrived. I always think about the hymn, *What a Day That Will Be.* It says, "What a day that will be when my Jesus I shall see. (I can envision Christopher seeing him.) And I look upon his face, the one who saved me by His grace. When he takes me by the hand and leads me through the promised land. What a day, glorious day, that will be."

That's where I've found my comfort. Even in the times when I thought we might lose Santiago, I thought, *if he leaves me too, his brother is going to be waiting for him.* Santiago knows he has a brother in heaven. Because we talk about Christopher, he knows he has his very own angel watching over him. When I look at Santiago now and consider everything he's been through, I remember how November 23 was the worst day of our lives, a day of excruciating sorrow each year because it is the anniversary of Chris's death. But God took the day we dreaded and made it into a miracle. Santiago could have been born two days before or a week later. But that day was the day God chose. On that day, God said, "I know the hurt you've been through; I've been there with you all the way. I will still be here, but here's your blessing. His name is Santiago."

Santiago has an active life!

Behind the Story

In January of 2018, Evonne's husband Robert passed away unexpectedly in his sleep of a heart attack. He was only 54.

Evonne says there are times she feels so much pain, she can't breathe. He was her rock and calming influence, "All Robert had to do was sit me down and tell me everything will be alright." Reading back through this story for RAISING WHEELS, Evonne says it's easy to see how much Robert loved her.

"He was in a good place when he passed away," Evonne recognizes. "Robert struggled with depression for several years after Chris's death. He felt he wasn't worthy of God's love. I would tell him, 'God loves us all. You are His child. I'm His child. The way we love the kids, that's how He loves you!'"

Over the last six months before Robert's death, he wanted to know more and more about God. He read his Bible morning and night and had Evonne create a playlist of Christian music. "I felt like Robert gained a peace he didn't have before," Evonne observes. "He went through so much pain with his back, but Robert took it in stride, as his cross to bear. It never stopped him from being with Santiago; but I could see he was hurting."

Evonne says it helps her to know Robert is free from his pain and is in a wonderful place, as though God said, "OK, Robert, you got it! It's time for the pain to end along with the depression you carried with you." Robert struggled when his back made him unable to work anymore, but he actually did so much more for the family. Evonne notes how he was always there for Santiago. "Robert was the one to send Santiago off to school and greet him when he came home and he never missed a doctor appointment. They were close."

Santiago has been upset, asking why his dad isn't there. At times the loss has caused great trauma and behavioral issues for Santiago, which the school and professional counselors have been helping him to overcome. At the same time, Evonne is amazed at her son's ability to have compassion on a mature level. "One day, Santiago touched my hand and said, 'I'm so sorry for your loss!'"

Evonne recalls how Robert would always comment on her strength and say, "I have to go before you. I can't be in this world without you!" Evonne would just reply, "Don't say things like that!" Now she is struggling to "find a new normal" in the midst of her grief, but says she can see a glimmer of light in the dark. "I know that God brought me through the hurt and back into the light when Christopher died. I didn't think I could get through it. I always had to look to God and pray for strength, and He brought me through." Evonne is certain that when Robert left his body, he was met with a familiar face, "Knowing Robert and Christopher are together makes me happy... and envious! What a beautiful reunion it must have been!"

Two years ago, Evonne shared with Robert a wish she had for a place to meditate. She told him how people create prayer closets or places of solitude to go spend time with God. Robert bought Evonne a beautiful statue of an angel to place in the backyard and found a bench which he carefully positioned across the back corner where he added the statue and a lattice with a cross hanging on it. Evonne now has a beautiful place to sit and look up at the stars when she's hurting, and it was prepared for her by Robert himself! Evonne has found great comfort in her beautiful memory garden and knows it is a sign God loves Her and that through Robert He prepared a place for her to heal ahead of her grief.

Evonne's Memory Garden

An Extraordinary Ordinary Girl

Allison Dickson

People tell me that I'm amazing, an inspiration. They say I've lived an exceptional life. I always blush. Although I do see where they may think that, to me it's just normal. I've never known life any differently. I guess you could say I've lived an extraordinary ordinary life. And I'm not done yet! The accomplishments I've achieved against many odds are based on my belief that anything is possible when you have enough love and support around you and the determination to never give up. My parents have empowered me to chase my dreams, and my mind has been opened to entertain and work hard to fulfill ambitions which often seem astonishing to those around me, perhaps because of my physical disabilities. Although I may have differences, we all do. Mine are just more visible than others. I believe we are more alike than different, yet in our diversity there is opportunity to see the beauty of life that surrounds us.

My parents, Joe and Johnnie Dickson, tried for years to have children and finally adopted my brother and sister, who are 12 and 14 years older than me. At 41 years old, my Mom was undergoing pre-op for a hysterectomy when her doctor walked in to visit with her. "Johnnie," he said. "You might want to rethink this procedure. You're pregnant!" My mother had unexpectedly conceived, and there I was.

My father was the administrator at Scott & White Hospital in Temple, Texas, and my parents were loved by the town as well as all the employees of the hospital. He was on the ground floor of establishing the small-town hospital and helping it grow into what it is today, Baylor Scott & White which is a major state-wide hospital corporation. Our neighbor was the Mayor, and my birth became somewhat of a community celebration as everyone was so happy for my parents. News of my arrival even reached friends in London!

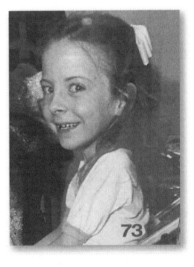

I was born by C-section on September 18th, 1979, and all appeared normal. As months went on, my parents noticed that I didn't put weight on my feet, and when I would crawl, it was army-style on my elbows. I would use my upper body, but not my legs. Since I was the baby, I was carried a lot, so it took a while for a serious suspicion that something wasn't right to be raised. At 15 months, I was diagnosed with a rare form of Muscular Dystrophy and my parents were told I might live a year. It's hard to imagine how they felt. I'm sure they had dreams and hopes for my future, which went on hold or ended all together. I've never asked very much about that time; I feel it's their experience and asking could awaken painful memories, so I really don't know much about it. What I do know is that they never gave up on me. My parents made sure I knew I could do anything I wanted, and they would go to any lengths to make it happen. I get my strength and determination from them.

In third grade it was a national Presidential election year, and to learn about the government, my class had a mock Presidential election.

I came home and told my Mom that I had been elected President! Our neighbor, the Mayor, even had a desk plate declaring my title made for me. Mom tells me, "I knew right then we'd better get our running shoes on, Allison is ready to go and she's not going to stop!" There were early signs of my drive and charisma with peers. I always had many friends and was generally accepted for who I was, just how I was. I'm not saying my classmates weren't ever mean or hurt my feelings, but it really was a typical childhood. I experienced the good and the bad like everyone else.

I was the Football Sweetheart my Senior year of high school and the first non-cheerleader to be honored with the title, as it usually goes to a cheerleader because they work so hard to support the team and travel with them. It was special they picked me that year which happened at the cross-town rivalry game on Halloween. The football players pick who they want as their sweetheart, and it was between me and two of my cheerleader friends. They usually announce the winner before the game, but the coach wanted to have everyone there to see the football sweetheart presentation and made sure it was done at halftime, just like at the homecoming game. From this change, I had a sense it might be me but didn't want to get my hopes up. I was thrilled and may have cried when the stadium announcer called out my name and a football player friend handed me a bouquet of roses as the newspaper photographer's lightbulbs flashed. At the party the night after the game, I was told that when I was announced the winner, the visitor's side behind me gave me a standing ovation right alongside the home crowd. It was a unifying moment. We also won in the last seconds with a field goal, beating our rival, Belton. Everyone stormed the field and the football players shouted over to me, "We did it for you!"

With the football boys!

As I continued through school, my classmates showed their love and respect for me through their friendship and acceptance. I believe this helped people be more aware and open to those with special needs. I was friends with a soccer player named Ivan and one day he randomly asked, "Allison, do you play soccer?" I was about to laugh, but I could see by his expression he wasn't joking; he was honestly asking if I was a soccer player like him. I glanced down at my feet and said, "No, but I'd like to!" I realized in that moment that to Ivan I wasn't "his friend Allison in a wheelchair." I was just his friend Allison. He didn't think of me as different or unable. He thought I could do anything. It was a profound and touching moment, but I didn't fully grasp it until much later. It was a simple question, but Ivan's five words changed not only how I thought about myself but also showed me how I could impact others. Looking back, I see that as the best compliment anyone could give me. My friends never really saw my wheelchair. They knew I could figure out how to do things. I adapt. We can all adapt.

Chad was a talented artist and another friend I made during high school. He was in one of my classes but never sat with or talked to anyone. He was quiet and to himself. For my 18th birthday, we had a big party at a coffee shop. I invited those I wanted to come, but also made it open for anyone. When I arrived, 75 people had already shown up, and I was there early. A painting was set up on display and when I asked about it, some friends told me that Chad had come earlier to put it up for me. He had wrapped it in brown paper and written "To Allison from Chad." It was the most amazing custom painting with a poem on the back that said "Find your own meaning in everything." The painting was named "The Bestowal Crow," and it had many various images blended together. In his painting class, all the students were amazed by this piece of art and wondered what Chad was painting it for and asked Chad if they could have it. He said, "This is for Allison, because when I walk down the hallway, she's the only person that looks at me and smiles." I never even thought twice about saying "hi" or

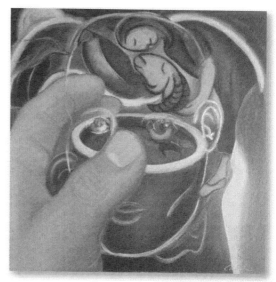

The Bestowal Crow

smiling at him. Everyone is worthy of kindness, and you just never know how much a smile and acknowledgment can mean to another person.

At the end of the party, as it was winding down, Chad showed up and we talked. He actually became quite popular after giving me his painting. He evolved to be more social and hosted parties. After his thoughtful gift, the cool girls wanted to date him. We are still friends and Chad has donated other artwork to support my fundraisers. He has borrowed "The Bestowal Crow" a few times to display at art shows. It's *that* good - and it matches my furniture! I took it with me to college at Southwestern University and then to Baylor Law School. I always found a wall to hang it on in my apartments. It is a good reminder to me of how you can make a difference in someone's life without even knowing it, simply by being kind.

At my high school there was never an accessible ramp in the front. All the years I attended, I went in the back door by the cafeteria. Near the end of my senior year, my parents decided to make it right, not so much for my sake, but for anyone who would need accessibility in the future. With permission, they gathered friends to design the ramp and a construction company donated its expertise to build it. By graduation, there was a ramp in the front, and it's still there today. The week before graduation, the local paper spotlighted senior students and decided to feature me on graduation day as the big finale. We did a photoshoot on the ramp,

and they told the story of how it was built. Even though I never got to use it, our purpose was to leave a legacy and help all those who would need the ramp in the future. I was fortunate to be very involved and connected to my high school when I was there. Putting in the ramp also became a way to raise awareness that ramps should always be a standard feature of a building. Accessibility isn't a luxury. It's a basic right we all deserve.

When it came time to graduate, the administration decided I wouldn't go across the stage but should have my diploma brought to me on the floor where I was sitting. There was a chair lift, so it was possible for me to get on the stage, so I'm not sure why these arrangements were planned. My parents knew that wasn't right and said, "No, that's not the way it's going to happen. Allison worked hard, came in third in her class, and deserves to go across that stage like everyone else!" They got their way, of course, as it was the RIGHT thing to do. My parents have always been great advocates. I know that's where my passion for helping others and making things right originates. After the ceremony, a friend observed how I received the biggest applause, and she was happy for me. It was a typical teenage milestone yet also an extraordinary accomplishment.

After high school, it was an unspoken understanding that I would go to college. I always hoped to have that experience and fully expected to further my education, but we never discussed the plan. I assumed I'd live at home and attend a local university. The internet wasn't big yet, so doing it online wasn't an option, and I began touring local college campuses. My parents would be an essential part of my success, so I needed to stay relatively close to home and my medical team at Scott & White. My Dad had retired, but continued consulting work which allowed him flexibility so that he was available to assist me. God knew what He was doing when He sent me to my parents when they were older! My Dad did a lot of commuting between his various jobs, our home caring for the animals, and school, where Mom stayed and helped me full-time. It was a lot of sacrifice on his part with a great deal of driving and long days.

I went to the Baylor preview day and knew very quickly the setup was not going to be feasible. The campus was too spread out; Mom couldn't drive right up to the buildings and get me out of our van if it was raining, and it happened to be raining the day of our tour, so we got a clear idea of what the struggle would be like on a bad day. My counselor suggested I look at Southwestern in Georgetown, a small liberal arts college with a strong academic reputation. I didn't want to go there; they didn't even have a football team! It was smaller than my high school. "No way!" I thought.

On our way back to Temple after visiting my sister in Pflugerville, my parents suggested we just stop in at Southwestern, not have an official visit, but wander around campus. Within ten minutes, all three of us knew this was the place. It had that welcoming feel of "home." All the students we met as we meandered around were friendly and genuine. Many of them said, "I hope to see you next year!" Two girls invited us to their dorm room to see the facilities and showed us that there was a handicap accessible room available on one of the floors. They wanted us to know that we could make it work! We went into the accessible room and then met everyone on that floor, who were especially friendly. My Mom called the Dean of Students the next day, introduced herself and told him about me and our situation. She asked if it would be possible to live in the dorm room with me. There was never a question if Mom and Dad would be with me to help with my physical needs, but how many 18-year-olds want to take their parents to college? This was going to be a unique situation.

Mom was told about some new apartments for upper class students with two bedrooms and two baths, a living room and kitchenette. It would be a great fit as it would be more of a family setting which sounded better than a one-room dorm room in an all-women's dorm. Everything fell right into place and we said, "Yes!" to Southwestern University. It was one of the best decisions I've made. Going there was life-changing: a new school with new people. I'd grown up in the same community all my life, so it was a little scary as I wondered if I'd be accepted and make friends as I had before. To help me meet and feel connected to my entering class, the Dean of Students assigned me to a first-year dorm floor, even though I lived in the upper classmen apartments. This arrangement allowed me to participate fully in all of the events and activities. I had good friends from all class levels as a result.

My parents made college possible. They were committed to helping me live out my fullest life. I toyed with the thought of telling people that they were my secret service protection. I realized quickly though that if the students didn't accept or like my parents being there, they were not people I'd want in my life anyway. My worries were soon alleviated as the students and employees warmly welcomed all three of us to Southwestern. They became the campus parents and when people missed home, hanging out with my Mom and Dad was the solution. Sometimes the college kids would stop by just to see how Dad was doing on his crossword puzzles or get a hug from Mom.

My majors were English and Psychology, and I was one class away from a Philosophy minor. My favorite professor in that field retired, so I was done. Two majors were enough anyway. I graduated with a 3.99 GPA... darn that one A- my sophomore year. I was named Outstanding Senior Leader and Outstanding Overall Leader on campus my senior year. I served in many organizations, and one of my favorites was Student Foundation in which I was Vice Chair. Whenever I was involved, I wasn't just a member, I was always an active leader and participated fully. I also received Student of the Year in both my majors, was inducted to the Phi Beta Kappa Honor Society, and graduated Summa Cum Laude with highest honors. During my junior year, I became part of the university's strategic planning committee. I was one of four students chosen to represent the student body. I met dignitaries and shared the goals, mission and vision of the university. I helped shape that dream; it was big and outside the box. From that experience, I realized I wanted to move things forward in my community, my major, career and in everything I touch. I always ask myself, "What can I do to advance this place and make it better?"

Another pivotal experience during this time was my sorority life. At Southwestern there are four sororities and in the Fall you get to know all four groups. I knew I wanted to join a sorority from the start; my Dad was in a fraternity and I'd heard his fun stories about Greek life. When I arrived on campus and started meeting all these amazing women in the sororities, I thought, "Yes, I want to be one of them!" They were the leaders on campus and the people I most admired. "If this is what it means to be in a sorority, sign me up!"

The first semester is an informal rush which includes lunches and events where everyone networks. All four sororities rushed me. I enjoyed each of them but felt the most connected to Tri Delta. It was my top pick. After going through their questions, explaining how I could participate and be involved, I felt confident I would be invited to join, but to tell a long story short, I wasn't offered a bid by Tri Delta. In the end, I wasn't given a bid by any of the sororities. This was shocking and devastating. It was the first moment I truly felt rejected. I had such idyllic circumstances growing up with everyone accepting and welcoming me, I just hadn't experienced much rejection in life. I didn't see it coming. Everyone appeared to like and want me, saying things like, "I hope you pick our sorority and join our chapter!"

It was a terrible day. The truth is, I almost transferred away from Southwestern, I was so hurt and embarrassed. I hadn't done anything wrong except maybe trusting too much and being naive. But transferring would have been the real tragedy. I learned more about myself from that experience than perhaps any other time in my life. It was eye opening in good and bad ways. I saw the positive and negative. When I didn't get a bid, it really rocked the campus. The reaction of my peers wasn't just "too bad," it was "What are y'all doing?! This is not right!" Those sororities were afraid to accept someone different into their chapters, afraid to adapt, grow and move forward.

After the fact, no one said I didn't receive a bid because I didn't fit the "ideal" image of a sorority woman, but I heard that there had been discussions such as, "What if we go over to the fraternity house and play Twister? Well, Allison can't play Twister!" That was the thought process they were all having, but what they didn't know is they lost out on the best spinner they could have had for their Twister games! My closest friends became Tri Deltas and were devastated that I wasn't joining their sisterhood. Some of them said they were just going to get out, but I told them not to do that for me. In my heart, I still wanted to be part of the sorority experience. I knew I'd enjoy it and make a difference. I wanted my friends to stay and make sure good prevails, but that year was very difficult seeing their involvement and being left out. I was friends with everyone on campus, as I enjoyed spending time with the athletes, the intellects, the artists and the party people equally. I connected with all groups. So, while it was painful to see my first-year friends having amazing sorority experiences, it was something time helped heal. I'll never forget that feeling of hurt and disappointment, however, I can look back and appreciate how it caused me to grow. I learned sometimes our circumstances are meant to show us our strengths.

The next year Tri Delta had new leadership, and I was a sophomore who was more established on campus. I had been involved in many different groups where I expanded my connections, excelled academically, and showed that I contributed to campus life. I went through recruitment all over again, as I still wanted that experience. All the sororities recruited me, causing deja'vu from the year before. This time though had a wonderful ending. I was given a bid by Tri Delta. Actually, it was more of a beginning than an ending, as Tri Delta would become a very important part of my life. I went to the academic mall where the new members join our chapters in a campus-wide celebration! I was moving slowly because I was emotionally and physically drained, so all the chapter sisters ran over to me shouting, "You're home!" They were crying, and I was crying. It was a magical night. It worked out! I got to know all the first-year women who joined with me, so it was a new group of friends. It turned out exactly how it should despite some bumps along the way. I find life often happens that way. You just stay strong and have faith that what's supposed to happen will, and life will work out as intended. I can say that my journey with Tri Delta was a life-changing experience.

The new leaders of Tri Delta were ready to look to the future, adapt, and see a world of different possibilities. They were "woke" before "woke" was even a thing. They were the ones who wanted me, and even now I'm involved with the chapter as an unofficial mentor and friend to the students. I know the chapter evolved and grew from my experience, and I hope I can continue to be a positive influence that helps them be the best, kindest version of themselves. I also have been the Alumnae Chapter President for Temple/Belton since 2010 and organize our local group into meetings and philanthropy events. I serve at a national level as an Alumnae Philanthropy Specialist, working with the Texas and Oklahoma chapters. I help them initiate events and serve as a liaison between national and alumnae chapters. I continue to serve on the national graduate scholarship committee where we award hundreds of thousands of dollars in scholarships. I received one to go to law school at Baylor, which was my next endeavor. So, I came full circle to be able to assist other graduates to receive aid from national. In college, Tri Delta was a big part of my experience, but it has continued to be important in my life afterwards.

I wasn't sure what would happen after college, but I had an interest in law. I thought about attending graduate school for Psychology, but worried it would be too narrow; generally, you can teach, counsel or research. I wanted to pursue a field of study that would give me options and open doors. With my parents getting older and my health constantly changing, there was no clear path to what the future held. I'm a very good writer and have a heart to serve others, so I started seriously thinking about going to law school and how that would give me a foundation for anything I could do in the future, whether advocacy work, government employment or philanthropy. I knew having a legal education would only be a positive step for whatever the future had in store for me and my family.

Once again, my parents recognized that I had the ability, intellectually, to continue my education. I'm a hard worker, committed and determined. I have faith that what is meant to be, will be, if I just allow myself to go down the path that's set out for me. My parents encouraged me to go to law school. We knew it would be the same set up, with my Dad commuting back and forth while my Mom stayed with me full-time at school. The University of Texas was an option, but would mean long drives for my Dad. When we visited the campus, I got the same feeling that it wasn't the right fit similar to when I first visited Baylor for undergraduate studies, although UT is a highly ranked law school and I was accepted   to the program. They welcomed me and were willing to do whatever it took to make my attendance possible. We asked where people live and they said, "Oh really close! Most people are only a 20-30-minute drive to campus." Clearly our definition of "close" wasn't the same. That just wasn't doable for our situation. I needed to be near my apartment for breathing treatments and other medical needs.

What didn't work at Baylor for undergraduate was the right set up for law school. I could live a few miles away from campus, and we could drive right up to the law building. It's strange how what was so wrong before worked perfectly for graduate studies. Like with Southwestern, when visiting Baylor Law School, it felt like "home."

I started law school but almost quit on the first day of orientation. We had a mock class to show us what law school would be like. The professor came in and had one of the male students stand to answer a question. After their exchange, the professor shook his head, so the student started to sit down. The second he hit the chair, the professor turned around and yelled, "I did not say you could sit! Stand up!" I had never experienced a setting that was so intense, but he was preparing us for the courtroom and an adversarial environment. The professors knew we wouldn't make it if we weren't tough.

I came home and cried, saying, "I'm not tough enough for this!" My parents could have grabbed onto my fear and self-doubt as an "easy out" opportunity, told me I was right and said, "Let's go home!" because law school wasn't going to be easy for them either. But instead they said, "Allison, of course you can do this. You've done everything you've ever set your mind to. You can do it!" In a nutshell, that basically sums up how we've always lived our lives. We have the belief system, dream big, work hard and make it happen!

I made up my mind I could meet the challenge of law school and completed my first quarter only to make my very first "B," which was an eye opener. It was actually a B- and I said, "What is this?!" It caused me to adjust my expectations. Everyone in law school is smart and driven. Baylor is on the quarter system, so the pace is full force. You are in class for 9 ½ weeks and then take your finals. You may have a final on a Friday only to start new classes the following Monday. The truth is, it did have some wear and tear on me. I would go for a quarter or two and then end up sick from working so hard, needing to take a quarter off. My Dad joked I crammed three years into five!

After three years, the people I started with were graduating and new students were in my classes. A whole new group of classmates, mostly younger, was an opportunity to make more friends. I was a little sad when my first friends moved on to their next stage and I was left behind, but some of my very best law school friends are people I met later who I would never have known had I graduated on time.

Law school was certainly a challenge, but I worked hard and made the Dean's List, the Law Review and was a Student Bar Association (student government) class representative as well as an Ambassador for Prospective Students. One of my favorite things to do when I wasn't studying was attending basketball and football games with my parents. My Dad got season tickets, and I had a student ticket. Sometimes I had too much homework, but Dad wouldn't miss a game. We will always be Baylor fans!

I became sick with pneumonia during my last quarter, but I returned to take my finals and finish up. A week before graduation, a spot was found on my Dad's lung. He hadn't been feeling well all year. He was diagnosed with lung cancer on the day I found out I was graduating first in my class, Valedictorian of 100 students. I experienced a huge high and a massive low all on the same day. That made it one of the strangest days of my life.

Because I had been so sick, I declined to give the speech. I just didn't think I was physically up to it, but I did write one. They asked if the Assistant Dean could give it on my behalf. During the graduation, I was on the stage when they announced the highest-ranking graduate and my speech was read by Dean Jackson. She began by explaining how I had been sick, but she would be giving my valedictorian address on my behalf. My parents were also recognized with a statue of a bear, thanking them for all they had done. As parents of the law school, I think people loved them more than me sometimes. The professor who gave the commencement address spoke about me and my determination, and I was given a standing ovation when I received my diploma. It was a memorable, touching day.

We were planning to stay in Waco to prepare for and take the Bar exam, but Dad was going through chemo and radiation, with some complications, so it was our turn to take care of him after all the driving he had done for nine years: four in undergrad and five in law school. So, I studied for the Bar at home with an iPod instead of taking a class, which allowed me to be there during his treatment. When it was time to take the Bar, I dictated my essays to a court reporter for the first time, with a proctor present. I wondered if that person was a lawyer and knew when I was getting things wrong and thought, "How did she get through law school? She's getting everything wrong!" It was stressful, but the proctor later expressed his admiration for my determination - and shared he was not in fact an attorney!

I was so nervous and physically drained after the first day of testing, I didn't want to go back. Mom said, "We're going to do this one time. If you pass, great. If not, that's ok too. Just do it one time and see it through." I passed of course. This was an important lesson to finish what you start. Even if I hadn't passed, at least I'd know I wasn't a quitter. We're definitely not quitters in this family.

After regrouping from the Bar, Baylor Law School contacted me about working for them as a Research Assistant helping professors with their research or writing, such as fact checking, editing, case law updates and preparing memos for presentations. It would be a by-the-hour job allowing me to work on the internet, which was more prevalent by then and meant I could work from home. I was excited to assist the professors, and they were very flexible with me, permitting work hours that fit with my life. As long as I completed the work, it didn't matter when I did it.

My Dad's health continued to decline, and he passed away 10 months after his cancer diagnosis. He had been sitting in a rocking chair, all of us chatting, when he got up suddenly to lay down. He hurried back to the bedroom and never got up again. We had intended to put him in hospice to receive the care he needed as he wasn't fully conscious, not talking or eating much, in the final stages of death. I believe Dad didn't want to go that way or become a stress on us, and in the end, he didn't have to. After a fall and trip to the ER, he peacefully passed away at Scott & White where he had built his career.

My last birthday with Dad

With Dad no longer with us, we started having aids come in, as Mom couldn't leave me, even to go to the store. I can't be by myself, ever. I never would be able to live independently because of my need for physical assistance. The aids were another pair of hands that allowed Mom to run errands or take a nap. It's a bit stressful to have someone new in the home, but if the person stays around, they become like family. There's high turnover because the pay is minimum wage. The aids need to have a servant-heart because frankly they could make more money working at a fast food restaurant. The system has its flaws. I never know if someone will be with us a week or a year. But I have to trust them, because I need help. It's an unusual situation, but you learn to adapt and move forward.

Life went on and I stayed busy working, active in my local Junior League where I served on the Board and was eventually elected President, as well as being involved with Tri Delta and my church. I was also dating someone and experiencing my first romantic relationship. But on February 4th, 2014, my life changed forever. I just wasn't feeling well and had a little fever. Our neighbor came over and said I should go to the ER, which I did. They ran tests and said my blood levels were slightly off, but it wasn't concerning. I know my body and could tell something was wrong. They said I could go home or stay and receive IV fluids as a precaution. I opted for the latter, as it seemed like a good idea to just stay the night and leave in the morning. I had no idea I wouldn't leave for five months. I call the first month of my illness "The Forgotten February" because after the decision to stay, I can honestly only remember bits and pieces of an entire month. What I can share about this early part of my illness is mainly what I was told by my friend, Tessa, who came to help, and not from my own recollection.

My Pulmonologist came in and I was almost nonresponsive. He knew that wasn't normal, so he ordered me to the ICU immediately. This decision probably saved my life. There was some panic as the doctors thought the medicine they had given me could be causing unusual side effects. They could see I was tired and sleepy, but still no one knew there was something seriously wrong. When my lips started turning blue and I went into respiratory failure followed by septic shock, they knew it was more dangerous. I had to be intubated and went on and off the vent three times during my stay in the hospital. I would start to do better and they'd optimistically take me off, then I'd relapse. I was completely conscious during one of the intubations, and it's not a pleasant process. I was told later though that I followed instructions very well! ("Keep your mouth open wide!") It's probably a blessing I don't remember much of this time because it was touch and go. Mom and Tessa would stand in the hallway watching the team struggle to keep me stabilized, crying, thinking it might be the end, as they were told to prepare for the worst.

While on life support, I couldn't talk, so Tessa made a little board with index cards and the alphabet for me to communicate. I'd point and spell out what I needed to tell them. I don't remember this, but Tessa says I talked to them through the board. She had to make ten different versions of the board as one was too big, another too little and they couldn't tell where I was pointing. Tessa spent every night for five weeks with me during this time. My Mom would come during the day and Tessa would drive the 20-minute trip to Salado where her parents lived to shower and sleep. They worked together to ensure I was never alone despite the excellent care of the nurses. Having family present even when you don't know they're there is different. It's an expression of love, protection, and faith. They never gave up on me. For that I'm forever thankful.

I spent most of the early part of my illness in the ICU. My condition would stabilize and they would move me down to a room, then I'd relapse. After the third intubation, the doctors recommended I get a tracheotomy. I had never had one, but it was becoming harder and harder to intubate me the more times they had to do it. With a trach they'd have the access needed. My anatomy is so unique that if the right people weren't there, they could injure me or not be able to do it at all, risking death. At first, they were talking about the trach being temporary, but it soon became obvious they intended it to be permanent. So, I got my trach and feeding tube, and I haven't had food or drink since. As of February of 2014, I have had nothing to eat or drink by mouth. All nutrition and medications enter my body through tubes. I like to think about what my first meal will be and ask others what theirs would be if in this situation. You'd be surprised at the answers!

Part of the issue is that my ability to swallow had deteriorated. Doctors don't know if it's from my Muscular Dystrophy or the intubations, or both. It's hard to comprehend that one day I was eating and drinking normally, and the next it was dangerous. The body does mysterious things. Doctors believed I would never breathe on my own again, and since I was on the vent, I would never speak again either. They even went so far as to warn

I might never go home. There was discussion about facilities that could meet my needs. I can't eat or drink, but today I can talk and breathe on my own. I am not supported by a vent, and I live at home, so I am blessed! We've come a long way, but there are challenges still ahead.

I was in the ICU from February to early March, five weeks, and then they

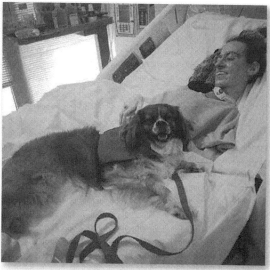

moved me to a different building, the Continuing Care Hospital, a step down from ICU, but I wasn't ready for a regular room. In ICU I had one-on-one care. A nurse was in the room with me at all times. Here, the nurses would have two or three patients. I still needed someone with me at all times because I couldn't yet speak and wasn't able to push the button for help, so friends set up a volunteer system for people to stay the night with me. Mom stayed during the day, then friends and siblings would spend the night. Again, I was never alone on this journey. The support of my family and friends was unwavering.

At this facility, there was personalized care, and they worked on weaning me off the vent and helping me become stronger. They helped me relearn how to sit in my wheelchair and drive it, as I had gone over a month not sitting up. I also had to practice using my laptop computer and remember all the log-in information for the first time in months. Can you imagine the emails and Facebook posts I had to catch up on?!

It was hard, but I slowly became stronger and learned I could still talk and breathe once the vent was removed. I moved from the Continuing Care Hospital to a rehab unit where I stayed for almost three months, until July 7th, 2014, when I could finally go home. There was a therapy dog named Toby who would visit once a week. I think I was definitely his favorite room to hang out in - but he probably made every patient feel that special. Toby was a bright light during a dark time. The weekend before going home,

I remember watching fireworks for the 4th of July from a hall window. I said to myself, *When I get home, I will watch fireworks live every year that I can!* Fireworks in July represent the dawn of freedom for our nation, and for me, it is a meaningful time to reflect on and celebrate overcoming a life-changing ordeal. Going home represented my personal freedom.

Since my illness, I have to fight the battle every day. My breathing is precarious. I've been admitted to the hospital numerous times. I've spent Christmas, New Years, Valentine's Day, Spring Break and summer vacation in the hospital. Some of those stays all in one year. I've had numerous hospitalizations because a simple cold turned into pneumonia or tracheitis. I have a fairly strict no-kid policy...they are adorable, but made of germs, which is sad because I'd love to be more a part of my friends' lives who have kids. But for my health I have to be so careful. It's an ongoing dilemma and bit of sadness.

I have never researched my condition. I don't want to put any expectations in my head of what may or may not happen. It's called "priming." For example, I might talk to you about Whataburger, and then you'll notice all the Whataburgers on your way home. Once something is in your mind, you subconsciously notice it or meet those expectations. I don't mind telling people what I have and if they want to research it, that's up to them, but it's not something I ever plan to do. Maybe it's a form of self-preservation. I live day by day and enjoy the time I have here. I don't want to read something that says someone with my condition never lives past

40. I don't need to know that, and I'm not the norm. I wasn't expected to live past three or accomplish the things I have. My will power, purpose and drive, as well as external factors such as my support system and medical care, have to be factored into any estimation of my potential life-span. In fact, no one knows when their time here may end. I'm really no different from everyone in that regard.

Even today, I take life as it comes. There are days when I'm coughing or have to do extra breathing treatments and be trach suctioned. Some days are really hard and others are good, but that's true for everyone. Mine might be different bad and different good, but everyone experiences life's ups and downs in their own way. We are all unique, with the commonality that we all have our own challenges to face, mine is just a little more visible.

As I began the process of recovering and adapting to the changes in my life, I started to formulate the idea of leaving a legacy and helping other people after I'm gone. For me, education is a passion and I believe it is empowerment. It opens doors and minds and moves us forward. If someone wants to pursue education, I want them to have that opportunity. I was fortunate to receive scholarships and financial aid to obtain my education, and I want other students to receive the help they need. I hope if a student is awarded one of my scholarships, they will come to know my story and say, "If she can do it, I can do it!" So many supported and believed in me, my scholarships are saying to them, "I believe in you! You go out and make a difference!"

I have three endowed scholarships, which will probably be the max. I started at Southwestern with the Tri Delta scholarship, which goes to up to three members of the chapter who have financial need as well as demonstrate academic excellence, service to the chapter and involvement in the community. I'd like it to be awarded to young women who excel in the areas I did. I would have appreciated such a scholarship. I couldn't afford college without assistance, so the scholarship qualifications are a mix of need and merit.

I wanted to turn that donation into a reward for the chapter. Southwestern pushed me to dream bigger, though, turning it into a more permanent and lasting legacy. In the Spring of 2015, a year after my illness, we launched a campaign to endow the Allison Dickson Delta Delta Delta Scholarship at Southwestern University. To fund an endowed scholarship that will last forever, a $25,000 minimum is required. It took only six weeks to raise that much. It gained momentum and went out on social media. People donated and wrote testimonials about how they knew me and were supporting it.

My Baylor friends got "jealous" and said there should be a scholarship in my name at Baylor Law, so a group of friends began the process, researching what it would take to create an endowed scholarship there as well, which was a $50,000

minimum. The Development Office gave us five years to raise the money, but it took just nine months! When I get on a mission, that is my focus and my innate drive takes over. These donations came from classmates, family, friends, supporters and even people I have never met, but who learned of my story and wanted to be part of the legacy.

The bulk of the funds for the Baylor Law Scholarship were raised from an event put on by my high school friend, Bill, who owns The Alamo Drafthouses in Dallas/Ft. Worth. He wanted to host something in Dallas, but knew I couldn't attend since travel is difficult, so he suggested bringing a "roadshow" to Temple. They set up an event with bounce houses and food vendors. We secured sponsors whose donations went 100% to the scholarship. We picked a movie, The Princess Bride, and called it the "As You Wish Movie Under the Stars." We had sword fighting demonstrations and activities for the kids that tied into the movie, and local businesses and families donated silent auction items. That one event raised $25,000, which reached our goal to endow the scholarship. My friend and partner-in-good, Bill, and I were able to announce together at the event that the scholarship was endowed!

In April of 2017, I decided I wanted to create one more scholarship to complete my educational journey. This scholarship would go to the Temple ISD Education Foundation. It's called the Allison Dickson Temple Proud Scholarship, and it is awarded to a graduating senior from my high school who will attend Temple College. I wanted it to be about hometown pride and helping young people in our community. In that same month, our state representative honored me with a proclamation, and at the presentation we launched the campaign to fund the Temple Proud Scholarship. After numerous fundraising events and the generosity of many, the scholarship was endowed with the $25,000 minimum in September of 2018.

In May 2018 I had the privilege of presenting a check to the first Temple Proud Scholarship recipient, a sweet young woman who wants to be a teacher and give back through educating the next generation. For me, the Tri Delta Scholarship was my first major philanthropic endeavor, so it's my baby, but I feel the Temple Proud Scholarship can be very impactful. Tuition at Temple College is much less, so it can go farther. It may pay for a full semester of school. It could be life changing for a student on the edge, not able to go without financial help. I want my legacy to be, in part, one of helping and encouraging students to keep going and learning. They are the future!

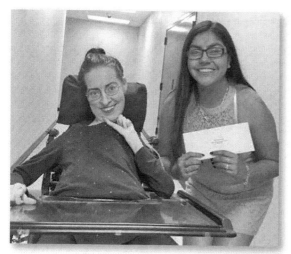

The First Temple Proud Scholarship Recipient

I believe there is purpose in everything, and there are reasons why this is my existence. God will use me for His purposes, to do good and hopefully make a difference. In a sense, I feel that my life is like the perfect storm - in a good way! I had the right parents, the right support system, strong beliefs and values as well as the determination to succeed. Hopefully I can inspire people to embrace their own plan and their own purpose to do great things with what they have been given. The beauty of life is that we are able to adapt to our unique circumstances. I hope I'm living that out, walking the walk (only metaphorically of course... hahaha). After my illness, it became apparent that life is short. I want to make the most impact with the time I'm given. I want to make a difference and pay it forward, leaving a legacy. I think we all want to leave a legacy, and we all do in our own ways! I'm fortunate to have been given the wake-up call to do it now, not wait five years down the road. Now is my moment; now is my time!

Behind the Story

Allison was featured in the January 2017 issue of a Lifestyle Magazine about new beginnings, focusing on her philanthropy work. She became friends with the photographer of the story, Julie Nabours Doughty, who suggested that while Allison can't travel easily, a cut-out version of her dubbed "Mini Alli" could be taken by friends to places that would be difficult for her to go. Allison thought that sounded like a fun idea, so the photographer made the Mini Alli photo statue and took it to the Waco zoo where she got a picture with it alongside an orangutan.

Allison was inspired by the concept and thought it would be fun to see what other adventures Mini Alli could have. So she had two Mini Alli's created with the plan to let people borrow them to take on their travels. She started with a picture of herself with Mini Alli and introduced it online to see what the response would be. The feedback was immediate and enthusiastic. At first Allison envisioned having a few that people could mail around to each other as "Traveling Mini Allis" but people wanted their own Mini Alli, not having to share and pass on. With ingenuity, Allison thought to turn the concept into a fundraiser where people could buy a Mini Alli and the funds would support the scholarships. Allison initially sold 75 Mini Allis and raised $750, with a $10 profit margin per statue. Mini Alli and #TeamAlliTravels is an ongoing endeavor and scholarship fundraiser.

Friends tell Allison that wherever they take Mini Alli, people ask about her and it creates opportunities to have conversations about abilities, differences, adaptations and perseverance. Mini Alli is an advocate and she's vocal! She's out there showing people that while Allison Dickson may not be able to go to Hawaii, nothing is stopping her from reaching there. Mini Alli has been on Willie Nelson's tour bus and with Luke

Pell from The Bachelorette. She's been to Vegas, Europe, South America, Australia and Canada. It's fun to see where Mini Alli ends up!

I was first introduced to Allison Dickson through Mini Alli. I was attending the Variety Children's Charity of Texas Gala where the Copp Family and the Raising Wheels Foundation received the Impact Award. Before the gala was a cinema industry trade show, as Cinemark is a sponsor of Variety Children's Charity, and they invited me to set up a display about this book to raise awareness at the table promoting Variety. They had a Mini Alli there and I picked it up, asking to get a picture with it. I didn't yet know who she was, or the significance of the statue. I was just drawn to the cheerful face.

After getting the photo, I was told her story, as Mini Alli has become a staple of the Variety Children's Charity of Texas displays. I told the vivacious Varity Children's Charity representatives that I haven't finished writing *RAISING WHEELS* and would love to include Allison in it.

Approximately two months later, I drove to Allison Dickson's house to interview her for this story. I had attended a seminar earlier the day we planned to meet, so I couldn't arrive until 6 p.m. that evening. Allison was gracious and beautiful as she greeted me. In front of her, and around the room, were tables stacked full of lipsticks, nail polishes and perfumes. Allison smelled wonderful and had a pink pouty smile. She gleefully said, "Nothing lifts the spirit like a little perfume and lipstick!" It was easy to see that Allison has many choices. I am quite certain that most of

Allison's table of cosmetics

Allison's table of cosmetics her options are gifts from the many people who come to hang out with her. She attracts regular visits from admirers as a result of her impressive ability to make friends. I asked Allison how she decides which perfume she wears from day to day, as I've never seen so many different perfume bottles in one place, including the perfume outlet stores! Allison told me that she picks just one and then wears it until gone. I find that fascinating!

As I sat down to begin transcribing, Allison let me know she was feeling quite fatigued as she had helped organize a fundraiser that week for her Tri Delta Scholarship and wasn't sure how long she would be able to work on the story. I assured her that it was alright, we'd work on what we could and would schedule another time if needed. Then Allison proceeded to tell her story for five hours straight! The more she talked, the more energized she became. As midnight approached, Allison was going strong, but her Mom and I were starting to pass out! I kept typing, though it was becoming illegible…LOL. There's so much more to Allison and her story, but this is a great introduction to who Allison is and all she has to teach. At the end of our storytelling session, Allison suggested she just may be interested in writing a full book. I believe she should, and hope to be able to match her storytelling endurance, assisting her to record it when that time comes.

PRINCESS ON WHEELS
Seeing the World through Wheelchair-Colored Glasses
Tiffany Elkins

I can remember the tears falling down my cheeks when the sonogram tech said, "It's a girl!" My husband and I had been married for 15 years and had boys ages 9 and 11 at the time. We loved raising our boys, but there was something so special about hearing that we were going to have a little girl. A little princess for her older brothers and us to love on.

Soon after that announcement, we heard words of concern that the ventricles in her brain were measuring just on the large side of normal and that we would need to come back for some follow-up ultrasounds. That feeling of pure joy combined with the fear of the unknown would be a common one for us many times in the future. At that moment, though, we had no idea we were in for the hardest but most amazing ride of our lives. The coming days would be filled with overwhelming experiences, many tears and some heartache, but the concurrent joy that we have experienced has made this road better than we could ever have imagined.

After that initial ultrasound, we had several others, all showing the same thing regarding the size of our baby girl's brain ventricles. After explaining to the doctors that large heads run in our families, the consensus was that they would monitor our baby right after she was born just to make sure there was no fluid on her brain, but that she probably just had a big head!

Our little girl arrived and looked just perfect. Molly Kate was the special name we had picked out for her. The doctors did an ultrasound of her head and told us that, despite the worries during the pregnancy, everything was ok. We took her home and settled into life with our new little princess. Watching her two older brothers with Molly Kate was so special, and we all loved life with our new baby girl.

Molly Kate was the most laid-back little baby. She loved to melt hearts with her smile and was so sweet. She didn't reach much for toys, but as third-time parents, we were not overly worried and didn't compare her too much to other little babies. After a few months went by, though, we began to think it was odd that she never tried to lift her head or push up on her arms. She also didn't have much interest in playing with toys. I made a note to ask the doctor about it, but since there were no other medical issues, even our doctor believed Molly Kate was just on her own schedule and that these milestones would come eventually.

When we went in for her six-month checkup, our pediatrician was immediately alarmed when Molly Kate's head size shot off the charts. It had continued to remain large after birth, but this time, it wasn't even on the growth curve. We were sent for a CT scan to check for hydrocephalus again, a tumor, or something else that could be contributing to this. We met with the pediatric neurologist after the CT scan and were so relieved when we got the news that they didn't see anything alarming. He determined that she had "benign familial macrocephaly"—a formal term for big heads that run in families. He believed that her motor skills were delayed because she was having to work so hard to keep her large head up and that she would probably catch up if we started some physical therapy.

We were relieved and thankful that we could get some help for her to catch up on her motor development. We were referred to Early Childhood Intervention in our state and went for an evaluation. My best friend has a son with Down Syndrome, and so ECI was an agency that I knew at least a little about. We went for the evaluation, and I remember realizing as they played with her and asked me if she could do certain things, that she really couldn't do many of the things on the list at all. I left feeling a little sad that she was so far behind.

A physical therapist came to our home to start therapy, and Molly Kate began to work on getting stronger. She loved her therapist, who ended up working with her from about eight months of age until she aged out of ECI at age three. To this day, we still count "Miss Mandy" as one of our dear friends. She loved Molly Kate, worked hard with her and became a good friend to me as we worked together every week. I didn't realize at the time that the therapists coming into our lives would become like family. In the months following, it was recommended that Molly Kate start occupational therapy as well as speech therapy, and again we gained some treasured friends.

We did therapy for several months, and Molly Kate did get stronger, but progress was very, very slow. She finally learned to lift her head while on her stomach, and she learned to tripod sit, but never to sit on her own. She worked on her hands and knees but was never able to get up on all fours. She made progress in occupational therapy, but she was still severely delayed and was unable to do many tasks. She worked on speech, but the sounds and words didn't come.

Before our twelve-month check-up, I remember having a conversation with our physical therapist about Molly Kate's progress, or lack thereof. It was becoming evident that something else was going on. I can remember Mandy nodding her head with a sweet smile on her face as I voiced my thoughts on this. She told me to let the doctor know that Molly Kate still wasn't sitting (usually about a six-month skill) and she wasn't bearing weight on her legs and feet.

When we got to our appointment, and I began talking, our doctor beat me to the punch and said that it was probably time for a trip to the geneticist. We were beginning to realize that something was, in the world's terms, "wrong."

It was October, and the first available genetics appointment wasn't until April. Our hearts sank at that news, and we began to pray. We already had a follow-up appointment on the books with the neurologist as a result of her six-month CT scan, so when we went to see him, he went ahead and scheduled an MRI. We told him that we couldn't get in to see the geneticist until April, so he said he would call and see if they might be able to work us in sooner. A few days later, the geneticist called and asked if we could come in that afternoon... five months before our appointment! We praised God for working things out.

The MRI was scheduled for a few weeks out, so they planned to do the bloodwork for the genetic testing while Molly Kate was sedated for it. When she woke from the MRI, she had been stuck in over 20 places as they were trying to get blood from her little veins. This would be the first of many blood draws, but the rest would usually be when she was awake, and both Molly Kate and mom would leave crying. We learned to ask for specific people to do that task to make it easier on her.

We anxiously awaited the results of the MRI, and finally, we got the phone call one evening from the neurologist who informed us that Molly Kate had something called Cerebellar Hypoplasia; her cerebellum didn't form correctly; it was much smaller than it should be. This brain malformation, he said, would cause issues with her learning, her hand/eye coordination and her gross and fine movements. I hurriedly jotted down what he was saying, assuming that we would go to see him in the next few days to find out what all this meant and what to do from here. Instead, he said they could schedule us for a 3-month follow-up. I hung up the phone in a daze, quickly telling my husband what he said as we rushed out the door to attend a concert for one of the boys at their school. We called our parents in the car on the way there to relay the news, put on our brave faces to act like everything was ok and entered the school. Right before the show started, a friend asked me how everything was going, and I immediately broke down in tears because of the devastating news we had just received. That phone call was the end of thinking that Molly Kate would be able to catch up and live a typical life and the beginning of realizing that this was something much bigger that she would struggle with her whole life. To this day, I still have the little scrap of paper on which I had hurriedly jotted down what the doctor relayed to me in that brief conversation that changed our lives.

The days following that night were scary. We didn't know what to expect. We researched everything we could about her brain condition but couldn't find a whole lot of information about it. We did learn that the cerebellum controls balance, and because of its effect on movement, it was definitely a factor in Molly Kate not being able to sit up unassisted. This would affect her ability to walk and could affect speech, eye movement as well as emotions. We did find a little YouTube video of a preteen girl who had Cerebellar Hypoplasia, and it gave us comfort to see this happy smiling girl who had learned to walk, albeit very wobbly, around age 10. The children with this condition had such varied abilities that it was tough to know what Molly Kate's future might look like. Some children learned to talk; some did not. Some learned to walk; some did not. There were no clear answers on what to expect. We knew right away, though, that we would do whatever it took to give our daughter the best life possible.

These days were scary, and I remember crying a lot, but our faith is what absolutely carried us through then and continues to today. We drew strength from God and knew that this was not a surprise to Him. We believe that God doesn't promise us days free of pain, but He does promise us that He will walk through the pain with us. I poured out my heart to Him during those early days and tears would pour down my face during church as I sang songs of praise to Him, even through the pain. Although we were hurting, we also knew that God was still there and that His promises hadn't changed. There were hundreds of friends and family praying for Molly Kate, and we saw God work in the smallest of details as we began to get appointments with different specialists and as friends began to support us in so many different ways.

After that initial phone call telling us that Molly Kate had Cerebellar Hypoplasia, our support system sprang into action and we got in to see some specialists in larger cities who had dealt with this condition before. We would begin the first of many trips to a hospital about three hours away to visit a developmental pediatrician and a neurologist, as well as other specialists after that as other needs arose.

Our new neurologist looked over Molly Kate's MRI and her symptoms and believed that there was an underlying genetic condition that had caused her cerebellar hypoplasia. The genetics tests began to come back, but nothing that really ever explained why she had this brain malformation. We would get the results of some of the tests, then go back for more blood draws, usually leaving in tears from watching her go through more "pokes" or from hearing about the prognosis of the conditions they were testing for next. We would wait on pins and needles to find out results, not wanting to get bad news, but at least wanting answers.

At one point, we were waiting on a blood test that had to be sent out and was supposed to return in 4-5 months to let us know if Molly Kate had a particular diagnosis. As with each test, we would research the diagnosis they were testing for and usually, after seeing the prognosis and life expectancy statistics, we would pray and pray that the test would come back negative. Such was this test, and after months of waiting, we called the hospital to see if they had the results. On what was still one of the most frustrating days of this journey, we found out that the hospital had "lost" her blood sample and no one ever realized the test hadn't been run. We were angry, upset, frustrated, and left wondering, on top of everything else, why and how this had happened. At that point, after some other difficulties with the same facility, we switched all of our care to the hospital where her other specialists were and began the long wait again. When we finally had exhausted all of the genetics tests the doctors could think of, we did the whole exome sequencing to look at all of Molly Kate's genes, but even those results came back inconclusive. Maybe one day, science will catch up to a diagnosis that is out there for Molly Kate, but maybe not. Some cases of Cerebellar Hypoplasia are thought to be a static event caused by a stroke in utero, but our physicians have always thought that Molly Kate's was caused by some other overarching diagnosis because of all of her symptoms combined. We will continue to search if other tests become available, but for now, we focus on how to best help our girl.

In between all of the doctor's appointments, we began to realize that our daily lives might never look the same. Multiple therapy appointments filled our days, and when we weren't doing that or taking care of Molly Kate, it seemed like I was constantly on the phone fighting with medical billing departments and insurance companies. Most of the time, Molly Kate would not sleep well at night, so the fatigue of being up during the night combined with our daily routine left us extremely exhausted.

The exhaustion and the emotions of slowly realizing that our lives were going to look so different than we had ever dreamed made for some really hard days. I can remember crying everywhere I went for the first year or two after receiving the news about Molly Kate's brain. I remember crying in the grocery store, in the car, and definitely at church. I love to shop for Molly Kate, and I can remember tears welling up in my eyes many times as I read the slogans on all of the cute t-shirts for sale for toddler girls her age that referenced running and jumping and dancing. Things that just seemed cruel when you had a daughter that couldn't run, dance, jump, or even sit.

Seeing milestones reached on social media of other children born around the time as Molly Kate was particularly hard. Sometimes I just had to stop looking. Well-meaning friends would tell us what their kids or grandkids that were of similar age to Molly Kate or younger, were accomplishing, and although I was happy for them, it would still hurt. Companies that sold baby products would send emails reminding me of which milestones Molly Kate should be reaching each month. Everywhere I looked, the world seemed to shout that my baby wasn't doing what she was supposed to be doing. I found some valuable Facebook support groups, but even those hurt to look at sometimes when children much younger than her with the same condition hit milestones that she wasn't even (and still isn't) close to.

As more therapists worked with Molly Kate, we were sent for a swallow study which determined she was aspirating a tiny bit on her liquids. This meant that we would need to start thickening her drinks and watching the textures of foods she was eating. Then one night, when she was sick, the seizures began. Neither my husband nor I had ever experienced watching a child have a seizure that we could remember. Molly Kate's first seizure was one of the scariest things we have ever witnessed. I have never felt such helplessness. That night would start a pattern of seizures each time she got sick. Thankfully, the seizures were short, and after many months, we found a dosage of medicine that has been able to control them. We don't know if we are forever out of the woods with seizures, but my heart reaches out to the moms and dads who deal with much more frequent ones than what we have. They are truly horrible.

Through the help of our ECI therapists, Molly Kate did eventually learn to bear weight on her legs with the use of a mobile stander. Her daddy built her a play table with toys hanging from it that stood upright in front her. She spent many hours in that stander and eventually could bear weight on her legs and feet, although she has yet to gain the core strength to stand independently. In a sweet and caring gesture, some of our friends from church collected money to purchase Molly Kate an Upsee, a device where she would be strapped upright to her daddy with her feet on his so that they could walk around together for short periods of time. As the time neared for her to age out of ECI and move on to the Public Preschool for Children with Disabilities (PPCD), our therapists began to talk about the need for a wheelchair.

Very early on in our journey, when Molly Kate was still a baby and before the doctors ever suspected anything, someone mentioned to me that Molly Kate looked like she might have a condition that would require a wheelchair. I remember at that time; I was very hurt by that. This was still during the stage when we were just thinking that Molly Kate was

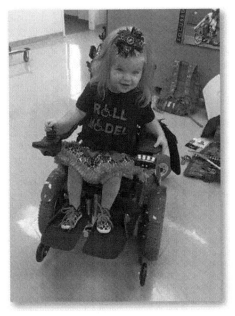

going to catch up to her peers and was just struggling with a big head. We had not yet even been told by the doctors to suspect a condition that wouldn't allow her to walk, so to hear those words so early on from an onlooker really tore me up. It wasn't that I was afraid of a wheelchair, I just wasn't even close at that point to thinking that we were dealing with a condition such as this. Fast forward a few years to when Molly Kate was nearing the start of age three preschool, and I couldn't have been more thrilled to start the process of getting a wheelchair! By this point, we had been carrying Molly Kate around constantly and we knew that when she started school, this wasn't going to be a possibility for her teachers. Some parents struggle, understandably, with feeling like getting a wheelchair is giving up on their child's ability to walk. We didn't feel like this at all, though. We were thrilled as we began to talk to our therapists about applying for a power wheelchair for Molly Kate. We knew she didn't have the stamina or strength to wheel a manual chair herself, and we were excited about the independence that a power chair would give her. We knew we would still work tirelessly to help Molly Kate get strong enough to walk, but we looked forward to seeing her have a way to get from point A to point B all on her own.

We were so excited the day that her chair came in. We had done the trials to prove she could learn to drive one and our equipment company had handled several insurance denials and reapplications for us, but it all finally came together. Of course, we ordered a chair in the color "pop star pink" for our little princess on wheels. We also purchased a little wheelchair for her doll to give to her on that day. Molly Kate is still learning to drive her chair proficiently --- mom and dad have even put a few scrapes on the walls ourselves with it—but nothing can replace the feeling of seeing your child do something independently when almost everything has to be done for her each day. Eventually, we also got a manual chair that we could push for times that places aren't accessible to her powerchair or for times that a chair has to be loaded into another family member's car. Now, four years later, I can't imagine life without a wheelchair. We still continue to work on strength for walking in therapy, but the wheelchairs have been such a blessing.

Molly Kate's speech difficulties, for me, have been the hardest parts of her condition. I long so much for her to be able to communicate and express herself. I can remember rocking her in her room for the first few years with tears streaming down my cheeks as I prayed that she would just be able to say or even babble "Mama." There's something in a mother's heart that longs to hear this word from their child. We would repeat words and sounds over and over to her, but she would always just look up at us and smile her precious smile.

Then, one night, a few months after she turned four years old, my son was recording me talking to her, once again trying to get her to say my name. She had recently been starting to put her mouth together like she was going to say something, and in the best moment ever, I heard that word that I had been praying to hear for so long. "Mama," she said, and then repeated it.

We cried tears of joy, as did the other family members, as she started to say "bubba," "dada," "Nana," and "Pappaw" over the next two months. At this time, these words, along with "ball" and "bye bye" are the extent of her spoken vocabulary, but we have taught her some signs to use for other family members, friends, and important words. I would love her just as much had I never heard her speak these special words, but it truly is a feeling I can't describe, nor will take for granted, ever again.

Molly Kate started school the day after her 3rd birthday. We were terrified to drop our baby off the first day with so many needs, but she has had wonderful teachers and teacher's aides that have taken such good care of her.

As many special needs parents find out from the get-go, you have to be an advocate for your child. Especially when you have a child with cognitive difficulties or that cannot speak; you HAVE to speak for them. Before Molly Kate started school, I attended seminars and support groups, read articles, and talked to friends that had been down this road before. I learned many useful tips that helped me to know what questions to ask and what things to request. I took the advice of asking for documents before meetings so that I could be prepared.

Molly Kate began to thrive in school. Although she could still only communicate with a few signs because of her limited fine motor control, she progressed academically and was able to show that she knew her colors and numbers. Her teachers had high expectations for her and we were always wowed by what she could show them. One of the best parts of school for her, was the social part. She loved her little friends and would get so excited if we ran into them outside of school.

Molly Kate is now six years old and continuing to surprise us. She sees a cerebellum specialist now who monitors her progress, and we continue to draw upon strength from God to help us with whatever challenges may arise. Although her progress is still slow from day-to-day, we see big changes from year to year. She now loves to wheel around the house in her wheeled stander and has learned to pull herself in a type of army crawl. It has been our delight to watch her "get into trouble" by digging in drawers and invading her brothers' rooms for the first time. We have learned to celebrate every single "inch-stone" but above all, we have learned that God has shown us a picture of His love for us as we love Molly Kate for who she is and not what she can do.

We have continued to work on finding ways for her to communicate. We tried many different communication methods and devices, but it was difficult because of her motor control issues. I knew that there had to be something out there for her, so we persevered over what seemed like a very long time and a lot of trial and error. Finally, with the help of one of her speech therapists, we found the right combination of an AAC device with a touch guard that has worked beautifully for her. She showed us that she is a fast learner and has 'wowed' us by quickly navigating through the screens to find what she wants to say. Hearing her tell her brothers "Stop drum" when they are playing the drums too loudly or "Molly Kate turn" for the TV has made us laugh and celebrate. She can tell us her wants, needs and what she did during the day, and it has been life changing. It has also confirmed that there is so much going on in that little head of hers, she just needed a way to express it. She has used her device to learn Bible verses for our Awanas program at church, and it has absolutely changed her educational experience at school now that she can more effectively communicate and respond to her teachers to show that she is learning the material they teach her. We look forward to her progress with this as she continues to develop her language skills.

Every morning now, we get up, lift her out of her safety bed and start the tasks of getting her ready for the day. These tasks involve thickening her milk because of her swallowing difficulties, changing her diaper, dressing her, giving her any needed medication, brushing her teeth, fixing her hair, and loading her into her wheelchair. We hope that one day she will be able to do some of these things on her own, but for now, this is

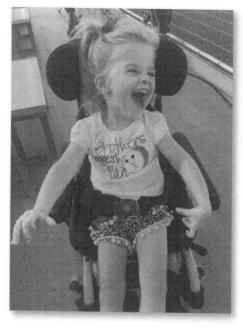

our morning routine. Throughout the day, we will be lifting and moving her many more times from floor to special chairs to stander to wheelchair depending on our day. She has six therapy appointments weekly, not including the therapy she receives at school.

In the evening, we shower and dress Molly Kate, then get her ready for bed. These daily tasks can totally exhaust a caregiver, and the hardest part for me is to know there is not an end in sight. With typical children, you know that each stage won't last forever—they will eventually potty-train, feed and dress themselves, and sleep through the night. With Molly Kate, we know that we may be helping her with many of these tasks for her whole life and that will become more and more difficult as she grows. Every time I become overwhelmed by this, I am prompted to remember that the God of the past is the God of the future and He goes before us. He knows just what I need today as well as years from now. This helps me with the big picture when I become paralyzed with fear and exhaustion. Even though it is easy to get overwhelmed, I have also always seen the daily care tasks that God has given us for Molly Kate as a privilege that has been bestowed upon us as her caretakers. It is hard; we are exhausted most of the time, but we are thankful that she is ours. She is a precious blessing.

Many of the things we dreaded when we first got Molly Kate's diagnosis became blessings by the time we needed them. I was in denial that she would need a wheelchair at the beginning, but when we got to that point, I couldn't wait for her chair to come in so that she could have independence. The initial idea of her wearing orthotics made me sad, but when the time came for us to get them, I was just so glad to have something that would help her stand correctly.

I will admit, as she has grown, it pierces my heart a little each time I see her peers doing new things, like starting ballet or soccer. There are some things she will most likely never be able to do in the typical way, and I've found that it's okay to grieve over that. However, I would tell parents on the same road to find other things your child can be involved in because we have received so much joy in watching Molly Kate do things through community programs for special needs individuals. This past year, she participated for the first time in our church's Buddy Bowling, where she bowled with a partner helping her. She had so much fun pushing the bowling ball down the ramp and being around all her friends.

Molly Kate has also participated for several years in our church's Buddy Cheerleading program, and I have coached. She and her friends cheer for our Buddy Basketball league. She has a buddy that helps her with her cheers and dances, and she loves to hold her megaphone. More recently, Molly Kate has decided that she wants to be on the court playing, so she has switched to basketball and has really enjoyed that too.

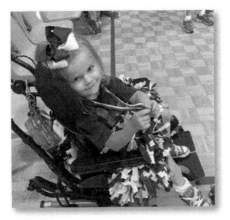
Showing off the medal for Buddy Cheerleading

Playing wheelchair soccer

192

She has participated several times in the special needs pageant in our area that celebrates the strengths and abilities of all children. Molly Kate loves getting her hair done, and I love dressing her up for the pageant. She has made some of the best friends of her life through college helpers she has met at this pageant. We get to pick a name for her to be crowned with each time, and our favorite one has been "Princess of Pure Joy."

We also participate in Easter egg hunts, Halloween carnivals, and other events put on by our local special needs organizations. These are not only fun for Molly Kate, but we get to see the other special needs families that have become "our people." Through them, we have made invaluable friends, we have learned how to advocate better, not just for ourselves, but for others, and we have met some of the most incredible parents on the planet.

Although Molly Kate can only verbally say a handful of words, her life has spoken volumes to us and to so many around her. Most of the time, she is so very happy. Her smile lights up a room, and you can read so much from her eyes and expressions. She has such a pure heart. Anytime a friend in her class gets admonished for something, Molly Kate's lip comes out, and she begins to cry for them. At home, if anyone raises their voice in anger, Molly Kate immediately gets her sad face and starts crying—she is our thermometer that reminds us when we need to speak more kindly to each other. She loves unconditionally and is a friend to anyone who speaks to her. We see so many qualities of God in her which brings to light the characteristics that we need to work on ourselves.

We have been asked many times, "What's wrong with Molly Kate?" While this is a common way of asking about her and is usually asked without any malicious intent, we have seen more and more that there is so much more "wrong" with us than there is with her. Do we wish that things were easier for her? Of course. We hate to see her struggle. But the most important things in life, she embodies every single day.

I could give countless stories that people have told me about how she has touched them just in her short five years. She had a special bond with a friend of ours with cancer. The way they brightened each other's day each time they saw each other was so beautiful. We have had friends write college papers about how Molly Kate has touched their lives. And then her former school teacher relayed these words to me and granted me permission to share them here:

"This past year I had two miscarriages. Both equally difficult, but in the midst of the heartache, there was Molly Kate. It's like somehow, she knew something was wrong without me telling her. She would sit with me and laugh with me, and through her gentle and sweet character, the Lord used her to help patch back together my broken heart. Molly Kate has impacted me by being a genuine light. She loves without question, and it's with pure innocence. I've never met a little one like Molly Kate, but I know that in her journey so far, she has already been the most beautiful witness of strength, courage, joy, and love than almost any other person I've ever met. I strive to love in a manner such as Molly Kate's."

Many have told us that when they are feeling tired or run down, they think of Molly Kate and how hard she has to work every day, and that gives them strength to continue.

We live near a university, and because of Molly Kate, students have gotten involved in special needs programs such as pageants and clubs that have touched their lives. They have learned that special needs children are not frightening, or individuals to stay away from, but rather children that love to play and interact as much as any other child.

Molly Kate has definitely impacted our family. Her brothers have learned much through having her as a sibling. They help without complaint and have become more compassionate to those with needs around them. They, too, advocate when they see things that could be better for individuals with special needs. The eyes of our whole family, including grandparents, aunts, uncles, and cousins, have been opened to the difficulties of people in wheelchairs and all of us have joined in the fight to educate and advocate in some way.

This year one of our high school-aged sons has become particularly passionate about helping others with special needs and has gotten very involved with both Special Olympics and a program at our local high school that partners typical students with students with special needs. He is an avid advocate, not only for his sister, but for many others, and was awarded a special service award at his high school this past Spring for his work in this area. Molly Kate has truly changed us all.

As for what we, as her parents, have learned, where do I begin? We have learned first and foremost that God's promises are true. He has walked with us every step of this journey and has not let us down once. He has provided for our every need, taught us to trust Him more, and comforted us in our grief through His word and through His people. He has taught us to be more compassionate to those around us and to remember that people are fighting battles every day that we can't see. He has taught us to work together as a couple better as we daily divide up the tasks we must do for Molly Kate. He has reinforced in me to remember all the ways He has taken care of us in the past when I am tempted to worry about what our future will look like with Molly Kate.

As I mentioned above, about 17 years ago, we became friends with a couple in our church right after both of our families had had our first child. We have continued to be the best of friends ever since. A few years after we met, I sat on the hospital bed with this dear friend of mine, as we cried together after she was given the news that her newly-born second child had Down Syndrome. It was shocking and unexpected news and they reacted the way most parents do when receiving the news that your child is not going to be like you expected. Of course, they, like us, would come to see the incredible blessings of their child's diagnosis, but the beginning was hard. I remember walking through those days with them, listening as she told me about ECI coming to her home and doing therapy with their little boy, and then the stories of him starting school, going to ARD meetings, and just the struggles, as well as the victories, of walking the road of special needs.

Fast forward nine years later, and this dear and precious friend sat on the bed with me after I delivered Molly Kate and was by my side a year later when we got the news of her condition. She was there as Molly Kate started with ECI. She was there as Molly Kate started school and we had our first ARD meeting. And she has been there as we have celebrated victories and cried over struggles. I am in awe of God's great providence that put this friend in my life years before I knew how much I would need her and her experience. He knew how much I would need her empathy and understanding when no one else could quite say they knew what I was going through. There are so many ways we can trace His hand on this road, but giving us these friends is one of the biggest. We joke that one day, when all of our other friends are empty nesters, the four of us, plus Molly Kate and James, will still be hanging out on Friday nights. God had a plan.

There are so many other ways that the Lord has provided for us. When we finally decided with our therapists that a power wheelchair would be the best option for Molly Kate because of several factors, one of the first questions was how we were going to transport it. As we began to look at the cost of wheelchair accessible vans, we were floored. The weight of medical and equipment bills was already such a burden at the time, and we couldn't fathom taking on a van payment for what they were selling for. Around this time, a friend who also happened to be our neighbor, started to talk to me about doing a fundraiser. At first, we were so hesitant to accept help, but as it became apparent that God had laid this on our neighbor's heart, we finally said yes.

I could write another book on how the fundraiser (which became known as the 5K for MK) came together and was carried out, but I will just say that once again, the Lord brought together many, many selfless people and the right circumstances to show us a beautiful picture of His love and His church reaching out to meet a need. Our church family, as well as many in our community, came together on a rainy Saturday in May and ran not only to raise money for a van but to show support for Molly Kate herself. We were so humbled, and the funds raised helped us purchase a van that was perfect for us. Another family was selling a van that they had custom-built for their daughter with similar needs to Molly Kate, and we were connected through friends of friends. This family even drove it several hours and delivered it to us. God could not have said more clearly, "Did I not tell you not to worry? Trust in Me and I will provide your every need." Although we have since traded that vehicle for one with a different type of ramp, to this day, our neighbors can look out their window and see a very tangible object that reminds us all that God provides. We were and still are humbled at the way our community served us in this way. We still see people, some that we don't even know, wearing their pink 5k t-shirts with Molly Kate's handprint on them around town, and each and every time, it makes me stop and give thanks.

A few years ago, some members of our church and other friends/family donated their time and resources to help us remodel our garage to provide an accessible bedroom and bathroom for Molly Kate. We live in an older home with narrow doorways making it hard to get her into a bathroom in her wheelchair. We know as she grows, it will be hard to carry her in and out of the bathroom and to lift her in and out of the tub. Providentially, there was a toilet and a sink in our garage when we moved in. We thought it was strange to have a bathroom in the garage, but again, God knew. It has become the perfect spot to close in and make an accessible room and bathroom.

Traveling is not easy with Molly Kate. The amount of equipment we need to load for any trip longer than a few hours is a lot. Many times, it is just easier to stay home. Over the past few years, though, we have taken a few long-distance trips with our sons and their youth group, not wanting to miss out on these opportunities with our boys. We were fearful about how difficult the travel, the arrangements, and the schedule of activities would be for Molly Kate, but each time we have done it, we have been so glad. It's been hard but worth it, and we have been able to make memories that our family will not forget.

We have learned many lessons along this journey, and I'm sure there are many more to come. Our eyes have also been opened to the reality that much of our world is not accessible to Molly Kate. Our hearts have been saddened at the abuse of handicapped parking spots and places that we go that are simply not accessible for a wheelchair. It's a tough feeling to realize that your child can't go somewhere or do something that other children can simply because they can't get there. The lack of changing stations in public restrooms for older children or adults with special needs means that they either have to be changed on a dirty bathroom floor or stay home. We know this challenge faces us more and more as Molly Kate grows. The positive side of this is that we are more aware   of these issues than we have ever been, so we are able to spread that awareness concerning why there are specially marked handicapped parking spots for vans and why schools need accessible playgrounds and push buttons and accessible curbs. We are able to advocate for changing spaces for all who need them. Sometimes the battle seems uphill and can be discouraging, but we press forward for our daughter and for others like her. It's also been so encouraging to watch our other children begin to become advocates for the disabled as their eyes have been opened to this world as well. Although we have definitely run into roadblocks, we have found that helping others see the world through "wheelchair-colored glasses" is sometimes the best way to promote change. We've learned   to ask for change and to educate schools, churches, and establishments rather than just complaining.

As far as advice I would give to others on this path; I would say to find a network of other parents traveling down this road. Facebook and other social media outlets can give you an online community of parents going through what you are going through. I have loved reading articles that others have shared online who just seem to "get it." The best, though, are those in-person relationships we have found with other special needs parents. Sometimes it is not easy to attend a support group in person, especially for those of us who can barely get out the door with our children and then have to worry about who will keep them and give them the care we would, but being surrounded by those who understand is so worth it. These people are your "tribe." I have looked to other moms with children in wheelchairs so many times for support and answers to my questions. It would be hard to do life without them.

We would also say to find a church with a special needs ministry. No church will be perfect in this area, but many are trying. Our church has provided special chairs for Molly Kate to sit in during her Sunday School class (before she had a wheelchair) so that she could be with her peers. They have purchased special toys that she is able to manipulate and have provided her with a one-on-one buddy that attends class with her as well as a room where individuals with special needs can go and be cared for during the church service. Our church offers activities for children with special needs as well as the Buddy Sports program mentioned above. Molly Kate also participates in a special needs choir for children and adults where she may not be able to sing the words out loud, but the joy on her face as she sits with her friends and raises her arms to the music is proof that she is loving every minute of it. Many churches are just now learning how to reach out to families such as ours, although some have been doing it for years. Asking for support and helping others see the world through the eyes of your family and child is key. Many times, churches may not realize the needs our families have and might be willing to support those if asked. Our church has done a great job with this and is an excellent support system to us.

I would also say, most importantly, to rely on God to walk with you day-by-day. He truly has given us hope through this journey. Through the trials of disability, we have been strengthened. We live a life that, if asked about beforehand, we would have probably said we couldn't do, but we have been given strength and joy. We still have incredibly hard days, but they make the good ones even better. Our lives have been so enriched by Molly Kate, and we look forward to more adventures with our Princess on Wheels!

The Elkins Family

Behind the Story

Tiffany is passionate about connecting families to churches with special needs ministries. She says, "Our church, First Baptist Church of Belton, has been really great about finding ways to include our whole family and giving Molly Kate a safe place to go and to learn while we have the chance to worship as well. Our faith has been integral to us on this journey. I know there are so many other parents like us who are weary and need hope."

People around the state approach Tiffany to ask what her church does, and she shares with them the ways churches can take the first steps, such as providing a buddy for a child with special needs. Tiffany notes, "The activities don't have to be big and elaborate, just do things that are inclusive." A way her church has increased inclusion is through the STARSS Ministry (Successfully Teaching and Reaching Someone Special). The Elkins family was involved in the STARSS Ministry even before they had Molly Kate.

In addition to weekly Sunday activities, the STARSS ministry also offers a Buddy Sports program which includes buddy bowling, buddy basketball and buddy cheerleading. A buddy is paired with a special needs child to help them as much as they need in order to participate. It was modeled after the Upwards Program, but is their church's own creation.

Since the Elkins family has been so involved, they are often asked to be representatives to speak in the community about the program and invite more people to be part of it. Tiffany explains, "Our church offers many activities that Molly Kate is able to be a part of such as a special needs choir, Vacation Bible School and age appropriate special needs Sunday School classes. Sometimes, she goes to the STARSS classes, while other times she attends classes with her typical peers and a buddy. Our church and special needs minister are great about talking with parents to find out what works best for each child."

Tiffany has come to recognize there's a large percentage of special needs families who don't attend church because they feel like they don't have a place for their child to go. To learn more about how your church can develop a special needs ministry, go to the special needs ministry page at: *www.FBCBelton.org.*

"We are passionate about advocating for accessibility throughout our community as well," says Tiffany. "We've been able to work with our local schools and district to obtain more accessible playgrounds, parking spots and ramps. It takes a lot of advocacy to raise the awareness, but we are passionate about change and are thankful for those who have come alongside of us to help with that vision!"

Life is About Choices

Jeff Rose

Life is a rollercoaster ride with ups and downs. For some, the coasters in their amusement-park-of-life are a bit more thrilling, with knuckle-whitening highs and nauseating lows. I was on the kiddie ride, sitting in a slow swirling tea cup or baby boat, going around and around, without too much to upset my system, until I turned eighteen. This was when I literally had my own personal earthquake. Running across the infield, I started missing pop flies because my physical world was being rocked on the inside. People thought I was stoned or drunk to be missing these easy catches, especially with my talent for baseball.

Frustrated with my challenges on the field, I retired my glove

Height: 6'1" Suit: 40L Shirt: 16.5/34 Waist: 32 Inseam: 33
Shoe: 11.5 Hair: Brown Eyes: Brown

and turned to the wrestling mat as an outlet for my competitive and athletic spirit. I wrestled all through high school and was terrible. I lost every match my sophomore year, won three my junior year, and five my senior year, to finish my wrestling career with eight wins and 52 losses.

At the same time, I was a relentless albeit not very impressive wrestler, I also became a runway model. The earthquakes that killed my baseball career (I wanted to go pro and play for the Minnesota Twins), stunted my modeling profession as well. My footwork on the runway was becoming awkward, and I started stumbling and falling off the ramp. I was invited to go to Milan, Italy, to model, but had to decline, not wanting to become a spectacle of how *not* to walk the runway.

Shortly after I graduated from high school, we lived in a split-level house. I would skip two or three steps going up and down the stairs, but when I could only skip one without stumbling and falling, my mom took notice. She is a nurse and knew enough to say, "Honey, let's get you a blood test." Two weeks later, the doctor said, "I regret to inform you, but you have a hereditary condition called Friedrich's Ataxia."

As I said, up to that point my life had been normal; I enjoyed high school, had many friends, and was the class clown of the school. The worse I became at sports, the more I developed my sense of humor. What could I do, but laugh at myself? Having that time to learn how to see the humor in life prepared me with a spirit of resilience for this disease.

Friedrich's Ataxia falls under the scope of muscular dystrophy. When I heard the diagnosis, I knew exactly what it meant because I had an aunt living with us who had the same disease. She was in a wheelchair full-time, had just gotten divorced, and moved from Florida to Washington state to live with us. All I had to do was look at her to see how much havoc Friedrich's Ataxia was going to play on my body. It is a genetic disease that causes difficulty walking, a loss of sensation in the arms and legs, and impaired speech. It's also referred to as *spinocerebellar degeneration*. The disease can cause damage to parts of the brain and spinal cord as well as affect the heart. There is no cure.

Initially, I didn't know I had a choice in my response, so I responded very negatively and reactively. I began smoking marijuana and drinking on a daily basis which lead to a D.U.I. arrest. I became depressed and even suicidal. As a young man in the prime of my life, it felt as if my life was already over. I knew what was coming, and I didn't want to accept it. For three and a half years I remained on a path of destruction. However, at 21 years of age, I was blessed with the knowledge of Christ and became a Christian. Someone came up to me and said, "Congratulations! You're a new creation!" At the time I didn't understand exactly what that meant. I strongly felt the disease in my body, so those words and my perception of self didn't match. This person gave me a Bible and said, "You are now defined by the man on the inside, not the man on the outside."

This message got my attention, and so I began reading the Bible with greater interest. As a result, I came to realize that, "I can do all things through [Christ] who strengthens me" (Phil 4:13). I also began to understand that with Christ in my life, I am more than a conqueror (Rom 8:37). Of course, I honestly didn't feel like a conqueror at all in my declining physical state, but then I read in the Bible where it says, "we walk by faith, not by sight" (2 Cor 5:7). Or in other words, we walk by what God says about us, not how we look or feel. In Deuteronomy 30:19, it says, "...I have set before you life and death, blessing and cursing: therefore choose life, that both thou and thy seed may live." Even God says we will have good and bad in our lives, but it is up to us to choose life and choose the good.

In the book of Joshua, God told Joshua to choose who he will serve. Meaning, he could choose to serve evil or virtue. In everything He does, God gives us a choice to follow or reject Him. We are allowed to choose righteousness or damnation. Some Christians don't understand this principle or get upset by it, but God has given us something called, "personal responsibility." It is vital to recognize the role we play in our response to everything in life, as our reaction to life, whether good or bad, is indeed a choice we can and must make!

In addition to the epiphany that I am a loved child of God, who is on earth for a purpose, I came across an equation that has perfectly explained this spiritual principle. I read about it in a book by Jack Canfield. Here is the equation:

$$E + R = O$$

In this formula, the "E" stands for "events." Events happen to everyone. I am a white male born into the Rose family. That was an event that occurred on my birthday, and I had no choice in it; it just happened. The "R" stands for "response." This refers to how you respond to an event that has happened to you. Initially, after my diagnosis, I didn't know I had a choice in my response, so I responded negatively, and my outcome (what the "O" stands for!) was equally negative. Once I came to understand this equation and apply it in my life, changing my response from negative to positive, my life was transformed and the outcome has filled my rollercoaster-ride-of-life with soaring vistas and expansive spectacles of all the blessings I have been given. Today, I speak to churches, schools, and many other groups, teaching this principle.

Life is actually about choices. It's about who or what we are going to identify with. For instance, I am not my body. My body is handicapped, but I'm not. Many people don't understand that they have a choice in what they feel about themselves. The Bible says there is power in agreement; whatever you agree with, you are given power over. Whether it be limitations or unlimited potential, good or bad, God has given us the authority to choose.

As I continued to read the Bible, a calm, relaxing peace would flow from my heart into the world. I learned to "think" with my heart. I anchored my heart to what God had already said, such as, "I am more than a conqueror," and, "I can do all things through [Christ] who strengthens me." My heart knew it was true, so I kept saying it. As I would daily disengage from negative external feelings, the truth in my heart was liberating desires that had been locked away for years.

Once I went from, "I can't" to "I can," I enrolled in school, and by the grace of God, got two B.A.s in California, then moved to Oklahoma and graduated from Rhema with a degree in Children's Ministry. After completing college, I joined a health and wellness direct sales organization and advanced to the top of the company. I share all this, not to boast about my personal accomplishments, but to show that life has nothing to do with conditions, and everything to do with decisions. Over the years, I have moved from a cane to a walker to being in a wheelchair full-time, but my life has gone in an upward spiral of success because I took responsibility for my choices. I don't allow external forces to dictate who I am or who I can become.

I have a disease with no cure or treatment, only drugs to manage the symptoms. For a while, I was given test drugs that were causing brain fog and making me miserable. I began feeling more and more terrible during the day because of these drugs and decided to be proactive and become a researcher. By the age of 33, even though I was on five different medications, I became my own doctor. In this process, I learned to alkalize my body. Furthermore, through my research, I learned that Japan was ranked #1 in the world for good health and the USA was #54. I dug in deeper to find out why Japan is number one and we are so low in good health rankings. As a result, I discovered that in Japan, doctors work on the body's P.H. when people are sick, reducing the acidity. Following this model, I learned how to alkalize my body and within two weeks I got off four of the five medications. Within a month, I was off all drugs. I don't need to take any now, and I'm very healthy. I exercise for two hours at a gym, five days a week. I don't have a six pack because I can't raise my legs, but I have a four pack!

I still don't have a choice in my diagnosis, but I can feel wonderful, maintain control over my health, and improve the functions of my body through exercise as well as what I eat and drink. I stopped eating fried foods and increased my intake of greens. I eat very little meat, preferring a mostly gluten-free and vegetarian diet. I also drink only alkalized water. It's funny, but through serendipity, God ordained me to find this water. I was very dehydrated because of all the medications I was on, and once He began hydrating me, I was able to start thinking clearly. The more hydrated I became, the more clearly I could think. When people go to the hospital, the first thing they do is hook them up to an IV to hydrate the body. It's essential to health.

The alkalized water helped my body rid itself of free radicals and began to neutralize a lot of the damage the disease was causing. The pills were making my body more acidic and full of these free radicals. Basically, the pills amplified the symptoms of the disease. The water doesn't heal the body, but allows it to return to a state in which the body can heal itself.

Now I own an alkaline water business because I am such a product of the product. I believe in it so much; I have sold over 150 water ionizer units to individuals and have watched all of my customers see improvements in their health. This has allowed me to pay for the nice apartment I live in with my sister, who was also diagnosed with Friedrich's Ataxia when she was 24. I am able to pay both her medical bills and mine and have the freedom to pursue any goal I set, including learning to surf and traveling.

"The Valley of Dry Bones" is a famous passage in Ezekiel 37. It is the story of how God raised an entire army from dry bones to full life, with muscles and skin. Everyone knows it as a picture of what God can do with something that was dead, as He brings them back to vibrant life. Yet, God did not make it happen by Himself. He told Ezekiel to *SPEAK* life to the bones. As Ezekiel *SPOKE*, only then was God moved. Every morning I *SPEAK* my goals out loud, and throughout the day, God moves to make them happen. Recently, God helped me advance to one of the top ranks of my company. But even when I was at the very bottom, I spoke like I was at the top. I have been in a wheelchair for the past nine years, and despite

negative circumstances, I have been able to overcome by speaking my goals every day. Through my journey, I realize that I am a powerful creator, not a passive observer of circumstance. Too many people are "praying" when they should be "saying." and throughout the day, God moves to make it happen.

To me, true health is being physically, mentally, and financially strong. I don't think people can fully recover from illness when they are always worried about paying bills. Today I have a housekeeper and a personal chef, and I pay them from the money I've made in my business. This happened because I chose not to agree with circumstances, but instead, chose to agree with who God said I was. That is where my power to prosper has come from. I don't share the success of my career in my story to promote my business or even convince people to believe in alkalized water, but to show that you can accomplish whatever you put your mind to when it's done with full faith.

I am also returning to the modeling profession of my youth. I made a video for an organization called *Changing the Face of Beauty*, which is a nonprofit corporation committed to equal representation of people with disabilities in advertising and media, worldwide. The words "disability" and "model" are almost never used in the same sentence. You rarely see them in advertising or on T.V. and, as a result, wherever we go, people don't really know how to deal with the handicapped. We

are unseen, hidden away from the public view, and undervalued. The more value you feel, the more you'll convey value to your community. The disability community is the number one minority in the world. I am rolling back in front of the camera as I strive to cut the path, lead the way, and allow the disability minority to become more mainstream and welcomed. In a way, I feel like God has put me here to be a type of Martin Luther King for the disability community, helping them rise up, be seen, accepted, and reach their dreams.

I began my story with the metaphor of life being a rollercoaster ride, but it is truly a joy ride because I choose to make it one. In reality, that is also one of my dreams; to develop an accessible amusement park full of roller coasters and healthy eating options, along with a spa and other ways that people can escape. It is easy to forget your difficulties when you are laughing and having fun. That is an opportunity I want to make available to everyone, and I have every reason to believe it will happen!

Three words to live by are *KEEP THE FAITH*. In the Bible, it says, "this is the victory that has overcome the world–our faith" (1 Jn 5:4). Keep your attention on your faith-vision. Keep your attention away from anything negative that the five senses may be presenting or exhibiting.

My life began to change when I realized that success was up to me. God gave mankind the authority to direct their own lives. The Bible says we are co-creators with God (1 Cor 3:9) and that our tongue is "the pen of a ready writer" (Ps 45:1). We are to write upon our hearts, His Words, and declare the magnificent promises that He has freely given us. In Joshua 1:8, God told Joshua, "This Book of the Law shall not depart from your mouth, but you shall meditate on it day and night so that you may be careful to do according to all that is written in it. For then you will make your way prosperous, and then you will have good success." This verse contains an important principle for success in life: The word of God must be embraced, spoken, and acted upon with full confidence that God will do what He has declared.

God had already done His part by giving Joshua His Law. It was up to Joshua to take personal responsibility and meditate. God told Joshua not to let it "depart from your *MOUTH*." In context, "meditation" refers to "speaking or talking about." The outcome? "YOU will make YOUR way prosperous." God didn't say, "I will make your way prosperous." It was up to Joshua to speak what God had already said.

When I began to place God's Word in my life, it became like an anchor to which my mind and soul could be tied. Even though outward circumstances would be stormy like the waves of the sea, I would not lose hold by affirming every day who I am in Christ. That is how I have achieved everything I have accomplished; because I didn't let the identity of circumstances replace the identity I have as a Child of God.

Behind the Story

Jeff won't let his disease define him nor allow himself to be limited. He has reached the top rank of Enagic.com, 6A, which is what an independent distributor can achieve when they have sold more than 100 medical devices (in Japan they are medical devices, the FDA in the US hasn't made any statements). This is not a multi-level marketing company, but direct sales. Jeff's distributor number is 8704038 for anyone interested in purchasing a device through him.

Jeff is working to raise awareness for *CureFA.org*, which is a nonprofit striving to support research for a cure for Fredrich's Ataxia. While many are waiting for a cure, Jeff says he isn't waiting around for a cure to live. He is enjoying life to the fullest every day.

Jeff recently spoke as a representative for CureFA at an event called *The Surfing Madonna Beach Run* with over 5,000 people in attendance. He shared his story including how he changed his response from negative to positive, creating an outcome where he could become a successful business owner living in San Diego, teaching people that their success has nothing to do with outward conditions, it's all about inward decisions. The purpose of the run is to donate 100% of the net funds raised to local ocean, beach and park related projects, including helping disabled people get in the water. This beach run is the world's largest. Last year the event set a Guinness Book of World Records for attendance. Jeff participated by being pushed in a beach wheelchair by his good friend, the president of CureFA, Robert Nichols in the 5K portion of the run.

My Reason Why

Ashley Ballew

"Thank God he was born today!" These were the only words my obstetrician spoke after she delivered my son and walked out of my hospital delivery room. When my thoughts take me to the day Benjamin was born, those words repeat so clearly in my head. A tidal wave of emotions hits me right in the heart, and depending on the day we've been having, the outcome may be tears, screams, guilt, anger, fear. At the same time, love is always mixed within the combination.

When I found out I was pregnant in late July 2001, I was elated! For as long as I can remember I have loved babies. I'm not sure if any of my family or friends know this, but I wanted to be a "baby doctor" when I grew up. Life is interesting, though. It's so strange how the smallest choices can have the largest impacts that ultimately change the path you are on. I believe that everything happens for a reason; that God has a purpose for each of us. Yes, even my son, who was diagnosed with cerebral palsy at eight months old.

My first doctor's appointment was on a naval base. During our marriage, my husband was in the Navy so we had to make our first appointment at the clinic on the base. After our initial visit, we were then sent to a civilian doctor. I mention this seemingly small detail because in our story it is one of those small actions that ends up making an enormous impact on our lives. When the doctor came into the room, he congratulated us and continued with the usual information and – the most exciting part

– my due date of February 29, 2002. A leap year baby! I thought that was so unique.

After just a month it was time for my appointment with the obstetrician who would be following me throughout my entire pregnancy. This visit did not go as smoothly as the previous. My doctor had trouble finding the baby's heartbeat, so she requested that we return the next day so I could have an ultrasound done. The next morning, as my husband and I drove 45 minutes to the doctor's office, there was an eerie feeling in the air. We passed an elementary school with its flags at half-staff and I remember wondering why.

As we arrived at the medical office and saw their TVs flashing in the lobby, we learned the first plane had hit the World Trade Center. Shock, fear, worry and confusion all invaded my mind at once. *What would this mean for my family?* We continued with the appointment, but with an expedited pace. My husband had to get back to the base, which was now on lockdown, on what was supposed to be his day off.

As I waited to see the very first image of my baby on that tiny black-and-white screen, my heart raced. I was overwhelmed with love for that tiny precious angel. First, I heard the heartbeat, then I saw the incredible image of my precious baby. At this point it was still too early to determine the gender. My doctor, however, surprised me when she asked which of us had the bigger head. "The baby's head is measuring ten weeks, but the body eight weeks. You're not as far along as you think you are," she said. This was a pivotal moment in our lives.

I tried explaining that I knew when my last menstrual cycle was and that I was a small baby at only five pounds, eight ounces. I was only 130 pounds at the time I became pregnant, so maybe the baby was just going to be small. But the doctor changed Benjamin's due date. She didn't just change it by a week or two. She went big and decided his due date should be April 1, 2002 – one entire month after the original due date. At that time, although I had been married for more than a year, I was just 21 years old. I'm not sure if my age led to her assuming I was naive and didn't know what I was talking about. I'm not completely sure why she based the due date solely on head circumference and did not factor in the other variables. My thought process was that I'd just go into labor earlier and prove the doctor wrong.

After the fact, my research indicated there is in fact a large majority of women who do not go into labor spontaneously. Unfortunately, I was part of that statistic. As my pregnancy progressed, the only problem I had was severe pain in my legs. I mentioned this at my visits and was told that it was normal. "Okay, you're my doctor." I didn't know any better nor was I able to get a second opinion. I was concerned that I wasn't feeling enough movement and was told to eat, lay on my left side and count how many times I felt the baby move. But I had already done this; that's how I could tell there wasn't much movement.

My doctor did not perform any extra tests and did not seem too concerned about the issues I brought to her. As the end of March approached, I continued to experience severe pain in my legs. On Monday, March 25 I asked to be induced. My induction was scheduled for Wednesday, March 27. My husband and I, along with my mom and sister, arrived at the hospital at 6:30 a.m. excited. The day I had dreamed of for so many years had finally arrived! I felt like a six-year-old on Christmas morning looking for her Barbie Dream House under the tree. All the preparations had been made: the tiny diapers, the blanket, the pink-and-blue-striped beanie. We were ready to welcome our son Benjamin Tyler Ullman into the world.

The morning slowly crept by and my doctor determined I would need to have an epidural. Unfortunately, on the first try the epidural did not work at all. On the second try, it worked only on the right side of my body. That was one of the strangest experiences I've ever had. So, we tried again and the third time was a charm. As my labor progressed, my doctor came in to break my water. To my surprise, my doctor casually announced that I had no water to break. She then turned to the nurse and told her she would be back when it was time for delivery.

Now, I can image what you're thinking because I was wondering the same thing. *What the heck was going on?* Hindsight is 20/20, and I know now from my extensive research that I should have been rushed for an emergency C-section. At 21, however, laying in a hospital bed, scared and confused, all I knew was she was the professional. She was the one who went to medical school. She knows what to do, right? The nurses scurried around, whispering. Occasionally I would get a half smile and be told everything was fine. The time had finally arrived. Benjamin was moments away from blessing our lives forever. My doctor asked my husband if he wanted to cut the cord, and like so many excited fathers before him he replied, "Yes!" Here we go, counting 1, 2, 3, one more push. He's here! Silence.

There was no cutting of the cord, no newborn tiger cry, no placing of my precious, tiny baby on my chest, no Hallmark tears of joy. Just those piercing words, "Thank God he was born today." With no explanation, she was gone. Wait, what do you mean? What's going on? I was so confused. I wanted my son! Strangely, I heard a nurse ask where the placenta was. Another nurse responded that it had already been thrown away (further research proves this is not typical practice).

I heard him cry, but it was so faint and weak that I didn't recognize the sound at first. I finally saw him. His face was wrinkled. His skin was dry and peeling, hanging like that of someone who had lost an enormous amount of weight. I recall telling my mom he looked like an old man. I was confused because my baby wasn't the typical pink, chubby cherub that you see in newborn nurseries on TV. I was waiting for the smiling faces of family members through the glass window. These are the pictures I'd dreamed about. These are the moments I was supposed to be experiencing. Instead I was lying unable to move, and no one was answering me. Nurses were moving all around. I felt confused, like I was at the scene of an accident rather than the birth of my baby.

I was constantly being reassured that everything was okay. The nurses and pediatrician were scattered around the room. I could hear chatter and murmurs, but nothing was clearly audible to me. My eyes were fixed on Benjamin. The nurse finished cleaning him up and tried giving him a small bottle of clear liquid. I wanted to know what she was giving him and why he wasn't taking it. She was trying to give him sugar water

– what hummingbirds love – because his glucose was low. I couldn't understand why his glucose was low. He wouldn't suck on the bottle because he was too weak. My eyes filled with tears. Why was my son too weak? He was supposed to be a strong, healthy baby boy. I hadn't had any health issues aside from the leg pains. I'd done everything I was supposed to.

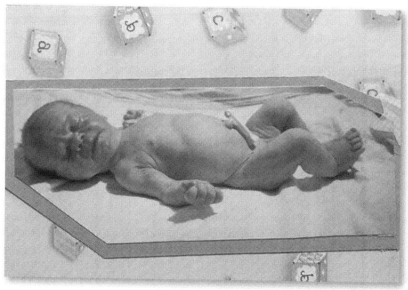

Benjamin at birth

At last, an hour and a half after the birth of my son, I was finally able to hold that precious angel I had been waiting so long to love. There are not enough words to express the love I had for him. I was with Benjamin for about two hours, along with my husband, my mom and my sister who were there also. A friendly nurse came in to take Benjamin to the nursery to have some tests done, and she said he would be back in a short while. The next thing I remember, the phone in my room rang and woke me. A nurse told me that she wouldn't be able to bring Benjamin back to my room because he needed to be monitored in the nursery. In the middle of the night, in a hospital room by myself, I just broke down in tears.

This was not how it was supposed to be! This is not what happens when you go to the hospital to have your baby! Benjamin was in the nursery for four days. I had been able to convince my insurance to allow me to stay in the hospital for two extra days, but then I had to leave. In my hospital room packing my things, I was angry, heartbroken and confused. I shoved clothes in a bag, threw things around, yelled at the wall and cried uncontrollably. I could not control my emotions. I couldn't leave my baby and go home without him; that's not supposed to happen. I just wanted someone to wrap their arms around me. Everyone just keep telling me it was okay, but it wasn't!

215

About that time, my sister came in to the room. Growing up, we hadn't been close. She grew up living with my dad, while my brother and I stayed with my mom. My sister said, "I don't know how you feel, but I imagine it must be pretty horrible. I just want you to know I am here for you." Those words have stuck with me for 15 years. So many people use the words "I know how you feel" in the wrong situations. Truth be told, no one actually knows how someone else feels. You might be able to relate, but you can't truly know how they feel. Most people are just trying to be nice. For me, in this situation, the words my sister used were the exact words I needed to be comforted and I appreciated them more than anything. Because of her, to this day, I try to be cautious of the way I try to comfort others.

As I was being discharged, my father and stepmother came to the hospital. The memory is as clear as yesterday. My father and I were standing in the hallway, admiring Benjamin lying in his incubator. He was too precious, wearing a white beanie with a University of Texas Longhorn logo on it with booties to match; he had received them as a gift. I tried to ignore the IV in his hand and the feeding tube in his nose, but at that moment, I started having a meltdown. Remember, I was just 21, scared and heartbroken. I would have loved for my father to just wrap his arms around me and tell me he loved me. Instead, he asked why I was crying which I found it to be an odd question. I told him that I did not want to have to go home and leave Benjamin at the hospital alone. "I know how you feel," he said. That just brought more tears. *How can you say that?* I thought. *You have no idea how I'm feeling! You have never given birth to a child! You have never had to leave your baby in the hospital alone and go home!* Getting in that truck with all the gifts and flowers, yet an empty car seat, was the second hardest day of my entire life. Hearing the neurologist say, "Your son has cerebral palsy" was definitely the most merciless.

Our house was 45 minutes from the hospital. Two days after I was discharged, as we were driving to the nursery to see Benjamin, I received a call from his doctor. There was a concern about a heart condition, and Benjamin was going to be transferred to the Children's Hospital. The transfer team was already in route. My husband and I arrived first. As we waited out of the way, we watched our son from across the room. Things were calm in the nursery; random machines beeped and babies cried. The transfer team arrived and approached Benjamin's incubator. A woman on the team suddenly yelled, "He's having a seizure!" My heart sank. I grabbed my husband's arm. The members of the team scrambled around in their bags grabbing tubes and different instruments. Huge plastic gadgets covered my tiny five-pound baby. The nurses in the room continued with their jobs like nothing was happening. My son had stopped breathing, turned red and was having a grand mal seizure. Surely this was no coincidence, my son having his first seizure the minute the transfer team arrived in the nursery. It made me wonder if he had had any seizures previously. Did anyone notice? This was the scariest thing I'd ever witnessed, and it was happening to my tiny baby! Help him!

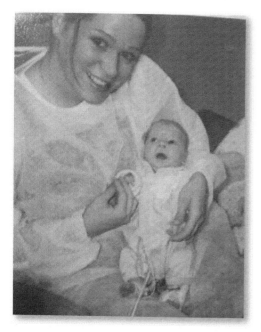

Benjamin had two more grand mal seizures in the ambulance on the 20-minute ride to the Children's Hospital. Four hours after the transfer team got their hands on him, he was settled in to the NICU at the Children's Hospital, and we were able to see him. Upon admission, his diagnoses were ventricular septal defect, grand mal seizures, hypoglycemia, aspiration and failure to eat. The NICU was a whole new experience I would not wish on my worst enemy. The heartache you see there is something that can never be erased. There are joys, though, on the days that babies finally get to go home, after months and months of being away from their families. Benjamin spent 45 days in the NICU. I went to see him twice a day every day he was there, driving 45 minutes each way. I would spend hours just holding him, staring at his face, kissing his head, praying he would get well so I could take him home. Some nights I would decide not to go and would call and check on him instead. The nurse would tell me that he was crying or that she had put him in the swing. I wouldn't be able to resist. I couldn't stand the thought of him being there alone without his mom, so I would go in the middle of the night; the time of day didn't matter. His father, on the other hand, only visited a handful of times. He claimed that he didn't like hospitals. *Well, friend, they aren't my number*

one hang out spot either, but this is your first-born son. He preferred going out to the nightclub instead. That's how he "handled it." Too bad he didn't handle his family life like he did his social life; our story would have taken a different turn.

During Benjamin's 45-day stay at the NICU, multiple tests were run every day from EEG's and EKG's, to glucose pricks every two hours. He had occupational therapists, physical therapists and feeding therapists come see him. The most frustrating part of the NICU stay was the lack of communication. I would arrive, scrub-in like a nurse preparing for surgery, put on my paper-thin yellow gown only to find Benjamin was not in his incubator or he was hooked up to 30 different wires. No one would inform me when this was going to take place or why.

When his seizures and glucose levels were finally under control, the only thing keeping him in the NICU was the fact that he was not eating. Benjamin had previously showed signs of aspiration; therefore, the doctors would not allow me to feed him traditionally. He had always been fed through the tube in his nose. Looking back, I feel like the hospital was trying to convince me to take the easy way out. Knowledge is power! You must educate yourself. Know something about everything and everything about something. This is where I failed. I was young, naive, selfish and uninformed. I wanted Benjamin home more than anything. One morning while visiting Benjamin, his nurse approached me. He told me that the doctor could insert a "G-tube" into Benjamin's stomach for feedings and then I could take him home.

Looking back, I obviously did not ask the right questions, but how was I supposed to know what questions to ask? I had no one to guide me. I had never been in this situation before nor had I known anyone who had. I was alone. Surely these professionals who work and live for this every day would be an advocate for me and my child. I prayed. I hadn't been to church in such a long time, but I prayed. I had the hospital chaplain come to the NICU and baptize my son.

Two days later, at two months old, Benjamin was in the operating room for the first time. He had a fundoplication to help with the aspiration and the placement of his G-tube. Fast forward 15 years, he still has his G-tube and he eats nothing by mouth, not even a sip of water. Benjamin lost his natural instinct to suck and swallow when he didn't get a bottle in his first two months. My regret is that I didn't educate myself. The guilt is debilitating. I am my son's only advocate; I cannot count on anyone else to take on that responsibility. I never should have left that NICU until he could eat on his own. Unfortunately, too often the lessons we learn come after the mistake.

Upon discharge, the doctor explained to me that Benjamin would be slower to develop than his peers and would take longer to reach his milestones. This seemed reasonable, due to his incredibly traumatic start in life. I was still confused though. As I reviewed the box full of discharge papers, I started my research. I learned that oligohydramnios meant low amniotic fluid, hypoglycemia, heart defects and hanging, peeling skin in newborns. My searches lead me to postmature babies. We've all heard of premature babies, but postmature babies are born after 42 weeks. Benjamin was born at 44 and a half weeks. (Remember my doctor changed the due date by a month.) Every single diagnosis that was on his discharge paperwork is a characteristic of a postmature baby, even the look of an "elderly man" was on the list.

The day had finally arrived! I was elated to bring my son home, and what better day than the day before Mother's Day? Motherhood was amazing. I enjoyed every moment with Benjamin. But my marriage was falling apart. My husband was not able to handle our son's difficult health problems. One evening we had gone out to eat at a restaurant, and I was getting ready to feed Benjamin through his feeding tube. My husband asked me why I didn't go feed him in the bathroom. I was appalled; how unsanitary! I could tell he was so embarrassed by the way his son had to be fed. This was the first of many battles we would have to fight concerning Benjamin.

Again, I prayed. We didn't go to church, even though there was one just across the street. When Benjamin was six months old, my husband came to me and said he was being deployed to California for six months. He told me it would be a good idea for Benjamin and me to move back to my hometown with my mother so she could help with Benjamin. I loved being a mother; I firmly believe that it is my gift. So when he presented this plan to me, I was not looking to accept help from anyone. However, with my husband gone, I really did not have any friends in the Navy town, so I packed up our things and headed back home. God has a plan for us all. I see this now.

With all of Benjamin's health issues, I had to find new doctors to take over his care. I found a highly recommended neurologist and made an appointment. When Benjamin was eight months old, I took him to see his new neurologist. I told his doctor a shortened version of what had happened as he examined Benjamin, stretching his arms and legs, moving his head back and forth, and having him try and grasp items in his hands. Just by listening to my speech and his examination, the doctor diagnosed Benjamin. I still recall the sound of his voice saying, "Your son has cerebral palsy."

My eyes glazed over. I could see my heart falling in slow motion to the floor. Then I could hear the loud shatter, like a glass window into a million pieces, just as the tears streamed down my face. Complete shock and bewilderment filled my body. *Why? Why did this happen to my son? I did everything right. What did I do to deserve this? Punish me, but not my son.* I had so many questions. There were so many unknowns. The doctors could not tell me anything else. Would he ever be able to eat? Would he sit up? Would he walk? Would he meet any of his milestones? They won't answer these questions because they don't want to be wrong, just like my doctor did not want to diagnose him because that would be accepting responsibility.

My mom always tells me, "Don't be sad; it could be worse." I really hate those words. That's like saying, "Don't be happy because someone else might have it better." I have a right to be sad. Several months later, I had a conversation with a doctor after an MRI. "He won't do anything he doesn't do now," she said. At that time, he was just smiling and laughing, but had no mobility at all. "Okay, so what do I do now?" I asked. "Therapy? Programs? What would help?" She told me I could put him in a place like a nursing home. Some parents do that. I was highly offended. I could not believe she had the nerve to suggest such an outlandish idea like that to me. Unfortunately, she would not be the last to do so.

More than six months had passed, and my husband had returned home. I had not. We grew apart. He enjoyed his bachelor lifestyle with his friends. The night before our divorce hearing, I called him crying, telling him I didn't think it was a good idea. He asked why I waited until then to tell him that. I didn't want my son to have a broken family. I wanted him to have a father.

Jeremiah 29:11 states, "For I know the plans I have for you declares the LORD, plans to prosper you and not to harm you. Plans to give you hope and a future."

At this time in my life, my hope was lost and my future seemed bleak. It would take years before I discovered what the Lord was accomplishing in our lives. My ex-husband remarried two months after our divorce was final. About a year later, they were blessed with twins and later another son. Benjamin, however, has not seen his father in 12 years. Benjamin is an incredible, funny, loving, spiritual and inspirational teenager. His father is the one who is missing out on the amazing blessings that Benjamin brings to everyone around him. I fear the day Benjamin comes to me and asks, "Why does my dad love his other kids more than he loves me?"

At the tender age of three, Benjamin was fitted for his first wheelchair. What a bittersweet day of emotions. In public, I would be constantly criticized for carrying my three-year-old because he "looked normal." He was too big for a stroller and people couldn't tell he was unable to walk. They just saw him, guessed his age, and assumed by society's standards he was too big for me to be carrying. So, they would comment, "You need to let that boy walk. He's too big for you to carry." Or, "Oh, he's not wearing shoes." I would politely say, "He has a medical condition and is unable to walk." "Can they fix it?" I would go to my car and break down in tears.

On the other hand, to see my tiny three-year-old in a wheelchair – something that I imagined only my fragile grandmother would use – was a very sobering image and made the cerebral palsy diagnosis that much more realistic. Again, the guilt and questions came. They always did at moments like these. *Why did this happen to my son? What did I do to cause this?* The fact that I can't take this pain away, that I can't fix this for him, breaks my heart. As a parent, you would do anything for your child, anything to make their life easier. Things like that happened quite often when he was younger. People are so quick to make comments without realizing the effect of what they might be saying. People in general don't take into account what it might take for others just to get out of bed in the morning. What a struggle it might be just to make it out of the house. I suppose it is the self-centered society we live in these days.

You know the saying, "Life doesn't come with instructions"? Well, neither does Raising Wheels Parenting! Seriously, someone needs to write a step-by-step book. Whose responsibility is it to help us? When our children are in the hospital, the doctors help medically. They get them stable enough to go home. But after the NICU stay, when our child is discharged, then we are on our own. Yes, of course we have at least one specialist appointment practically every month. They keep our children healthy, try to keep them out of pain, and schedule a surgery every year or so. Therapy is a must because they have to get out of their wheelchairs and get some movement in their muscles. My planner is as thick as a phonebook, but where is the knowledge? I need the study guide!

Then there's the school system. Who is there to guide us through that? They have a language all to themselves. ARDs, PLAFS, PPCD, EPCD; the acronyms are endless. You need a dictionary just to fill out the enrollment form! Who is in charge of educating us on the school lingo? Or, what about grants, scholarships, wait lists, community programs, etc.? Not to mention, all the equipment, camps and services that insurance won't pay for?

I've found that there is no one place with the wealth of information and opportunities that are out there for our children. Instead, most of my knowledge has come by word of mouth from parents who have come across the information by accident. In some areas communication has gotten better; Benjamin and I have been in this "special community" for 15 years now. It has taken a long time to acquire such information, which is a very sad fact in my opinion. Our job as parents is challenging enough. There are programs, grants and scholarships available, but it shouldn't be so hard for our children to obtain them.

Benjamin suffers through pain every day. Some days are better than others, but to see your child suffer and be unable to do anything about it is heart wrenching. He manages to have a smile on his face 95% of the time. He is a typical teenager when it comes to moodiness, though. He is a social butterfly and loves to make people laugh. He makes sure to pray for all the people in his life, even strangers. Benjamin enjoys music and loves Christian songs.

One of his most unique and treasured traits is his love for the Lord. Several years ago, Benjamin and I started visiting churches. We enjoyed them, but never felt at home. One of Benjamin's good friends at school asked us if we would like to attend his church. Of course, we would try it. This is where our story starts to come together. One morning, as I was getting Benjamin dressed, he told me, "I seek God," at least, that's what I thought he said. I said that's good Ben, God wants you to seek him. He said, "No I see, saw God." "You did? When?" "When I was born," he said. I stood there for a moment, not saying anything, just processing what he had said. Benjamin

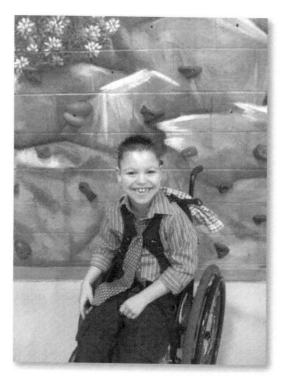

doesn't know what "being born" means. We've never talked about that or God being there. Although I have no doubt He was there that day, there is no way Benjamin could be making this up.

As we entered the church, everyone was so welcoming. They were excited we were there, and they spoke to Ben. I had never felt so close to the Lord as I did when I walked in to that building that morning. I knew we were home. A few months had passed and I had questions about Benjamin's salvation. I knew Benjamin had a strong connection with the Lord. I emailed my pastor about the questions I had. He is very knowledgeable and quickly replied with Scripture, explanation and interpretation. Then I read the next-to-last scripture he had included. He must have known all the guilt I'd felt, all the years of questioning I had experienced. I hadn't asked for it, and I didn't know it was there but, after waiting ten years, I finally got my answer:

John 9:1-3 "And as Jesus passed by, he saw a man which was blind from his birth. And his disciples asked him, saying, Master, who did sin, this man, or his parents, that he was born blind? Jesus answered, neither hath this man sinned, nor his parents: but that the works of God should be made manifest in him."

You see, it wasn't my sin. It wasn't my fault. The Lord has a plan for everyone. Benjamin was born with a very specific purpose. You can see the Lord's light shine through him. What a blessing it is to be his mother! I was entrusted with this precious child to make sure he is able to fulfill his purpose. The moment I learned this; the guilt was lifted.

Raising a child on wheels comes with a new set of challenges. Parking has got to be one of the biggest issues for wheelchair users. When people illegally park on the stripes, over the lines or in a handicap accessible spot with no tag, it is infuriating. I wish everyone understood that it's not because we want to park close to the store; we just want to be able to get our kids in and out of the vehicle! When you park too close, we can't open the door wide enough to get our child out or have enough room for the wheelchair. This happens at least a couple times a week. The excuse is almost always, "I was only in there for a minute." Okay, well, we stood here in the parking lot for ten minutes waiting because we couldn't get our ramp down because your car was in the way.

Also, when it rains and you are trying to get your child in the car, we both end up soaking wet and so does the chair. Grocery shopping has also been a difficult task for me as a single mother. Pushing Ben and pulling the cart as he is trying to grab things off the shelf is a challenge. Other shoppers huff at our little train like it's an inconvenience to them. Going to other people's houses is quite the challenge because they are not set up to be wheelchair friendly, even the homes of family members. All my family lives in two-story houses. Of course, I don't expect them to go buy new ones, just be considerate of our needs when asking why we never come over to visit.

Also, we don't go to parties for friends because he can't eat cake or get out of his wheelchair. Also, most parties these days are at fancy party spots with activities not very accommodating to wheelchair users. Again, I'm not complaining, just stating facts. Traveling requires extra packing of all supplies, medications, milk for feedings. We do travel on occasion, but it's just not easy. People don't realize we can't just grab a bag and hop in the car. It's more like packing for a seven-day cruise just for a two-day trip.

Public places have minimal accessibility, and sometimes it is hard to maneuver and be included in activities. Benjamin is incontinent, but there is nowhere in a public restroom for me to change him. I refuse to put him on the floor. Every day we get up early, and Benjamin goes to public school while I go to work. Benjamin is a high school sophomore now, and after a long day he typically has physical, occupational and speech therapy. He works so hard, but is completely exhausted by the time we get home. He participates in fun activities as well like music class, sports and other weekend things. I work in special education at an elementary school, and

I feel I bring a different side to the classroom because I'm not only an educator, but also a special needs parent.

At the same time, that means I don't get a break from this world. It's 24/7 for me. At times this can be emotionally, mentally and physically draining. I was recently diagnosed with fibromyalgia, which drastically affects my body on a daily basis – not a great condition to have when you constantly lift, dress, move and entertain a 75-pound, 15-year-old child. In June of 2012, I had surgery on my shoulder, due to the continuous lifting. When I spoke to my father and stepmother about my upcoming surgery, I expected them to ask what they could do to help. Instead, they said, "Benjamin is your whole world, and your life revolves around him. I wish there was a place where you could take him and leave him but you could go visit on the weekends." I was speechless. I literally had no words. They have always told me what I should do and how I should do things. But have they ever once said, "Hey, one day a month we will come over and watch Ben so you can..." Now, in my time of need they are telling me I need to put my 10-year-old in a home. *Excuse me? You have no idea what I do every day.*

Raising Wheels inside an apartment is next to impossible, but some of us have done it. I pick up my 75-pound child out of a bathtub backwards because the insurance company says a bath chair is a "luxury" not a "necessity." When I wanted to buy a house, my brother asked why I didn't like the apartment. I wanted my own house! Or when he says, "Don't worry sis, you can have another kid." No, it's about my heart being broken for my son, knowing I can't fix it for him.

Every day I worry about Benjamin. I worry about his safety, his health, his happiness. I worry what will happen to him if something happens to me. I am his sole caregiver. If something happened to me, the state would automatically give him to his dad who hasn't seen Benjamin in over 12 years. His father would not know the first thing to do in order to take care of him. I struggle when I hear friends' stories of their kids. They are getting their licenses to drive, getting married, going off to college – things that I know my son will not be able to do. So, I celebrate all Benjamin's accomplishments big and small.

Benjamin and I have been blessed with a beautiful home. A home that was built with diligent prayer for over two years. We unexpectedly were able to purchase a wheelchair-accessible van, which makes transferring so much easier. Over the last 15 years, we have formed countless friendships that have provided support, strength and courage during times of heartache, trials and joy. Our lives and story have touched other families and friends. Our church family has been our biggest support and comfort. We would not be able to triumph over our tragedy without the love, care and devotion from Fellowship Bible Church.

We all have a story. You may be able to find someone with a similar story, but they are all unique. If you've found yourself or a friend in one of these storylines, breathe. Yes, there are going to be difficult times. There are going to be very tough decisions to be made. You will make them and then wonder if they are the right choices, just like we all do. You will second-guess yourself and that's okay too. It is okay to cry; in fact, it is healthy to a point. You have the right to any emotion that you feel and no one should tell you otherwise. Don't leave the hospital empty handed. If you have to leave your baby, take a blanket or a stuffed animal home with you.

For you mothers: God gave you a mother's instinct; always listen to it. If you feel something is not right with your child and you get an answer that doesn't sit well with you, ask for a second opinion. Ask questions; if you don't know what questions to ask, research questions to ask. Never leave without asking questions. Learn early on how to become the best advocate you can for your child. This will make the rest of your life much easier. You will be fighting for the rest of your life. Learn about as many programs as you can and get on wait-lists as early as possible; they are years long, but you will need them.

Remember that some of your friends will not understand this new life you're living. They will not be able to relate to your world; it will scare them. Be prepared to lose some of those friends, not because they don't care about you, but for the simple fact that your world is much more complicated than anything they are prepared to take part in. You will quickly realize who your true friends are and who you can count on. You will, however, find a new world of friends. Friends you will share joys, laughs, accomplishments, embarrassments, even silent crying sessions with. These friends will be like your own secret society. A circle that can relate and understand when the outside world has no clue what you're going through. Don't deny or resist this circle because it will be a comfort to you. They will understand.

Learn not to care what other people think. When you are in public and receive stares and gawks, shake it off. Always remember there will be a thousand critics without credentials; learn to ignore them. So many people will offer unsolicited advice, but they don't walk in your shoes. Learn to forgive yourself. You will also have to learn to forgive others, even those who are not sorry and whose apologies have not been given. Forgiveness is a process, a choice that we must make over and over each day until we are free from hurt.

For far too many years, I held on to the excruciating pain of the life that I had envisioned for my future and the future of my family. I've had to forgive my obstetrician for not acknowledging and accepting the responsibility of changing my son's due date, which in turn caused his cerebral palsy. This fact changed the lives of me, my son, my family and my friends. I've learned to forgive my ex-husband for not meeting the expectations I set for him. The hardest hurt to overcome is that of my family. The isolation, suggestion of placement, and lack of understanding are the things that hurt the most. These things too I forgive. They don't live in our world, so they don't comprehend what it is on a daily basis, 24 hours a day, 7 days a week, 365 days a year. The forgiveness, though, that's really for me. I forgave so I can move on. Wear your tragedies as armor, not shackles.

Behind the Story

After writing this story, and realizing the usefulness of an instruction guide for newly diagnosed special needs parents, Ashely has begun working on that book. It is titled, *What I Wish I Knew: A Guide for Newly Diagnosed Special Needs.* Ashley says, "I wish I had known the right questions to ask! I wish I would have known the right places to go to get the help and the information I needed. I wish I would have known where to get support that is needed." These are the answers which will be outlined in her guide. Watch for its release date to be announced when it will be available at: *www.RaisingWheels.com.*

Ashley also intends to promote cerebral palsy awareness. She points out that Autism receives a great deal of awareness, while we don't hear about cerebral palsy nearly as much and there are many who have it.

Ashley earned an Associate's Degree in child development and has managed to maintain a full-time job while taking care of Ben by herself.

Benjamin and Ashley

It Takes a Metropolis
A Village is Not Nearly Big Enough
Janice and Rick Mason

Welcome to The Starting Line of An Unexpected Race

Janice:

When I step back and look at my family, I see so many blessings. I feel that my journey has given me "God glasses." When I look at the world, it's so easy to focus on all the negative. I never expected that God would give me one child with disabilities, let alone two. At the beginning, I was so focused on "fixing" the challenges. Yet, amidst the struggles of raising my special needs kiddos, I learned to wear my "God glasses" and see His graces. I realized that there is nothing imperfect with my children; I love them for who they are, and they have made our family's lives much richer than we could have possibly imagined.

In 1997, my husband, Rick, and I were blessed to relocate to beautiful Sydney, Australia. Prior to that, he had been traveling there for weeks on end. The company he worked for then decided it would be best for us to simply move there.

We had been trying for over a year to conceive. However, with his travel schedule things weren't very "fruitful." Prior to our move, I had been working at a large computer company based in Austin, Texas. However, we decided that in order to best maximize the enjoyment of our move from Texas, I wouldn't work outside the home in Sydney. Within a few months, we were pregnant. I was overjoyed. I felt we were beginning a new journey together.

Since it took us so long to conceive, I'd had plenty of time to ponder if I'd wanted a daughter or a son. Having grown up with three older brothers and just one sister, I really was hoping for a baby girl. I envisioned she'd be a little athlete like I had been. I could see her with a blonde ponytail running around a soccer field, or wearing a first- place blue ribbon from her swim meet.

But God had different plans. We found out our baby was a boy. I quickly adapted to that. Having grown up with brothers, I knew a thing or two about the opposite sex. I just focused on taking great care of myself and my little guy. My pregnancy was completely uneventful except for the fact that my husband was now traveling to Tokyo most every week. At the 35-week point, my doctor jokingly threatened to take away his passport if he didn't stay home.

> *Rick:*
>
> *I was working hard, travelling all over the Asia Pacific region, but loving the life we had in "Oz" as the Australians call it. Every weekend we would do something new or go into Sydney, even if only for a run out to the Sydney Opera House. Sometimes I would slap myself because I couldn't believe our good fortune to be living there.*

At my 36th week, we hosted a party for my husband's co-workers. During the party my lower back started hurting. I thought perhaps I had just lifted incorrectly at the pump class earlier that morning. However, my husband's colleague had a different thought. While walking out the door, she hugged me and said, "I think you're in labor. That would explain the lower back pain."

Since this was my first child, I needed some guidance, so I called the hospital to ask for advice. They asked me when was the last time I felt him kick. Up until that point, he had been quite active. However, as I thought about it, I realized it had been hours. The hospital staff suggested we come to the hospital right away. The contractions continued while the nurse hooked up the fetal monitor. My baby's heart rate was not changing even after they broke my water. The moment my doctor walked into the room, he took one look at the monitor output and said, "This bub's got to come out right away."

I was immediately being prepped for an emergency C-section. Of course, I was terrified. Here we were in a foreign country, away from friends and family, and suddenly going in for an emergency C-section. We had attended the usual birthing classes. Never once did I entertain the idea of a C-section. Being a lifelong athlete, a vaginal birth was always my expectation. While being wheeled into the operating room, I felt so out of control. I was very afraid of what was about to happen. While holding Rick's hand, I told him to get married again if anything happened to me.

> *This was a small hospital by U.S. standards. Very few folks were working in the middle of the night. Our doctor said to me, as we were wheeling Janice into the operating room, that he needed me to stay inside at the door,* 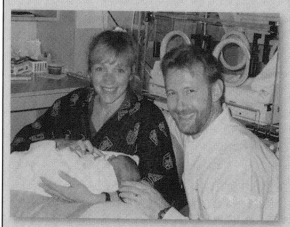 *which was the entrance to the operating room. It would automatically lock. He had called in the head of pediatrics and explained that I needed to stay there to let him in! Yikes, here we were a half a world away from home and suddenly I'm scared to death that I am about to lose my wife and unborn son.*
>
> *I paced and prayed, paced and prayed until the pediatrician arrived and I let him in. Then I went back to pacing and praying that all would be ok until our doctor finally came out and said both were ok. It had been touch-and-go for our baby, but the doctor said he thought that after some time, he would be fine.*

I woke up in the recovery room and soon we were visiting our sweet baby boy, Connor Sloan Mason, in the NICU. The moment I saw him, I told my husband, "He's beautiful. Let's make another one!" My husband just laughed.

A few hours later, the head pediatrician of the hospital visited my husband and me. He told us Connor was a very lucky baby. He said had we not come to the hospital when we did, Connor probably would have died.

The doctor explained that the umbilical cord was coming away from the placenta. My baby had been in distress, and I didn't even know it. As I look back on my husband's colleague and her message that I was in labor, I truly believe it was the Holy Spirit looking out for my son. Had she not said what she did, I probably would have tried to just endure the pain since I was still four weeks from my due date.

The next several months were spent recovering from the C-section, breast feeding and surviving on very little sleep. Fortunately, my mom couldn't wait to come stay with us and help. She could never get enough of her grandbabies, especially as newborns. I am the youngest of five kids, and my mom had blessed each of my siblings and their spouses with her help for their children. Now it was my turn.

A few months later, my husband was offered a position back in Austin. While I loved living in Sydney and the experience it offered us, I was ready to be back in Texas and close to my family. Like they say, "You can take the girl out of Texas. But you can't take Texas out of the girl."

Janice and I loved Sydney. It was a magical place for us. The city, the people, the weather, all of it, was so fun and relaxing. That was the lifestyle we enjoyed. But try as I may, I could not convince Janice we should stay. So, with a 6-month old baby we moved back to the U.S. and I took a new job.

Prior to our move home, I took Connor to the pediatrician. I mentioned he didn't seem to be developing at the same rate as the babies of two friends I'd met in the birthing classes. The doctor didn't seem too concerned. He simply said Connor might benefit from some physical therapy once we got settled back home.

After moving back to Austin, I returned to work at the same computer company for which I worked prior to our move. When I mentioned my concerns to his new pediatrician, he thought Connor was just a big baby and would eventually catch up. However, on my insistence, he prescribed physical therapy sessions.

Soon after starting the sessions, a dear friend of mine and her husband were visiting us. She was an experienced speech therapist and offered to accompany Connor and me to one of his sessions. She asked his therapist if she felt Connor's issues were developmental or neurological. At the time, I didn't realize the huge impact her answer would have on our family's life. The physical therapist paused for a moment, gently hugged my sweet son, and graciously said, "neurological." At that moment, I didn't have much of an emotional response because I didn't realize just what neurological meant.

That night at dinner our friend explained to Rick and me what the physical therapist's answer really meant. With that conversation, the realization of Connor's condition began to set in. Along with it came the emotions of pain, anxiety, grief, fear, anger and a host of others.

Connor's diagnosis of cerebral palsy (CP) was confirmed a short time later with an MRI. More specifically, we learned he had spastic quadriplegia; both his arms and legs are affected. The neurologist couldn't predict whether Connor would ever walk.

I immediately went out and bought all the books I could find on Cerebral Palsy. I needed to find out what was this thing our baby had and how we would beat it. I quickly learned there was a wide spectrum of this condition. More importantly, there was no beating it; there was only adjusting to what Connor could and couldn't do.

The good news was that it is as bad as it is going to be; in other words, the damage was done and it wouldn't get worse. I decided that I would focus on what Connor could do rather than what he couldn't.

With Connor's diagnosis, him clearly missing developmental milestones, the physical therapist's thoughts about his issues being neurological rather than developmental and finally the confirmation of his condition with the MRI, I began to question our pediatrician's statement that Connor was behind simply because he was a big baby. Boy, did he miss the mark! I knew in my gut that something was wrong. I felt he just dismissed my premonition. He didn't even suggest any type of diagnostic testing.

I also began to question why the pediatrician in Sydney didn't say anything to us about his condition. Rather than wonder, I decided to call and ask. His answer was simple. He knew I would act upon his suggestion of physical therapy and that path would lead to a diagnosis. Knowing how difficult the news would be to handle, he felt it best that we were told once we were home with the love and support of family and friends. At first, I was upset with him. But as time went on, I knew his decision not to tell us had been the right one.

Where Do We Go from Here?

During the months following the diagnosis, having the support of loved ones was the crutch I would need to make it through. My mother was incredibly supportive from the very beginning. When we would visit her in Houston, she worked to implement all the strategies to help Connor be the best he could be. These strategies included everything from seating chairs to rolling towels which were placed under his armpits for tummy-time to adapted sippy cups. Her support was relentless and encouraged me to be the best version of a mom I could for Connor.

I began to read up on his diagnosis and what therapies he would need. The twice-a-week physical therapy sessions became our top priority. Many times, he would cry for the entire session. He'd fall asleep in his car seat before we even left the parking lot. At home, I tried to facilitate all the stretches with Connor that I observed his therapist doing. His crying during his mom-therapy sessions quickly became too much for me to bear. We would both end up in tears.

I shared this with his physical therapist. She graciously said to me, "Janice, it's time you let me be his therapist and you just be his *Mom*." Those words really resonated with me. I had wanted to fix Connor. I figured if some therapy was good, then more therapy would be even better. This was the beginning of a relationship with his therapist that continues to this day. She and I don't always agree on things; however, we always mutually respect one another.

The first two years were tough for me emotionally and spiritually. Having lost my father suddenly at the young age of 13, and then divorcing my first husband because of abuse, I felt that marrying my second husband and having a baby would finally give me the life I had planned. I never gave any thought to having a child with a disability. Frankly, I was angry with God. But I didn't know if for a while. I realized I had been trying to fix Connor's disability. I couldn't help thinking, maybe if I tried hard enough, I could make his cerebral palsy go away. One day I found myself in my closet crying. Finally, the moment had come for me to surrender to what I recognized was God's plan for me. I had been trying to be Connor's mom without the strength I would soon find from Him. I told God that I would quit trying to do it my way and asked for the strength to be the mom He wanted me to be for Connor. With that prayer, my heart began to feel a sense of peace. I started to trust that things would be okay. I learned to focus on the things Connor could do, rather than those things he couldn't. It was a big shift for me.

> ## GOD DOESN'T GIVE US WHAT WE CAN HANDLE, GOD HELPS US HANDLE WHAT WE ARE GIVEN.

Janice and I agreed we would figure a way for Connor to do whatever he wanted to do in life. It might not look the same as other children, but we would find a way for him to experience whatever it was that he sought. Thus, we started a long line of activities like baseball, horseback riding, flying as the copilot in a small plane, even making a tv commercial, all before he was six years old.

Once my husband and I wrapped our heads around our new normal, we began to discuss having another child. Since Rick had two children from his previous marriage, he was content. Plus, he was anxious about the possibility of having another child with special needs. I certainly didn't blame him. However, knowing the irreplaceable love of my brothers and sister, I wanted to give Connor a sibling. Rick finally acquiesced, and we were blessed to conceive his younger brother, Brice Patrick Mason.

At that time I was 38 years old and considered of "advanced maternal age," so my obstetrician watched me more closely than normal. Thankfully, each of my monthly appointments and ultrasounds were uneventful. At times I would start to get anxious if my baby would have special needs like Connor. Each time my thoughts wandered that way, I'd quickly commit to trusting in God's plan.

On May 5, 2002, while sitting in church, I realized things felt different in my hip area. The pressure had changed. I told my husband I thought we needed to go to the hospital. It was nice to not be caught by surprise this time. My doctor and I agreed another C-section would be the safest choice. Rick doesn't do well with blood, so my sister wanted to be there when her nephew was to be born. When Brice Patrick was born later that day, both my sister and I were in tears. He came out kicking and screaming. She just kept saying, "He's beautiful, Janice. He's just beautiful."

For the next few days, Brice and I remained in the hospital together. I kept thinking of one of my favorite scripture passages "Therefore, since we are justified by faith, we have peace with God through our Lord Jesus Christ. Through him we have obtained access to this grace in which we stand, and we rejoice in our hope of sharing the glory of God. *More than that, we rejoice in our suffering, knowing that suffering produces endurance, and endurance produces character, and character produces hope, and hope does not disappoint us.*" (Romans 5:1-5, Revised Standard Version of the Bible-Second Catholic Edition)

That sense of hope helped me recover quickly. The nursing staff was impressed to see how quickly I was standing upright after undergoing a C-section. I was anxious to bring Brice home and enjoy time with Connor and Rick.

My mom stayed with us for several weeks getting what she always called her "grandbaby fix." Having a newborn in the house was a lot of work, but I was so relieved to finally hold Brice and know everything had turned out just fine. God was good. In a matter of months. though, Brice too would need physical therapy for a condition called torticollis. Congenital torticollis occurs when the neck muscle that runs up and toward the back of the baby's neck is shortened. It caused Brice to constantly turn his head to one side. It also led to temporary strabismus, which is a misalignment of the eyes. However, both issues were resolved in a matter of months with physical therapy from Connor's therapist.

By now, Connor was three years old and in the Preschool Program for Children With Disabilities (PPCD) classroom. My journey of navigating the annual school meetings with teachers and therapists had begun. In Texas, this type of meeting is referred to as an ARD, or Admission, Review and Dismissal. The purpose of the ARD meeting is to provide an opportunity for parents and educators to discuss and develop an individual education plan (IEP) for the student.

It was while he was in the PPCD classroom that we experienced our first wheelchair assessment. It was clear that Connor would not be walking anytime soon, so a wheelchair became a necessity. While the gentleman who performed the assessment could not have been kinder, the idea of my son needing a wheelchair was difficult to embrace. Although his seating system was my favorite color, green, and was embroidered with my husband's nickname for Connor, C-Man, the delivery of his chair was a challenging moment I will never forget.

Up until that point, we could camouflage his inability to walk by putting him in a stroller or grocery cart (with gallons of milk placed next to him to keep him upright). Seeing Connor in a wheelchair made his diagnosis a reality more than ever. It was a visual reminder that my son was different. That was hard for me to get used to. But, like with all other hardships up to that point, I just kept "putting one foot in front of the other."

One day I was talking to one of his adaptive physical education coaches. She shared with me that she too had a son with cerebral palsy. Her son was much older than Connor. I confided in her that I struggled with all the things required of me as his mom and asked how she endured it all. I will never forget her response. She said she often saw God's grace when watching people interact with her son. She saw kindness, patience and love. While I had not yet experienced that very much myself, I stored away her words of wisdom.

When Connor was five years old, I received a call from my oldest brother. He wanted to donate one of his horses to a therapeutic riding program. I did a little research and found one near our home called ROCK (Ride On Center for Kids). I picked up the phone to inquire about their program and spoke with the founder and executive director. She could not have been kinder or more patient with me while answering all my questions.

It just so happened that she and her colleagues would be travelling to Houston for a special needs horse show in a couple of weeks and could pick up my brother's horse on the way back. This exchange of one of God's amazing creatures, a horse named Blanca, would change our lives forever.

Connor started his new adventure of therapeutic horseback riding! While he lacked the strength to sit up independently, with a side walker on both sides of him for safety and a horse handler to control the horse, Connor's horseback riding career began. He's been riding for over 15 years now. More importantly, he's competed in many horse shows for individuals with special needs and won many first-place belt buckles, just like the real cowboys in the Austin Livestock Show and Rodeo. It is a sport he has grown to love!

Remember the words of wisdom from the mother of the older boy with CP? They rang true at the Ride on Center for Kids. From Nancy, the founder, to every volunteer at the program, we have experienced such kindness. They treat all their riders and families with incredible dignity and grace.

If You Can't Stand Up, Stand Out!

Shortly after Connor began riding, Nancy insisted I meet her sister-in-law, Erin. She felt we would really get along well. Nancy was right. Erin and I clicked. She too has a child in a wheelchair. One of Erin's passions is interior design, and she felt her daughter's chair needed some "snazzing up." She created some fabric spoke guard covers with huge pink flowers on them. When Connor saw those covers, he said, "Mom, I want some of those but with fire trucks on them!" Erin looked at me and suggested we start a business together. With that, *Wheels of Fun* was born. Our mission is to allow children to express their personalities on wheels. The covers put people at ease and give everyone a safe topic of conversation. They make a difference and put smiles on faces.

Starting *Wheels of Fun* was an exciting adventure. Erin and I kept a journal of moments when we saw God's hand in things. Many times, when we needed guidance, it was obvious He had shown us the way. I've always felt a sense of pride when discussing our wonderful product with people. When people see children in wheelchairs, they feel empathy and want to say something. However, out of fear of saying the wrong thing, many times they'll simply look the other way. Our covers make it simple; if you see a precious little girl in a chair with pink butterfly covers on her wheels, all you need to do is smile and say, "I love butterflies too!" The smiles and feelings of joy are immediate. It's as simple as that.

Throughout the 14 years since co-founding *Wheels of Fun*, there have been many occasions when I wanted to simply stop doing it when I felt my 'plate was just too full'. Whenever I have felt that way, I have received a sign that it's not time. That sign has come in a variety of ways: an emotionally charged email from a customer, an unexpected large order, or an order from a long-time customer who calls and says she's so thankful we're still in business.

While running the business has been stressful at times, it certainly has brought me many blessings. While I couldn't change Connor's diagnosis or give him the ability to walk on his own, it has allowed me to brighten the lives of others. I can help bring smiles to the faces of so many children in wheelchairs around the world; and if you make a child happy, just think of the joy you bring to their loved ones!

From the moment we realized the impact of Connor's condition, I made the decision to give up my full-time job in the corporate world. Not only did we give up the salary, but along with that decision went my promotions, positive performance reviews and feelings of belonging in the workplace. I felt that to be Connor's best advocate, I needed to be the one attending his therapy sessions and communicating with his teachers. I decided that no one is going to be a better advocate for my son than me.

> *I also realized things needed to change. I was consulting and travelling most weeks. With a son in a wheelchair, that wasn't going to work any longer. It was going to take both of us to make our new life work, so I changed jobs once again, this time from the highest paying job I had ever held to a new one with a huge pay cut to boot. But we both knew it was what needed to happen. I loved travelling but this was so much more important.*

When I looked at my priorities, being the best mom possible for my kids always came out on top. I missed the paychecks and all the other positive things about working outside the home. But, since we were blessed for Rick to make a salary to allow me to stay home, the answer was clear.

Being a stay-at-home mom would be much more pleasing to God.

Wheels of Fun filled some of the emotional holes I felt being a stay-at-home mom. It gave me a way to interact with other adults using my role as Connor's mom to bring joy to others. I am a mother of a child in a chair, so I "get" my customers. I'm not simply selling them a product.

Connor with his Wheels of Fun soccer ball covers

239

Help from Above (in a Leer Jet)

One of the issues with cerebral palsy is that the muscles do not lengthen along with bone growth. Specifically with Connor, the interior rotation in the muscles in his hip area was causing concern for the doctors. In the fall of 2007, his orthopedist was concerned his femurs were going to come out of the hip sockets. We tentatively scheduled an invasive surgery to be done in Dallas the following summer.

I discussed this condition with one of my best friends. She mentioned a friend of hers, whose son also has cerebral palsy, had found an amazing doctor in New Jersey. They lived in Dallas at the time but traveled to New Jersey and couldn't say enough positive things about their results.

I didn't give this doctor much thought because I couldn't imagine traveling that far. However, my friend was insistent I check into him. Obviously, this was meant to be. A rare snow day in Texas meant that Connor's therapy sessions were canceled. I took a chance and called the doctor in New Jersey to see if he could talk with his physical therapist and me.. He was not in surgery that day and happened to be free to consult with us. The three of us spoke about Connor's condition and what he thought would be the best course of action. Connor's physical therapist has many years' experience in pediatrics and is not easily talked into things, especially an operation only performed by one surgeon in the world.

However, by the end of the call, we all agreed traveling to New Jersey for the doctor's unique surgical procedure was the right thing to do. I couldn't believe I had a sense of peace about it. I had never met this man before, but I trusted in this decision.

After the surgery, Connor would be in a body cast from his ankles to his chest. The challenge would be how to transport him home from New Jersey. I quickly learned we could not fly on a commercial airline due to Connor's cast. I researched medical transport companies and even with our insurance, our out-of-pocket cost would be close to $10,000. Needless to say, I was getting anxious.

A good friend of my brother's is in the medical field and well-connected in the Dallas area. My husband emailed him and asked for suggestions about getting Connor home. Being a man of few words, his response was simply, "I'll be in touch." One morning after my daily readings and pleading with

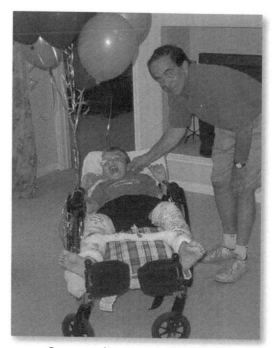

Connor with Jim Swartz, President
and CEO of Careflite

God for a solution, I closed my Bible and the phone rang. I knew it was my answer. When I picked up the call, the voice on the other end said, "I hear Connor needs a ride home from New Jersey." It was the CEO of Careflite. He proceeded to tell me they would pick Connor up at the New Jersey hospital and fly us via private jet home to Austin. The amazing part is we had no out-of-pocket costs for the trip. We would not be paying $10,000 to come home. I knew this was the answer to my prayers! This just solidified in my heart that we were making the right decision.

The day before the surgery, we met the doctor and his team for the first time, face to face. We hit it off with him and his staff right away. He is essentially a Renaissance kind of man. Not only was he a world-renowned surgeon inventing the very surgery he was to perform on Connor, but he was also an inventor and a poet.

As we were leaving that day, I was talking to one of his staff. They shared how the insurance company had called that day to say they were not going to pay anything for the air ambulance to get us home because they said we could have obtained this surgery from a surgeon in Texas. Then, unbeknownst to us, our Renaissance doctor in New Jersey called the head of the insurance claim department and explained there was no one in the whole world certified to do the surgery except him. The surgeon the insurance company had said could have performed the surgery in Texas was actually being trained by our doctor and was not yet certified. (Wow!) The insurance company changed its mind and we were back on!

We arranged for Brice to stay with my sister while we traveled for Connor's surgery. While in the hospital for the seven days post-surgery, the thoughts and prayers posted on the Caringbridge website for Connor were overwhelming. When it came time to go home, I knew we would be met with love and compassion. I was right; our neighbors had cleaned our home and stocked our refrigerator with fresh food. Additionally, for weeks to come, we received home cooked dinners delivered to our frontdoor.

On the first Saturday morning after returning home, Rick and I were having a moment alone over a hot cup of coffee in our kitchen. He was at a loss for words as he watched through the window as a friend from church mowed our lawn.

Just prior to Connor's surgery, I was watching television and heard some profound words from a well-known talk show host. She said, "Allowing someone to do something for you is an act of love." In other words, it's difficult to let others serve you, but letting them do so allows them to show their love. I shared those words with my husband and he agreed. The wife of the kind man who mowed our lawn was expecting at the time. My husband immediately added, "Once their baby arrives, I'll be the first one to mow their lawn." He was true to his word.

> *This is just one of the many lessons I have learned along this journey. Letting someone else "do for me" was difficult since I am a "take care of my own" kind of guy. Receiving was so much harder than giving. But letting others help you is a blessing for you as well as them.*

With Connor's cast, it was imperative we change his body positioning every two hours, 24 hours a day. We had to set our alarm to two-hour intervals during the night to re-position him. I must admit, it was more sleep depriving than breast feeding him as a newborn had been.

During this time, we were blessed to have a former nurse as a caregiver for Connor. Since he would be in the body cast for a month, the helping hands of a nurse in the house were a gift from God. I vividly remember opening my bedroom door one morning with Connor lying on our living room floor and his caregiver by his side. Before I was even through the doorway, he began to ask me a question. She immediately said to him, "Leave your mother alone!" Then she smiled at me saying, "You go back to bed. I've got this!" I did an about-face and slept for several hours. A nap had never felt so good.

The purpose of this surgery was to prevent hip dislocation. We have x-rayed his hips each year since then and are so pleased that 10 years later, his hips still look great. On a daily basis, mothers make countless decisions throughout the day. The success of this surgery gives me the confidence to trust in God and His providence. It reminds me of Philippians 4:13, "I can do all things through Him who strengthens me."

One of our favorite family outings was attending the Round Rock Express baseball games in our community. They are a Triple-A farm team. Not only is the stadium beautiful, but an evening at the ballpark is fun for the entire family. Since it was the middle of the summer in Austin, we certainly couldn't take Connor to a game to roast in his body cast.

So I contacted the CEO of the baseball team, Reid Ryan, who we had come to know personally from regularly attending the games. We also met the rest of his family through the Ride On Center for Kids. Connor rode with Reid's son, Jackson, while Brice played with Jackson's younger sister. When Connor and I both were getting a little cabin fever, I called Reid, spoke with him about Connor's surgery, and asked if there might be an open suite at an evening game. It would make him so happy to be able to attend a baseball game. Reid insisted we watch the game from their family's suite.

When arriving at the ball park, I found myself walking in with Ruth Ryan, wife of Hall of Fame pitcher Nolan Ryan. She recalled when Reid was young, he was hit by a car. He too was in a body cast for a while. She and I talked like two mothers simply sharing stories about their kids. She could not have been more gracious. That evening, she made sure Connor had all the ice cream he could stand.

When I think of that night, I reflect on the dedication of a mother. The nurturing attention and love we show not only to our own children but to others as well. We show our love through kind words and endless acts of service. My mother is an amazing example of this type of love. The strength I possess to endure the challenges and obstacles in life is a direct gift from my mother. The adversity I witnessed her face and overcome gives me courage every day to accept my difficulties and tackle them with confidence, knowing that they will only make me stronger. My mom became powerful as she suffered early widowhood and supported her family with industrious determination. She didn't finish college, but that didn't stop mom from being a successful sole breadwinner for us all, after she lost our father. Mom also made certain that her children had the opportunity to go to college; it wasn't a question of if we would go, only which university we would attend. Even though my dad wasn't there to help with the college plans they had made for us, mom did everything in her power to make it possible.

Not only was my mother a great example of perseverance, but she was also a charitable woman, continually showing her love for others through acts of service. Even when she retired, mom never stopped giving back and making life easier for those around her. She volunteered at a local hospital, serving in the nursery, and loved every minute of it until her diagnosis of Alzheimer's. Such news was devastating to mom and all her loved ones, but even then, she handled this life event the same way she had my father's death, with amazing grace and courage.

When people would ask my mother how she handled everything with such strength, her answer was, "What choice did I have?" Her words often resonate with me and the faith she possessed has given me the same conviction. She was an inspiration to all who knew her and I hope to honor her by continuing mom's legacy of courage in the face of adversity.

My Three Sons

In the summer of 2009, life threw us another curve ball. At the age of 46, I found out we were expecting our third child. With both Connor and Brice, Rick and I tried to conceive for almost a year. Given our ages of 46 and 59 respectively, we were thinking more about retirement than childbirth. However, God had a different plan. When I took the home pregnancy test, my husband was reading the fine print of the instruction booklet, looking for the "false positive results" section. No such section existed, even in the fine print. He sat beside me and told me the test was positive. I was indeed pregnant. I looked at him, smiled, and told him he was going to have to keep working until he was 104.

244

When I called my Ob/Gyn, she was quick to tell me she didn't feel I was actually pregnant. It wasn't until she performed an ultrasound and saw a heartbeat that she believed it. She pulled out an age/conception chart and explained that at my age, we had less than a one percent chance of conception. We all agreed this baby was meant to be. My obstetrician began calling him her "Miracle Baby" from that moment on.

At the regularly scheduled 20-week ultrasound, the doctor shared with me that he noticed a white coloring in our baby's intestinal area (called bright bowel). He said it could indicate one of several things including Down syndrome and cystic fibrosis. He suggested we schedule an appointment right away with a geneticist. I asked why I would want to see a geneticist and he replied, "Because you're at 20 weeks and still have options." By "options," he meant abortion.

I calmly looked at him and said, "I already have one son with cerebral palsy. Even if my baby has either one of those conditions, he's still my baby and I would *NEVER* abort him just because he too might have special needs." The doctor reiterated that I should consult a geneticist. Needless to say, I was in a state of disbelief.

After discussing things with my doctor, we scheduled another ultrasound with a different clinic. This doctor saw the same whiteness and mentioned meeting with a geneticist as well. It was like hitting the replay button for me.

> *I remember the conversation like it was yesterday. I questioned him regarding what exactly a geneticist would do. The doctor said he would perform an amniocentesis and then we would know if there was an "issue" with the fetus. I asked if there was any risk with the procedure. He said, "Yes, but a small one," well worth the risk in his opinion. I said, "Why would we put our baby at risk for data that would not change our decision?" He looked at us in total disbelief.*

Within a matter of weeks, I was seeing a Perinatologist in addition to my regular Ob/Gyn. When she performed my next ultrasound, she did not see any bright bowel condition. Instead, she noticed a small hole in the wall of our baby's heart and a buildup of fluid around it. At that point, she too mentioned the option of abortion. My husband and I reassured her that we intended to carry our baby to term. She was very respectful of our plans, and we began the journey of the next 20 weeks together.

> *We had a whole army of prayer warriors praying for our baby in no time. Friends and neighbors would stop us and tell us how they were praying for us and our "little one."*

With our first two sons, agreeing on a name did not come quickly. However, with this one the perfect name was readily apparent to both Rick and me. In the book of Genesis when Abraham and Sarah learned they would be having a child in their advanced years, they both laughed. In Hebrew, the name Isaac means laughter. Since I was 46 and Rick had just turned 59, it seemed appropriate for our little unexpected miracle to be named Isaac.

I quickly formed a trusting relationship with my Perinatologist. With each passing examination and ultrasound, she reported that things looked good. The fluid was diminishing and the hole did not increase in size. Beginning with 35 weeks' gestation, I planned to have weekly ultrasounds. However, on the morning of my 36-week ultrasound, I woke up and immediately called my sister. I told her, "I don't know how I know this, but I'll be having the baby today." She said she'd get her things together and come to town.

During that morning's ultrasound, Rick and I were chatting while the fetal monitor was recording our baby's information. I noticed his heart beat was just not right. Moments later, my doctor determined I had very little amniotic fluid left. She said she'd call my obstetrician to meet us at the hospital. She instructed us to go straight to the ER.

Isaac was delivered within a matter of minutes by C-section. His heart was examined by a pediatric cardiologist and by God's grace, both the hole and the fluid issues had completely resolved themselves. Of course, Rick and I were so relieved. That was only until the medical staff started mentioning the possibility of Down syndrome. Some felt he had it, while others didn't. He had a couple of the physical characteristics including the simian crease (line across his hand) and the gap between his big toe and the rest of his toes. However, his facial features were

not as obvious as most newborns with Down syndrome. I told Rick I wanted a definitive answer, so our new baby boy's blood sample was tested.

While I was resting in my hospital bed the neonatologist delivered the news that Isaac did, in fact, have Trisomy 21, aka Down syndrome. I laughed out loud. Was my cross not heavy enough already? Was I not serving Him well enough? I was not asking these questions of God with a sense of humor, but rather in disbelief. I was very angry and felt betrayed. I couldn't believe it. I struggled to manage our life with one child with a disability. How in the world could I manage another? I didn't *want* to manage another.

I then immediately thought about Brice and how unfair it was for him to be sandwiched between two brothers with special needs. How would he cope? While I was processing all these thoughts and emotions, the doctor continued to speak.

I will never forget what else he shared with us. He suggested we focus on what Isaac had already accomplished. His heart had healed on its own. He was also successful in latching on to breast feed on the first attempt. Most babies are not able to do that, much less a newborn with Down syndrome who typically struggles due to low muscle tone in the mouth. The next words still resonate in my mind: "Rather than focusing on his diagnosis, focus on how amazing he is with his diagnosis!" While I found his words encouraging at the time, the thought of raising another child with special needs was absolutely overwhelming to me. With the enormous hormonal changes, sleep deprivation and the diagnosis, I struggled to be joyous about the arrival of our baby boy. As a matter of fact, I spent my time either sleeping or crying. My feelings were those of despair. My sister, who was staying with our other two boys, was visiting Rick and me at the hospital just hours after receiving the news. Through tears, I told her I didn't want to live anymore. This was just too much for me to bear. Of course, she immediately pleaded with me to not talk like that. She said we would get through this together helping in any way she could.

The next few months were very difficult for me. I didn't want to tell anyone about Isaac's diagnosis, not even his brothers. I didn't want peoples' sympathy, questions or thoughts on our "new normal." I had to come to grips with it first.

I learned with Connor's diagnosis of cerebral palsy to stay away from the Internet! A diagnosis does not define a child. I didn't want to learn *everything* about Down syndrome, but only what applied to Isaac.

> *I, on the other hand, went back to the book store. Just like with Connor, I devoured all the material I could to prepare. I decided I would have the same 'can do' attitude with Isaac, whatever he wanted in life, we would find a way.*

It took several weeks before Rick and I were ready to discuss the news with his brothers. I was anxious about how the conversation would go. They were playing a video game together when I walked into the room. I began the conversation with the medical description of Down syndrome. I quickly followed it up with how amazing Isaac is with his diagnosis. We then discussed how we all love Connor with his CP and Brice with the things that make him a little quirky. Isaac would be his special self. God has a plan and we should just all love one another as they were created. The boys paused for a moment, said "Okay, mom," and went back to playing their game. They were completely unphased by the news. Isaac was their precious baby brother, and that was all that mattered to them.

Since our other two boys were already established clients of a therapy clinic, it was easy to add Isaac to the mix. He soon began both physical and speech therapy. Since he was at home with me during the day, his disability didn't change the logistics of our day-to-day life at that point.

When he was two years old, his physical therapist suggested we consider enrolling him at the Rise School of Austin, whose mission is to provide the highest quality early childhood education for all children. Rick and I researched the school and immediately enrolled Isaac. Many of the students have Down syndrome, so we quickly felt like we had found a community.

Isaac loved attending the Rise School. The teachers, therapists and administration were fantastic. However, he aged out and we moved on to our neighborhood public elementary school.

One night when I was lying next to Isaac in his bed and we had finished our nighttime prayers, he dozed off. I began stroking his hair, tears filled my eyes and I thought if everyone in this world were as sweet, caring, non-judgmental and empathetic as him, then the world would be such a better place.

It amazes me how my son has always touched peoples' hearts in special ways. For example, when he was just months old, my sister's neighbor was babysitting him so she and I could go out to dinner. Her neighbor is very strong in her faith. When I returned to get him, through her tears she told me, she felt that when she held Isaac, she felt as if she was holding Jesus in her arms.

On a daily basis, he makes us laugh. He's only nine years old and there have been countless people in our lives who've told us about how much joy he brings them.

Isaac is a blessing beyond compare. When folks ask me about him, I have a simple answer. I tell them I don't know what I did to deserve Isaac, but whatever it was, I am sure glad I did!! He is the bright spot in my day, every day!

What About Me?

Another coping mechanism for me is exercise. During my childhood, I participated on the neighborhood swim team. Then in middle and high school, I was on the volleyball team. In college I played in the United States Volleyball Association team formed at the University of Texas. While studying for the CPA exam my senior year, I took up running. In my 20's I also incorporated weight training.

Too often I witness mothers setting aside their needs and interests, feeling it is the right approach to fully serving their families. This can be especially true with special needs parents. The requirement for more attention and assistance can leave parents feeling that their every waking moment should be focused on their child's needs. The truth is that parents can better handle the stresses of life when they have outlets for and sources of personal joy and accomplishment.

While Connor was just a newborn, a friend in Australia suggested I compete in a sprint triathlon. I had no idea there were triathlons shorter than those in the Olympics. I had always held an interest in competing, but had pushed the idea aside, thinking it wasn't possible given the demands of my life at the time.

However, I followed her suggestion and soon caught the triathlon bug, participating in several races a year. One of my biggest personal accomplishments was the completion of a half Ironman near Houston, TX, when I was 39 years old. A friend of mine trained and competed with me. It was a day I'll never forget. It took us more than six hours to cross the finish line, and we were elated! My mother was there waiting for me at the finish line that day, which made it even more special.

Throughout all my years of competing in triathlons, Rick was my best fan. He made sure all arrangements were made so I could compete; he cheered me on throughout the course, and was at the finish line with a congratulatory hug.

I haven't competed in a triathlon in several years now, but exercise is still one of my top priorities. When people ask me how I have the energy or discipline to work out, I simply explain to them that it's my physical, mental and spiritual therapy. It allows me time to pray and get mentally organized for my day. Plus I feel so much better when I'm done.

Janice at the finish line after completing the USA Triathlon National Championships in Oct 2015, in Milwaukee, Wisconsin.

Always Wearing Our God-Glasses

I had concerns for our son Brice when we received Isaac's diagnosis. I worried it would be difficult for him to cope being in between one brother with cerebral palsy and another with Down syndrome. Would he feel cheated or embarrassed? Brice has always had such a gracious heart. Nothing changed with Isaac's birth. He helps Connor's caregivers in so many ways. He shows unconditional love to both brothers, which absolutely refills my heart.

Just the other day, he received $20 from a pet-sitting job he had. He immediately took that money and gave it to his niece for a birthday gift. For his English assignment he wrote a poem describing himself as "devoted to his two brothers with disabilities." God created Brice with a special heart not only for his brothers but special needs individuals as a whole. He doesn't measure people according to their abilities. He just sees them all as children of God.

Like most of us, I go through my daily routine without paying a lot of attention to all that I deal with: therapy appointments, insurance denials, managing caregivers for Connor, the paperwork for the medical waiver program he's on, and durable medical equipment repairs. This list is endless. That doesn't even include the physical demands of raising a child who cannot dress himself, walk, or even get himself to the toilet.

Then, when you add in another child with an intellectual disability, the demands change. Every day I realize how different they are. Parenting a child with a physical disability is so different. For so long, that's the world I lived in. Rick and I are only beginning to navigate the academic world for Isaac. I don't anticipate it to be an easy journey.

The other day I met a neurologist from Chicago. He's the uncle of a young girl with cerebral palsy. We were talking and sharing stories about his patients and my life with Connor. Towards the end of the conversation, he paused, looked off into the distance and quietly said to me, "People don't realize the chronic stress placed on parents of children with special needs."

For a moment, I reflected on what he said. I then told him I try not to think about it. When Connor was young, I would focus on all the things he couldn't do. Year after year I would list the milestones that Connor had missed. It made my glass half empty all the time. I then decided to focus on the things he could do! I apply that same approach to raising Isaac. Each day when he says new phrases or shares new feelings, it makes me smile. He is developing on "Isaac time.

"What have I learned in this journey? Many things, but one hits me all the time, life is what you make it. Call it making lemonade out of lemons, or seeing the glass as half full. Whatever metaphor works for you. I like Scott Hamilton's quote, "The only disability in life is a bad attitude."

Raising children with disabilities isn't easy. Many marriages don't survive it. The divorce rate is even higher than the average divorce rate in America. But we firmly believe that God equips you for whatever challenges come your way in life. It's just how will you respond. If you will only open your heart, He will be there for you.

I certainly have my days where I just want to "Pick up my ball and go home. I don't want to play anymore!" I want to be like a turtle, pull in my head and legs and make the world go away. But then I think of my mom and her perseverance. On my bathroom counter is a picture of my amazing mom holding Isaac as a newborn. Her Alzheimer's had progressed and her arms were unsteady. I knew I wouldn't have any more opportunities for pictures with her youngest grandchild. So my sister and I stood by very close to ensure she didn't drop him. Her loving smile in the photo is so illustrative of the love she had for her children and grandchildren. The frame reads "My mom...my strength." With my faith in God, the loving support of my husband, family and friends, I continue to walk this journey called life. I may stumble along the way. But, without struggle, there is no TRIUMPH.

When I reflect on Connor's life, I think of all the things he's been able to experience through the love and support of his family and others. He's been riding horses since he was five and competed in many horse shows along the way. He was a founding member of the Astros with the Miracle League of Austin. He attended Camp Smiles at Camp for All from the age of 7 until 14. Since then he's gone to Camp Most, which is the weekend camp for individuals who age out of Camp Smiles.

Rick and I purchased a lake house with my sister and her husband when Connor was just two years old. Connor enjoys riding on the Wave Runner and boat, going down the slide, tubing and fishing with his uncles.

We've also rented an RV on three occasions and visited the Grand Canyon, Colorado, and traveled to the East coast to see family. Connor's been with us every mile.

He's also enjoyed University of Texas Longhorn football games along with Texas Stars hockey games.

And for several years now, Connor has served as an altar server at our church.

Ever since Connor was little, Rick and I assured him we would help him do anything he wanted. We also told him it was his job to work hard and be the best he can be. In the spring of his senior year, he decided he wanted to walk to receive his high school diploma. He practiced for months with a walker during his adaptive physical education class.

On June 2, 2017, a beaming Connor Sloan Mason proudly walked across the graduation stage while being honored by a standing ovation by not only his classmates but virtually everyone in attendance, numbering over 7,000 . I don't know who was prouder, my husband and me or Connor. Since then, he's been attending classes at Austin Community College. We're excited to see Connor continue with his college education and what the future holds.

Our family has not treated him any differently. With his family and others to help him, Connor can do anything he sets his mind to. We feel that way for each of our children.

The Mason Family

Behind the Story

Today, Janice spends her time advocating for Isaac to ensure he receives the education all children deserve, as described by the IDEA law. Prior to this focus, she was a passionate sidewalk counselor, praying for the unborn and speaking with mothers and fathers during a crisis pregnancy about her children and the value they add to her life. So many babies diagnosed in utero with potential challenges are aborted.

40 Days for Life is a campaign that takes a focused and peaceful approach to raising awareness of the sanctity of life. Janice can see how much special needs children are devalued in society and feels called to be active in showing how fulfilling life is with her precious sons. Bringing her young adult in a wheelchair and 9-year-old with Down syndrome to *40 Days for Life* campaign events paints a positive picture of kids with disabilities and helps those who are considering abortion to recognize how special their babies truly are. Just their presence is powerful for those entering the clinic as well as those driving by. It helps people see that clinical medicine's recommendation to kill any human who isn't perfect according to society's standards is highly flawed, to say the least.

While the Mason family has loved their pro-life activism, Janice has found advocating for Isaac's education has become critical. Because educating children with special needs is expensive, many school districts prefer to place them all in a self-contained classroom. School districts say they are about education, but in the end, many today are about funding and not spending for the betterment of the children with special needs. Many parents are ill-informed of their children's rights. School districts don't promote educating the parents seemingly because the more parents become informed, the more empowered and vocal they become. There is hope on the horizon, however. For example, Janice is encouraged by the newly elected members of the Board of Trustees, one of which has a child with Down syndrome and understands the challenges that face both parents and children as they navigate through public schools. Janice says, "I will be working with this trustee and hopefully the rest of the Board to evaluate areas for improvement within the district. I am hopeful that honest discussions about some of the inequities which exist for our children will result in change, not only for Isaac but those who will come after him. I know God is calling me to use my voice to help bring about change."

A Life Fully Lived

Stacy Zoern Goad

I have a physical disability. It seems severe to some, less so to others. I use a power wheelchair and rely on a team of caregivers for most of my daily needs. I can't wash my own hair or dress myself. But I can eat on my own, breathe on my own, and use a toilet normally (once someone transfers me). With this set of circumstances, I moved away from home to go to college and live in a dormitory, went to law school, lived alone in an apartment (with caregivers that came in throughout the day and slept over at night), got a dog, drove a van, traveled extensively, started my own company, got married, and gave birth to my son (via C-section). I've done a lot more in my 38 years, obviously, but those are the big ones. So how was I raised in such a way that I had the confidence, skills and support to make this all happen? To live a *normal* life? That's what we all want for our children, wheels or not. It is our job to prepare our babies for the real world.

Stacy and Jason on their honeymoon in Costa Rica

Stacy eight months pregnant with their son Jude

My parents never treated me as if I were special (aside from the way every parent does). I wasn't coddled; my parents had high expectations for me, and the focus was never on my disability. Don't get me wrong, my mother (like most mothers) is a worrier. I get this now, as a mother, more than ever. I also imagine that having a child with a disability accentuates this. However, my mother wasn't selfish in her worrying. She didn't sacrifice my experiences, adventures or independence to satisfy her own sense of comfort. I think this was huge. I was sick more than the average kid, and when I was sick, it was more dangerous since pneumonia is the number one killer of people with my disability. My strength has always been very limited, so I had to rely on others *a lot*. But despite these limitations, I still played outside, even down the street with the other neighborhood kids. My mom (reluctantly) let me start coming home alone after school in the fourth grade. We had to be creative. I couldn't operate the key, so I carried the garage door opener. I was in the mainstream as much as physically possible.

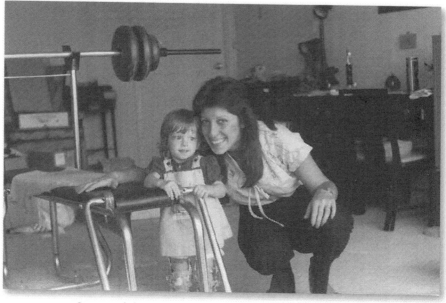

Stacy with her mom in 1980, wearing long-legged braces
before being diagnosed with Spinal Muscular Atrophy the following year

For instance, my parents thought it was important that I play a musical instrument. I couldn't hold anything heavy, and I didn't have normal lung capacity, so we settled on the piano. I could only reach the keys in front of me, and my fingers were so weak I often used two fingers to play a key, but I took lessons for five years and played in countless recitals. This taught me discipline, routine and patience, helped me overcome performance anxiety in front of a crowd, and aided my brain development.

I went to summer camp every year for one week, from the ages of 6 to 21. It was a camp for children with my disability, and each child had an able-bodied counselor. It was scary for my parents letting me go at such a young age, but I thrived. Disability was normal at camp, and that was important to experience. It allowed me to spread my wings in a comfortable environment and to gain independence. I made lifelong friends there. And it gave my parents a much-needed break too.

My parents both worked full time, so by necessity they had to entrust others with my care. I think this was also crucial for the psychological well-being of everyone in our family. Parents of children with disabilities tend to differentiate their child from others, to confirm in their own mind that the child's needs are more severe, complicated or dangerous than others, thus excusing or explaining their *need* to be the child's sole caregiver or their *need* to be over-protective. In many cases, however, this is merely a way of thinking, a worldview created by the parents. Remember, before you had a child with a disability, you wouldn't have known the first thing about how to care for your child either. You have *learned.* And so must others for your well-being and for the well-being of your child. No one else knows your child or her needs the way you do, but that's okay. Only in very extreme circumstances is this special knowledge a matter of life and death. So let your kiddo go to that sleepover, that field trip (without you!) or summer camp.

I always excelled in school and was involved in extracurricular activities, but it wasn't easy. It meant a lot of sacrifice by my parents and a lot of effort. Unlike other kids with working parents who can carpool, no one else could pick me up in my power wheelchair, so my parents were constantly the ones providing transportation. I was in all honors classes in high school, and my parents often had to physically help me with projects like building a spaghetti bridge for geometry. When I was voted student council president, my parents figured out a way to get me to school early for meetings, stay late for special events, and attend weekend activities. When I wanted to go to a student council retreat in another city for a weekend without their help, I found a friend in school who agreed to be my caregiver for the weekend, and I went.

These experiences built my character and shaped me into the woman I am today. I had to learn about my limitations and my capabilities myself. I had to take risks and learn from mistakes. I had to learn how to advocate for myself, how to explain my needs and how to ask for help. None of this would have happened had I been sheltered. And when it was time to graduate high school, my accomplishments made me a competitive candidate for universities all over the country. My parents had prepared me well. They knew they would not be around forever, and it was imperative I learn the skills to take care of myself one day. By supporting my educational endeavors so I would be competitive for college, they ensured I would someday be employable. With income, I could support myself and my needs. What they didn't want for me, nor I for myself, was a life dependent on government assistance, merely crossing the poverty line, unable to control my own life. I could, and would, create and successfully maintain my own safety net. I didn't need my parents to do that. I didn't need the government to do it either.

I don't mean to oversimplify raising a child with a disability. Life with a disability is a struggle. However, in my 38 years of living with a disability, I have learned that *society* is much more disabling than my medical diagnosis. So what if I am unable to move my body without help? That's what paid caregivers are for. However, the architectural and attitudinal barriers persist, and they can be crippling. I think the most important thing parents of children with disabilities can do is recognize these societal absurdities. Teach your child ways to alleviate obstacles rather than compound their impact. There is a fine line between realism and complacency.

By way of demonstration, consider airplane travel. Domestic flights do not have accessible bathrooms. International flights claim to have accessible bathrooms, but they are nearly impossible to use because of their small size. We are forced to leave our wheelchairs during air travel, and our wheelchairs (which can cost upwards of $70,000) are treated no better than luggage by minimum-wage employees who have not received specialized training on medical equipment. Often, our chairs (our "legs"!) are damaged in flight. Airplane seats are not made for us, so the trip is uncomfortable at best and usually pain inducing. Some people must bring their own straps and seat attachments just to remain upright in these horrendous airplane seats. Getting on and off the plane is no picnic either. I prefer to be carried on the plane by a companion, because I find the aisle chairs to be impossible to transfer out of, dangerous and demeaning. Being lifted into the seat takes a lot of space, space only provided by the bulkhead, yet many airlines restrict access to these seats, even for those of us who need them. In fact, American Airlines has recently adopted a nonsensical policy that allows only people with service dogs or unbendable knees to reserve the bulkhead. I am thus forced to decide between spending 1-2 hours on the phone climbing my way up the decision-making tree to get managerial approval to make the reservation or to simply lie. Given these seemingly unsurmountable obstacles, why on earth would I ever fly? Because like you, I am human, and I want to experience the world in this life I have been given. I am just forced to try a lot harder. It sucks, but it does build character. All these little obstacles force you to be creative in problem solving, be an advocate for yourself and develop a healthy amount of stubbornness.

So how do I do it? Well, whichever path I choose, depending on my mood, I get the reservation for the bulkhead. I plan my flights in 4-hour increments, so I don't need to use the restroom. I dehydrate myself. I avoid layovers, but if they are necessary, I give myself at least two hours between flights. If traveling internationally, I get a sleeping pill from my doctor, take it when I get on the plane and then sleep (extending my bathroom time by several hours). I know the weight and battery type of my wheelchair, so when I arrive at the airport, I am informed. I also know my rights. For instance, I am not required to remove the dry-cell batteries from my wheelchair. I know to remove loose or easily damaged components of my chair before flight. I have laminated signs taped to my seat and footrest explaining ways to handle the chair. I demand my chair be brought to the door of the plane upon arrival, so I can avoid more discomfort in their shitty hospital manual chairs. I use the restroom immediately prior to boarding the plane. I let them know I must be pre-boarded and need 5-10 minutes before anyone else gets on the plane. And I bring the contact information of a wheelchair repair shop at my destination just in case.

The craziest thing is that all of these obstacles and all the hoops I must jump through are completely unnecessary. The history of our country could have just as easily included air travel as covered by the Americans with Disabilities Act; people could have given a shit with commercial plane design; planes could have accessible bathrooms, and places to sit in our own wheelchairs, tied down, just as we do on trains, in cars and on boats. Air travel is not a nightmare because of my disability, it is a nightmare because people have made it that way.

But this is the world we live in. I take every opportunity I can to normalize disability in our culture. Disability is a normal part of the human condition. It should not be something feared or pitied. Your child with a physical disability will have all the same desires, dreams and goals as you did when you were young. They will face the same temptations, so they should be taught good decision-making skills. You can't assume they won't ever drink alcohol, try drugs or have sex just because of their disability. Educate them on these topics as you would any other child. The pervasive stereotypical assumption in our society that people with disabilities are asexual continues to this day, even in the medical field. There are many women I know who use wheelchairs who are not tested for STDs or cervical cancer in their yearly gynecological exams. Their doctors are often surprised to hear the wheelchair user is sexually active. These are the attitudes we must work to change.

Similarly, significant numbers of people with disabilities are historically undervalued in the work force and are not encouraged to pursue a career. This is often perpetuated by the infantile treatment many people with disabilities receive, even well into their adulthood. We may not have control over the disability, but we do have control over the impact we let it have. For instance, my disability does not affect my bladder control. However, I am immobile on my own. So the only way for me to toilet "normally" is for someone to help me undress and transfer me to the toilet. My parent's potty trained me as a toddler, just as my nondisabled peers were taught by their parents. Thank you, Mom and Dad. Other parents of children with my very same disability choose to avoid the effort of potty training and keep their children in diapers unnecessarily. This "convenience" ends up being a source of embarrassment for the older child/adult, an unnecessary expense, a limitation to their social and sexual life and is un-called for infantile treatment.

This infantile treatment extends to financial dependence, leading to a vicious cycle. The child is never allowed to grow up, does not gain the confidence necessary to enter or succeed in the work force and thus remains financially, and often physically, dependent. Interestingly, our society is seeing a trend in this parenting style across the board, and even children without disabilities are not learning responsibilities or basic skills. You may have heard people complaining of parents with attachment issues or children/young adults with entitlement issues. When it comes to children with disabilities though, we simply can't afford to adopt this parenting style. We can't afford to underestimate children with disabilities just because they are "different."

As a successful adult with a physical disability, I know I am an inspiration to some. I think that is a good thing, but I am also an advocate and understand the dangers of being "inspirational." As a parent of a child with a disability, it is good to know a bit about the history of disability advocacy. An emotionally difficult but profoundly informational read is *No Pity: People with Disabilities Forging a New Civil Rights Movement* by Joseph P. Shapiro. If there could be a mandatory reading list for parents of children with disabilities, this would be on it. As with other civil rights movements, it has been a long, hard struggle for people with disabilities to have the same basic rights others take for granted, like education, housing and architectural access. As Shapiro's book illustrates, we have come a very long way, and the passage of the Americans with Disabilities Act in 1990 was crucial landmark legislation. But as you and your child will come to realize (if you haven't already), we have a very long way yet to go.

There is a phrase we use in disability advocacy called "inspiration porn." Stella Young gave an incredible TED Talk on this topic, entitled "I'm not your inspiration, thank you very much." People with disabilities define the term "inspiration" in different ways. Some think it is something that makes able-bodied people feel good about themselves, like when you see a news story applauding someone for helping a stranger who has a disability and the focus is on the disability not the human factor of being kind to strangers. Other people think of it as a type of objectification which reduces their existence to having a disability, so that one's accomplishments inspire. Often this takes shape when someone with a disability is praised for doing something ordinary. Regardless of how it is defined, "inspiration porn," the primary way in which disability is represented in the media, negatively impacts the advancement of the rights of people with disabilities in our society. There is no harm in finding something inspirational to be so, but there is harm in underestimating that segment of society as a whole and then praising commonplace interactions or accomplishments. This is an important distinction of which parents of children with disabilities should be aware. This is why I take caution when people refer to me as "inspirational."

When I was in elementary school, there was a field day each year. While I suppose it was fun to get outside of the classroom and be outside all day, I remember feeling bored. I was not able to physically participate in any of the activities. At the end of field day, the entire school gathered in the auditorium for the awards ceremony. And each year the teachers in charge would wait until the end of the ceremony to give me the final award. Though the reason varied year to year, such as "best cheerleader," I always "won" a blue ribbon. But the truth was that I knew I had literally been sitting there all day doing nothing. I knew that everyone else knew I had been sitting there all day doing nothing. I didn't appreciate being included in a superficial, unauthentic way. Even at such a young age - 8 or 9 years old - I would have rather had the teachers come up with activities for me to participate in, and then only provide me with an award if one was earned. I didn't deserve a blue ribbon. Not everyone gets a blue ribbon. Their intentions were pure; no harm was meant. But it *was* harmful, both in the way I viewed myself and how the other children grew up viewing disability.

It is experiences such as that which often result in youth with disabilities, myself included, going through a phase of self-loathing. Not necessarily overt self-loathing but certainly a sense of shame for your differences and a desire to be as inconspicuous as possible. These feelings, which are sometimes unavoidable to an immature mind in a society where disability is perceived so negatively, can be overcome by embracing one's disability. As an adult, I recognized a gratitude for my disability for providing me a life with a richness in friendships unmatched by "normal" people; a depth of love, empathy, compassion, communication and understanding in my marriage that many people will never experience; a son who will learn firsthand that obstacles are no reason to give up and that judgments made superficially will cause you to miss out on incredible people and experiences. Disability rights aren't just about laws and regulations. They are about an acceptance of disability as a completely normal part of the human experience. "Disability" is not a bad word; use it proudly! People deal with poverty, unemployment, the death of loved ones, illness, stress. These are all difficult but normal parts of life and so is disability. When people go through difficult circumstances, we should support them, encourage them, be there for them, but not pity them. We should not excuse them from living life to the fullest. Disability should be no different.

It is this negative perception of disability, often labeled "ableism," that is one of the most limiting aspects of having a disability. It is the view of "other" that perpetuates a society not built for us. This view is constantly reinforced by the smallest gestures, vocabulary and assumptions, but that cumulatively prevent people with disabilities from being seen as and treated as equal. I have never been one to take offense for the language used, but the disability advocacy community legitimately has concerns about terms such as "confined," "wheelchair-bound" and "suffer." It isn't about political correctness. It is about an underlying attitude toward disability. We are not our wheelchairs. We are people. We are not our limitations. We are children. We are not our struggles. We are wives, friends, daughters, moms. I am not confined or bound by my wheelchair; I am freed by it. Likewise, I am annoyed when strangers make comments to me such as "Hey there, hot rod," or "Slow down, you're going to get a ticket." Just the other day someone commented to me, "Wow, you're really good at driving that thing." I wanted to respond, "Wow, you're really good at walking." It literally feels that absurd to me, because driving my wheelchair is such a normal part of my existence – as is walking for someone who has always walked. We can only obliterate this ignorance by teaching by example, by being out there in the world, living ordinary lives. I remember visiting Berkeley when I was in my mid-twenties. Berkeley, the home of the disability rights movement, is home to a disproportionate number of wheelchair users. Wheelchairs are everywhere you look. People don't stare. It is normalized. It is awesome.

As long as you don't box your child in and define them by this difference, your child will grow into a capable, incredible adult. As much as my own parents were a supportive force in my life, they had tremendous concerns all along the way. When I was diagnosed at one year old, they feared a childhood of ridicule. That never happened. They feared my getting a dog when I lived alone would be too much to handle. It wasn't. Most of all, they feared I would never find romantic love, and they assumed I would never have a child. They were wrong. I suppose those fears are normal, and even based in reality to some extent, but they didn't let those fears control my life. And I've experienced everything I've ever hoped to experience.

No one ever said life was easy. To quote one of my favorite movies, *The Princess Bride*, "Life is pain. Anyone who says otherwise is selling something." How we react to the pain, though, is our choice. I choose to experience life. I try my hardest not to be ruled by fear. I feel the sadness, the frustration, the anger, and then I move on to a solution. I'm creative. I'm stubborn. I'm grateful. I find a way. I find the strength and the power within to persevere. And I never feel sorry for myself. It could always be so much worse.

Stacy and Jude

Behind the Story

Stacy wrote a book when she was twenty years old and published it seven years later. It's titled, *I like to Run Too: Two Decades of Sitting*. Stacy teaches that it's important for society to see the differences between people who are sitting and who are standing and to recognize that there's not that much of a difference at all. "In the ways that matter, we are all the same." She says. "People don't realize the struggles and obstacles society has placed on those with disabilities. We need more awareness. We can't improve accessibility in this world unless the general public sees the need for it."

Stacy feels the general public won't make an effort to make the world more accessible until they recognize how similar we actually are, "Right now it's easy for people to not care about it because we are the 'other.' There is a disconnect. As long as it doesn't impact them, and it's someone else's problem, it's easy to turn a blind eye to the frustrations I wrote about in this chapter." Stacy is striving to bridge the gap so that it's not "us and them" but rather, we are all in this together, and should have, and could easily have, a universal design.

Stacy points out that anyone from any walk of life can become disabled, "A disabling injury can happen to any person at any moment, so it's interesting that this minority still faces so much attitudinal and societal discrimination when anyone can become a member of that group in the blink of an eye."

These days Stacy is all about her three-year-old, as he is all consuming. She expresses that it's a wonderful, normal life! She has a caregiver who has been with her for a while now, so that stability has been nice. Stacy and her husband love games and having friends over for game nights. They are also big Netflix watchers. Stacy laments, "I used to be an avid reader, but haven't been since I've had a child."

Stacy practiced law for six years, then quit to start a company that she ran for another six years; Kenguru, an electric vehicle for people in wheelchairs. "We sold the company in 2015, and the following year, the company that bought us filed Chapter 11, the team was laid off and the project ended. We never brought the vehicle to market." Stacy had just given birth to

Jude which was terrible timing to become unemployed, but a blessing to stay home and spend that first year with her son. In contemplating what's next, Stacy decided she didn't want to go back to the practice of law, as she enjoyed the business development and social networking that was part of building Kenguru. Recently, Stacy started working as a legal recruiter, recruiting attorneys for corporate legal positions. She enjoys helping people find their dream jobs. It has been fulfilling as well as challenging as it's a very niche position. Stacy says, "There are not many legal recruiters specializing in in-house recruiting, and I'm able to work from home, which is great for my personal circumstances as well. It's the perfect job for me."

Stacy presenting her company, Kenguru, to President Obama

Everybody Can Ride
The Story of Project Mobility
Hal Honeyman

Once upon a time, in a bike store, it all began. Julie came in to prepare for a biking trip across Europe, riding from Luxemburg City to Copenhagen Denmark. Being a lifelong cyclist, having spent a few months riding through Europe myself, I was sold on her while she bought a bike from me. A few weeks later, Julie came back and asked for "that red haired guy." Apparently, I hadn't done a very good job marketing myself, only the bike, but fortunately she didn't need to know my name for me to have made an impression.

Together we biked everywhere, all the time. We were immersed in all things bike until suddenly we found ourselves married. In 1975 I worked at a store called The Bike Rack that was for sale. My parents bought that store and now, here we are over 44 years later, still working with our parents, Dale and Nancy in our family business.

Our oldest son went on his first bike ride in utero on a ride called Bicycler Across Magnificent Miles of Illinois (BAMMI). This was a Chicago Lung Association Fundraiser, which we participated in for ten years. We actually rode as support, fixing the bikes that broke down along the ride. We had brought a van and mechanic and took turns riding, making it a mixture of work and play. Once my son, Dane, was born, we regularly loaded him in a trailer and biked all over the country. Basically, we are a biking family.

The triplets were our, "Let's have one more." They were born at 27 weeks: two girls, Clare and Emily, and their brother, Jacob. We spent three months in the neonatal intensive care unit. When Jacob was a few days old, he had a brain bleed. As a result of the bleed and complications from prematurity, he was diagnosed with cerebral palsy. At the age of three, Clare and Emily started riding bikes. This is when we realized the importance of finding a way for Jacob to ride as well. We found an adaptive bike in Canada called Freedom Concepts which Jacob was able to ride successfully. The first five times he rode, he wasn't pedaling on his own, but on the sixth time he learned how to pedal on the down stroke which caused his eyes to light up, realizing he could propel the bike on his own power!

This is really where it all started. We explored the variety of adaptive bikes available and began selling them at The Bike Rack. We would take a group of bikes to hospitals, camps and clinics to let people try them out. We did this for a few years and the whole time we continued to expand the range of bikes we offered as we encountered different needs and abilities. We also got into wheelchairs and sports equipment, anything for people with physical limitations to stay active and moving.

In 2008, we were approached by an organization bringing a group of 25 injured veterans and their significant others from Walter Reed Hospital to Long Beach, California to participate in an event called Summer Fest, a week-long program of sports and physical activities. As I began doing the math on the costs of getting a trailer and bringing the bikes to support the event, I realized that starting a nonprofit would be necessary. Disabled Sports USA provided the funding to support Summer Fest, which were adaptive sports activities such as cycling, climbing, water sports, sailing, skiing, and "everything you can think of outdoors." Our parents hauled a trailer full of adaptive bikes from Illinois to California and we spent a week getting people on bikes. The event launched *Project Mobility*.

Up to this point, we had been doing events at hospitals, but after Summer Fest, we were approached about bringing the bikes to Walter Reed Hospital and doing a bike clinic there for the wounded veterans. We would pull men and women out of the hospital and put them on bikes. That's where we met people from Wounded Warrior Project who asked us to consider supporting a ride going from Miami to Key West. That snowballed into upwards of 50 events per year over the course of 13 years. Essentially, we put 9,000 people on bikes in that time period. Of the thousands we helped, no one ever came to a Soldier Ride and left unable to participate.

We customized and adapted a bike to work for everyone we met. Our role was to work with manufacturers to get bikes at a discount, or donated, and select the various equipment needed for the rides. Then we went on the rides, tuning up and prepping all the bikes, making sure they were mechanically safe and ready to ride. Once the prep work was done, the warriors would come and we'd fit bikes to their abilities, as many as 50 in a day. Then we would support the ride itself with a U-Haul, guiding them through the ride, providing mechanical and moral support. Sometimes we helped push riders up the hill while riding a bike, if they needed a little more support. Some would be struggling, but wouldn't let us touch their bikes while others welcomed the added push. In the course of these events, I went to the White House ten different times and met three Presidents.

It was a great experience working with the vets, but the largest portion of our time is spent working with kids. We started going to hospitals and would conduct events for children, going to therapy centers, doing in-service teaching therapists how to identify what works for different abilities. My favorite summer camp was Camp Independence at St. Louis Children's Hospital. They have one of the best cerebral palsy clinics in the world. Jacob was a patient there for many years.

Cerebral Palsy Clinic at St. Louis Children's Hospital was started by Dr. Janice Brunstrom. She is a pediatric neurologist and has cerebral palsy herself. She accepted a job at the hospital as a neurologist and announced that she intended to start one of the best cerebral palsy clinics. In each specialty area, they brought in the best doctors in the world. Camp Independence is a week-long period during which they help kids participate in two activities each day: martial arts, dance, etc. with cycling as the grand finale. The idea is to help each kid find a sport they love and take it home, to carry it on. Project Mobility goes five times every summer. On each trip, we try to collaborate with other events as well as meet veterans and kids.

The Shirley Ryan Ability Lab in Chicago is another place we've done a lot of work with kids and adults with disabilities. The goal is to get them on an adaptive bike for a first-time experience. We team up with therapists to see what works and also find ways to provide bikes, either through Project Mobility or another organization. We really get the ball, or wheel, rolling.

Adaptive cycling provides many benefits for children, both physical and emotional. It's physically strengthening and provides improved range of motion/flexibility, which transfers to enhanced daily activity such as walking or getting in and out of wheelchairs. Other physical benefits are cardiovascular. Kids get into their teens and gain weight. The big enemy for someone with physical limitations is lack of movement leading to muscle tightening and spasticity. Getting kids on bikes provides the movement needed to prevent these conditions. Emotional benefits include self-esteem, confidence and a sense of freedom. It helps them to integrate with their peers and other people. It can be done as a family, which strengthens bonds.

The reciprocal motion of pedaling is powerful brain development. I've seen it with kids and adults who have traumatic brain injuries as well as stroke patients. It helps their brains make new pathways and connections. One of my favorite stories from the Ability Lab is of Mark Stephens, who had a bicycle accident which caused him to go over the handle bars and have a C-5 spinal cord injury. He was told he'd never walk again. Before the accident, Mark was a driven person, a competitive bike racer and successful financial trader and the injury didn't change this about his personality.

One day, Mark came to visit me at the bike store, pulling up in a VW Beetle. I watched him getting his wheelchair out of his vehicle and walked up to help. He let me know that no help was needed. Five minutes later, he got his chair out and came in to introduce himself. He told me he intended to ride across the country to raise a million dollars for the Ability Lab. I said, "Game On! Let's Go!" We fitted him for a recumbent bike with substantial modifications. We did trouble shooting, figuring out how to make it work with his injuries. Mark successfully rode it across the country and indeed raised a million dollars. He's gone on to do many other great things, proving that you can overcome and not let an injury define you. WLS TV in Chicago has a video of him leaving the hospital with a walker, when he had been told he would never walk again. The best thing about what we do is meeting people like Mark Stephens along the way, seeing the adversity they've faced and overcome.

The Bike Rack has grown from 900 square feet to over 10,000 square feet of space in our own building. We have indoor and outdoor training, which accommodates all forms of bikes. Jacob is happy and healthy. He rides with us in many of our events. The mission of Project Mobility is to make a positive difference in the lives of children, adults and wounded soldiers with disabilities. Project Mobility was started to put on events, but we also provide bikes to children and adults. We gave away 14 bikes in 2018 alone.

One day before Christmas, a girl named Riley came in looking for a bike for her dad. She watched a video about project mobility and decided she didn't want anything for Christmas for herself, instead she wanted to help a child with physical challenges receive a bike. The story got out in the local Chicago media and donations came pouring in. We were able to give way 3 bikes that year! This has evolved and now we give away over a dozen adaptive bikes every year to children and injured vets. We hold fundraisers for these gifts and a number of bikes clubs have begun stepping up to help raise the funds. We give bikes away at all our events as well. Aldi Corporation is the presenting sponsor of our signature fundraising and adaptive-inclusive event, *Everybody Rides*. We have able-bodied people coming out and supporting those riding adaptive bikes. These are big events that bring the entire community together!

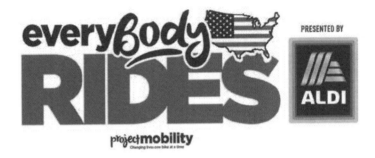

Behind the Story

Hal Honeyman is the older brother of Tamara Simmons, author of **The Funding Guide for Children with Disabilities**. I had the chance to visit The Bike Rack in St. Charles when I was in town working with Tammy, introducing her *Funding Guide* at the Abilities Expo in Chicago. It is a busy, happy place where Jacob can often be seen smiling and encouraging all who enter.

Veteran's Mobility Initiative is the project Hal Honeyman is currently working on, seeking funding to provide one-day clinics at VA hospitals or Warrior Transition Units. It consists of an event where they bring bikes to a park near a VA hospital and recruit injured veterans to come out and ride. Recently, they had 25 men and women participate in an adaptive cycling clinic. The adaptive bike techs from Project Mobility fitted all 25 people for bikes and led them on a ride. It was a six-mile ride along Lake Monona. At the end of the ride, there was lunch and a Q&A session. Project Mobility is seeking funding to replicate this experience all over the country. The idea is to expose veterans to the equipment and how it works, and then provide the experience of riding and engaging with other veterans. The final piece of the Veteran's Mobility Initiative is to raise funds in order to give them their bikes as well. To learn more visit: *www.ProjectMobility.org.*

Everybody Rides 2018 adaptive bike recipients, Frankie, Mia and Dallas, at Aldi Corporate Headquarters, who sponsored the event

Conclusion
Raising Wheels:
How You Can Too!

There are many reasons you may have read this book. As the parent of a differently abled child, I hope you found encouragement, inspiration and resources which you might not have been previously taught. As someone living life on wheels yourself, may you recognize all the ways you are unique, yet not alone, and the great value of your life. Perhaps you picked up this book to gain strength from the indomitable spirits of those who shared their stories in order to face your own daily challenges. **The Triumph Book: RAISING WHEELS** is the platform for a community of encouragers, whether an author in this book or a reader who will carry the messages beyond the pages, changing the world as we join together in Raising Wheels, with an emphasis on *RAISING!*

Melissa and Jody Copp lead the way, paying it forward through the Raising Wheels Foundation®, an organization supporting parents in RAISING differently abled children and RAISING awareness of the need for accessibility. After receiving the gift of accessibility through a 100% accessible home for their boys, they wanted to have other parents see the joy of accessibility not just in their own homes but in the community, they are RAISING their differently abled children in. Melissa says, "Our story is like so many others. We try every way possible to triumph over tragedy when faced with impossible challenges; but they are possible to overcome with the support of others. We are here to be the support system required to overcome these challenges. Accessibility isn't a luxury. The Raising Wheels Foundation's mission is to improve accessibility everywhere for everyone. Come roll with us!" (For more information about their initiatives, visit: *www.RaisingWheelsFoundation.org.*)

Ashley Ballew shares, "Living a life on wheels is a definite challenge in the society we live in today. Knowledge is power and to educate our communities is to empower our children, spouses and friends that are living and 'Raising Wheels.' I love the following quote by Rick Hansen: *The wheelchair should not be a symbol of disability. A wheelchair is a vehicle to liberation and freedom; a chariot for independence.*"

We can all do little things to participate in the movement of RAISING WHEELS, as Janice Mason observes, "It's not a secret that parenting can be a tough job. Although there are countless blessings along the way, raising a child who uses a wheelchair to access their world adds to those challenges on a daily basis. If you find yourself in a situation in which you become impatient or frustrated with a parent/caregiver accompanying a child in a wheelchair, please pause and take a deep breath. Rather than sharing your frustration through an impolite comment or gesture, give them a smile instead. It won't cost you a penny, but will be a sweet gift to everyone involved."

Erin Kiltz lifts our perspectives to recognize what an opportunity it is RAISING WHEELS. She concludes, "We have the rare privilege of educating our communities through everyday interactions, the way we love and respect our children and our gentle responses to honest, yet sometimes awkward questions. I feel as though our daughter Gracie was here 26 short years for such a time as this -for the world to see her as well as every other individual with special abilities for who they are, 'fearfully and wonderfully made' with gifts to contribute. It is our hope through the stories of *Raising Wheels*, there is a true paradigm shift in how each of you see our children."

As someone who has truly excelled in life, Allison Dickson now uses her example of conquering all odds to lift as many people as she can reach, encouraging them with powerful words she makes every effort to share. It has become her purpose in life to lift you and me. Allison states, "I hope readers are moved by the journeys shared by each person in this book. If one person better understands that anything is possible through determination, faith and support of loved ones, then the purpose of this book is fulfilled. Our differences make us unique, and our uniqueness makes each of us beautiful. Let's embrace and celebrate our uniqueness through love, respect, empathy, compassion, empowerment, inclusiveness and kindness.

On Allison's social media, she likes to share a Quote of the Day (#QOTD), something that speaks to or inspires her. She hopes by sharing these quotes that the messages may reach you where you are and touch you heart too. Here are a couple of my favorites, which are most applicable to the message of this book:

Our lives are steered by uncertainties, many of which are disruptive or even daunting; but if we persevere and remain generous of heart, we may be granted a moment of supreme lucidity - a moment in which all that has happened to us suddenly comes into focus as a necessary course of events, even as we find ourselves on the threshold of a bold new life that we had been meant to lead all along.

- Amor Towles

Beauty is many different things: knowledge, music, dance, art, photography. Beauty is laughter. Beauty is honor, loyalty and your word meaning something to others. We are all full of so much beauty. We all have a beautiful light that we have to work at keeping lit. Beauty is seen in being compassionate. Find what you love. Believe in your dreams. Set goals. Make it happen. Have backup plans. Work hard. Love life; love the life you live. Love others, but love yourself too.

- Unknown

I think the best conclusion for this book comes from David Farber, who simply says, "Embrace your life and the plans God has for you! *'For I know the plans I have for you,' says the LORD. 'They are plans for good and not for evil, to give you a future and a hope."* -Jeremiah 29:11.

About the Authors

Melanie Davis

After suffering the loss of her seven-month old daughter, Brynn, to SIDS, Melanie found healing and purpose by sharing her story with those who could be encouraged and inspired by the wisdom and purpose she found in her daughter's death. She developed *The Triumph Program* to assist others to discover write and share their own Triumph Stories and went on to become the founder of *Triumph Press*, which publishes *The Triumph Book Series*, as well as the books and stories of others who have overcome adversity. She is the publisher of *The Funding Guide for Children with Disabilities* and attended many Abilities Expos around the country, helping people with their fundraising plans. At the Houston Abilities Expo she met the Copp Family and they developed a strong connection. From this meeting, they decided to co-author *The Triumph Book: RAISING WHEELS* and create a platform to connect parents of uniquely abled children, assisting them to discover life-changing products and lift one another. *The Triumph Book: RAISING WHEELS* is the third in *The Triumph Book Series*.

Melissa Copp

Melissa Copp resides in Waco, Texas and is the Founder and Executive Director of the Raising Wheels Foundation®. After receiving her business degree from Texas A&M University in 2001 and her Masters in Legal Studies from Texas State University in 2006, she traded in big city life in Austin to the slower paced town of Waco, Texas. She moved there with her husband in hopes of starting a family. Their first son, Calan, arrived in August of 2008, but parenthood came with a slew of hardships including developmental delays, genetic testing, brain scans, specialists, and countless other issues. All while battling these hardships and moving along without a diagnosis, they welcomed a second son, Lawson, in March of 2012. Life repeated itself and their world was thrown once again into the revolving door of specialists after Lawson demonstrated similar symptoms. In April 2015, both her boys were diagnosed with a rare and life-threatening Mitochondrial condition caused by a PNPT1 genetic mutation with two other known cases in the United States and about a dozen worldwide with no cure or treatment plan. Although raising two differently abled sons has its challenges, Melissa has focused on the beauty that is RAISING WHEELS and has dedicated herself to advocating for the differently abled community and championing for change for better accessibility in homes and public places.

Her love and passion for her boys on wheels led her to focus on the need for a 100% accessible home for her boys and in January 2018, her and her family were featured on Season 5 of HGTV's "Fixer Upper." They were gifted a fully renovated home from Chip and Joanna Gaines, Tim Tebow, Make-A-Wish and countless others so their differently abled boys could finally feel what it was like to wash their own hands, race down a hallway or play in a backyard. Melissa used that life changing event as motivation to pay it forward through the Raising Wheels Foundation® to help provide resources to other families raising differently abled children.

Read the first two books in
The Triumph Book Series

Stories of people who found purpose
and joy in life because of their tragedies

*"These are not stories crafted by the authors,
they are authors crafted by their stories"*

*"As I read the conclusion, I was flooded with emotion.
Some of it may have been healing from my own experiences
and some of it may have been realizing that there is always
hope and ways to get through life's adversities."*

Epic first-person stories which increase appreciation and support for our veterans while helping them win their battles after the war

"Every American should read this book."

"Heart touching tribute and history lesson in one!"

"From those who were there."

Featuring Tuskegee Airman
Lt. Calvin J. Spann

COMING FALL 2020!

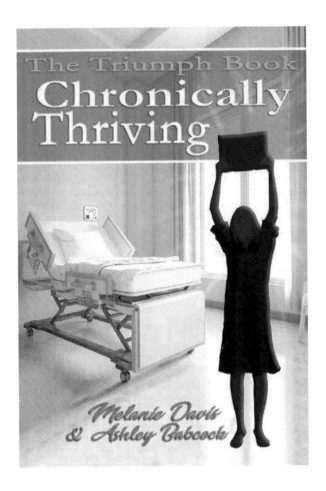

Stories from those who not only survive, but thrive with chronic illnesses

A much-needed guide for all those who may be suffering with invisible illnesses in isolation, where they can find hope and healing and know they are not alone.

Books that Find Joy
Amidst Adversity

When tragedy presses down
And you feel the pain of impending darkness,
We have walked the road from tragedy to triumph.

Follow us and see the mist clear!

TriumphPress.com

Made in the USA
Lexington, KY
27 October 2019

56086637R00164